FROM HERE TO PARIS

FROM HERE TO PARIS

To my lovely wife and first mate, Linda.
And in loving memory of my dad and the ones who didn't
make it to the end of the voyage.

All artwork, including drawings, cartoons,
and paintings are done by the author.

To see more original artwork go to:
www.rainbowsend-cartoons.com
www.hammondfineart.net

ISBN – 13: 978-0615918587
ISBN – 10: 0615918581

Cover art and design by the author.
Davenator Press
U.S.A.

FROM HERE TO PARIS

Get Laid Off.

Buy a Barge in France.

Take it to Paris.

A Memoir by

Cris Hammond

Prologue

The budding young Vice President of Human Resources patted me on the shoulder and said, "Have a nice life." Then he turned and walked back into the building.

Standing there in the parking lot with my personal possessions in a cardboard box and my severance papers stuffed in my pocket, I thought, "Why the hell not?"

My inner John Belushi was urging me to go back into the building and play Samurai Chef with the copy machine, but instead I went to Starbucks. By the time I got there, my cocky attitude had vanished, replaced by a hysterical voice inside my head, screaming, Ohmygod! You're screwed! You're really screwed!

I was in my mid-fifties. My hair was graying. My belly was softening and my feet hurt. And now I was unemployed. This was not in the plan. This was a crisis. It was as if I'd been merrily driving the shiny new company car at 90 mph and suddenly it slammed to a halt, launching me into a whole new reality. It seemed like a really good time to panic.

On the other hand, it was a gorgeous day. I looked around and noticed how warm the sun felt on my face. Embracing my new, unemployed status, I turned my cell phone off for the first time in months. I even started to feel a little sorry for that young fellow who had to go back into his drab office on such a nice day. As I sat there sipping a cappuccino in the sun glinting off San Francisco Bay, it came to me that sometimes your life falls apart just enough to allow you to put it back together in an entirely different way.

Chapter One

"How vain it is to sit down to write when you have
not stood up to live."

\- Henry David Thoreau

Like most people who've passed their half-century mark, I've left an uneven wake, littered with big plans and once shiny dreams. First, I thought I'd be a cowboy, going everywhere at a gallop and constantly saving runaway stagecoaches. I got as far as tearing around the house with a six-gun flapping at my knee and lassoing the dog. Then one day I saw Gorgeous George, the dirtiest, most vile wrestler of his day, take on Haystack Calhoun on TV. I put aside my six-gun and began leaping off the couch onto my little brother. My father, noting a fearless, and perhaps villainous tendency in his first-born son, began encouraging me to be President of the United States, but I really saw nothing wrong with growing up to own a used car lot, like him. While my friends' dads were all driving around in Ford station wagons, he'd drop me off at school in a red and white Corvette, or a Thunderbird with glass-pack mufflers and spinner hubcaps. President Eisenhower never did cool stuff like that. But then one night, fate supplied an unknown arsonist who burned the car lot down and those dreams, quite literally, went up in smoke.

I was a mostly broke painter in 1994 when a friend of mine, whom I hadn't seen for years, called me out of the blue with an offer. He had a unique idea for a business and had lined up some money to fund it but the money was running out. If he didn't figure out how to make it work, and make a big sale soon, his backers would shut him down. For some unknown reason, he felt that my experience as a cartoonist and artist was just what he needed to help him pull this thing off.

Sometimes fate sends an arsonist to change your life, and sometimes it's a bounced check. Earlier that same morning, a client had called to tell me that the check she had sent me for two of my paintings was going to bounce. With that phone call, my rent had vanished. By the end of the second phone call, I was reborn as the vice president of a two-person company, ambitiously christened America's Best Employer, or ABE for short.

A week later, wearing a shiny new blue suit fresh from The Men's Warehouse and a pinching pair of black loafers, I was introducing myself as an expert on an arcane section of employment law that pertains to the use of independent contractors. In record-breaking time, I had gone from a struggling artist to a briefcase-toting, jive-talking, Independent Contractor Compliance Evaluation Expert. I was also collecting a regular paycheck, covered by health insurance, and becoming acquainted with life in the corporate zone.

Over the following years, the artist in me gradually faded away. I began to feel more comfortable with that briefcase in my hand than a paintbrush. My imagination focused more on sales strategies than on the subtle tones in the shadows cast by the afternoon sun. I had a steady salary and a mortgage, and I could actually pay it. The transformation from shaggy artist to buttoned-down exec having been achieved, I lived comfortably within the illusion that this new-found security was permanent. Little did I realize that a perky V.P. of Human Resources and my equally perky wife were on separate tracks to prove that nothing in this life is permanent.

The VP of H.R. had been dispatched to hand me my walking papers by the President of the company, my immediate release from ABE being necessitated by my recent request for a bonus. It was a sudden separation, but well planned, right down to the cardboard box he provided for my personal effects. With six weeks severance pay, unused sick and vacation pay, and a promised commission settlement due, some day, I joined the trickle that would soon become the river of the newly unemployed. Meanwhile, my wife Linda was turning fifty-five, and to make matters worse, she'd found a gray hair. Youth was gone! Her auburn hair would turn to snow, her green eyes would grow pale and dim, and her cute little teeth would soon be falling out. In short, decrepitude lay just ahead. She had begun walking around the house saying things like, "When are we gonna start having some fun around here? All we do is work! I want to live! It's now or never, baby."

Chapter Two

"A man needs a little madness or he never does
cut the rope and be free."

- Zorba

"It's now or never." There's some swagger to that phrase when you're young. But when you realize that your friends now look like the people your parents used to play bridge with, "It's now or never" starts to pack more of a wallop. A sense of urgency sets in. You start to ask yourself, how much time, really, do I have left?

Until the day that I sat down at my computer, punched in my password and discovered I'd been locked out, there'd been no pressing reason to start questioning my odds of survival. But having your password rejected first thing in the morning can send your day off in a whole new direction. After that VP had clarified my situation and deposited me in the parking lot, a little voice inside my head started asking questions like: How much money do we have? How long is that gonna last? What if we sell the house? Would it be enough to retire on? How long will we live? We're pretty healthy; maybe too healthy. What if we outlive our money? I could work part time. *'Welcome to Wal-Mart, can I help you?'*

That voice wouldn't stop. Actually there were two voices battling inside my brain in an internal debate that made me long for a psychic mute button. On one side was a bon-vivant urging me to declare victory, call it retirement, and play for the rest of my days and on the other an insufferable accountant screaming, "It's not enough! You need more. It's not enough! You need more." I don't usually drink before nine-thirty in the morning, but standing there, staring back at my old office, I was sorely tempted.

A few months before, while I was still being paid to come up with gems of Contractor Compliance Evaluation expertise, an idea had begun to grow in my mind. Linda and I could move down to the British Virgin Islands, buy a speedboat and a camera, and zoom around taking pictures of vacationers as they sailed about in chartered sailboats. They'd be so thrilled to have their seafaring adventure memorialized that they would rush to my cool new website as soon as they got home and buy loads of 8x10 glossies. Profits would roll in, more than enough to keep Linda and me in sun-block and rum punch. I had spent hours hunched over my computer, surfing the Internet, researching fast inflatable boats and digital cameras. During weekly sales meetings, I would doodle plans for my new yacht photography website and cover quarterly reports with sketches of fanciful logos depicting a dashing photographer atop a flying fish. But that was doodling and sketching, entirely different than sitting in my car wondering what people do at nine-thirty in the morning on a Thursday when they're unemployed.

Fear, relief, anger, elation, fear, confusion, joy, fear, fear, panic. So passed the first days of my post-employment life. As things calmed down, it became obvious that neither Linda nor I was ready for retirement. Maybe it was the deeply ingrained habit of incessant working. We were like gophers accustomed to digging in our tunnels, never feeling safe on the surface long enough to stop and really take a look around. Whatever it was, we weren't able, weren't ready, weren't willing, to entirely let go. I became determined, however, to take this opportunity, if indeed it was one, to change the way we lived and restructure things to maximize the amount of joy and minimize the degree of stress in the next chapter of our lives.

We had some savings set aside, plus there was that small severance package coming. Our two daughters, Nicole and Krista, were grown and on their own. Linda worked at a real estate office in town and had a deal or two in the pipeline, so we had a little breathing room while I pondered what to do next. One afternoon while I was thus pondering and looking at San Francisco Bay, it came to me. I couldn't wait to tell Linda.

"How about a martini, dear?" I said when she came home from a hard day of placing 'For Sale' signs on people's front lawns.

She looked me up and down. "Love one. What's up?"

"I think I know what I'm gonna do next," I said. "Vodka? Two olives?"

"You're wearing your Hawaiian shirt. Is it that yacht photography thing again?"

"I'm going to call it Paparazzi-H2O. Get it?"

"Cute. Does that mean that you're going to live on an island in the Caribbean?"

"Nope. Don't need to. I'll do it right here. On the Bay." I gave her my most brilliant smile, then stabbed two olives and plopped them into her drink.

"Will it make any money?"

"Tons. I'll build it up, go public, sell it to Microsoft or Nikon for ten million, then we'll go kick it on an island."

"That isn't your first martini, is it."

"Oh, and I think I've found a really cool boat to take the pictures from."

"You're not a photographer."

"It's got a 250 horsepower motor."

"We're gonna need more vodka."

The severance package went for a down payment on a boat, a custom built rigid inflatable boat (RIB) that was ideal for the job. Thirty feet long, it had a welded aluminum hull surrounded by bright blue inflatable tubes that made it look like a big floating bumper car with a 250 horsepower engine. It had a stand-up steering console with a small windshield that kept my glasses from being ripped right off my face when we got up to speed. Since I had to learn to handle it in all conditions, I spent the next month zooming wildly around the Bay and tempting my gainfully employed friends out for midday spins in my new office.

This was all great fun, but Linda had put her finger on a major weakness in my plan: I knew nothing about photography. It rapidly became apparent that this needed to be addressed. I knew how to handle a boat, but when it came time to pull out the camera and aim it, I displayed all the finesse of Woody Allen juggling a Smith and Wesson. I was going to need a professional.

I posted an ad at all the local colleges and art schools asking for anyone who wanted to try their hand at a little action photography. I was inundated. The next few weekends were spent taking prospective photographers out on kamikaze missions to see if they could handle a camera from a slippery perch on the bow of a hot-rod boat as we careened through the hordes of Sunday sailors on San Francisco Bay. Only two prospects lasted a whole day and one did it by giving up on the camera entirely and simply hanging on to the life-lines and shrieking like a lunatic every time a wave crashed over her. Her enthusiasm and delight were astonishing, but she didn't produce any useable pictures. The other survivor was a tough young British ex-pat named Ben Ashe. He was about 32, six feet tall with close-cropped hair, and a very steady hand. He could somehow frame a shot, set the focus and lighting, then hit the shutter at exactly the right moment while the boat under him was banging off wave tops at forty miles per hour. Ben had legs like springs and a completely disjointed body so that his head and hands stayed calm and focused while the rest of him bounced around like a tap dancer on cocaine. He became the yacht photographer. I became the boat driver.

The boat driver was not an unimportant figure in all this. The plan called for us to approach a boat that was sailing along peacefully, show our unsuspecting customers the camera, then race around them and shoot the scene from all angles. That was the easy part. It got delicate when we had to drive up close enough to toss them a little rubber stress-ball with our website address on it so they could find their pictures and buy them. All this had to be accomplished while they continued sailing and without ramming and sinking them.

As a business plan, it was dead simple and that's what I liked about it. It called for us to work only weekends during the peak sailing season, about seven or eight months a year. I had one boat, one camera, one computer and one part-time photographer. The markup on the pictures was stupendous, and my customers would love them. If the numbers worked out, I'd cover my costs and, if Linda sold a house or two, together we'd make just enough to allow us to keep the roof over our heads. This wasn't my ultimate vision of retirement but it was fun, so we were moving in the right direction.

The day finally came when Ben and I launched our business onto the bay. We'd practiced shooting and tossing the ball with a friend who had a sailboat, but this time we were going to try it on total strangers and ask for their money. It was a hazy Saturday morning in late March and we were standing at the steering console with the big, fuel-injected engine idling behind us. Covered from head to toe in foul weather gear including gloves and rubber boots, we were still shivering from the chill and the anticipation. Across the Bay, the Golden Gate Bridge glowed red from the sun that was still low on the horizon. Through the thinning mist, we could see a few boats creeping out from Sausalito and Tiburon, just beginning to raise their sails in the shifting breeze. We could just make out their crews, dressed in bright yellow jumpsuits and hats, scurrying around the decks, never suspecting that they were being watched and evaluated by a pair of eager entrepreneurs.

Ben pointed to a pretty blue sailboat with all her sails up that was catching a little wind about a thousand yards away and said, "How about them?"

Pushing the throttle forward I hollered, "Hold on." The engine barked and roared and the boat reared up and shot us forward as if we'd been launched from a slingshot.

Someone on the sailboat noticed this apparition bearing down on them like a hungry cheetah and raised the alarm. All heads turned toward us and froze in attitudes that said, "What the hell?" When we were about fifty yards off, Ben clawed his way forward, raised the camera and pointed it at them. That's all it took. Everyone aboard started posing, smiling, and waving. The captain ran around trimming his sails and cleaning up his decks for his photo shoot. I circled behind them then pulled on ahead and stopped then let them sail past us with Ben all the while shooting pictures. When we were done, we came along side and prepared to toss the ball. "Where can we get copies of those pictures?" called the crew.

"The website is on the ball. They'll be up there on Monday morning," I yelled as Ben tossed the ball into their cockpit and we pulled away.

"Well, I'd say that went pretty well, wouldn't you?" I said to Ben as he came back and dried off the camera.

"Yeah. Wanna try another one?" he asked. I looked out toward the San Francisco skyline and saw that at least fifty more boats had come onto the bay, sailing in all directions.

"That one. Right there." I pointed at a boat a hundred yards off, hit the throttle, and off we roared.

We shot twenty-four boats that day and the same the next. We'd shoot until noon, take a break to eat lunch and warm up a little, then head back out. By the end of the day, we were wet, hungry and tired, but good tired. Sunday evening, I went over all the shots we'd taken, did a little Photoshop tweaking and straightening, and then sent the photos up to the website. Monday morning, the orders started appearing via email. It was working! All that first week, I'd eagerly open up my email box and count the orders. They just kept coming. Money was flowing in the right direction again and I was thrilled. It wasn't much, mind you, but it was enough to feel good about the project.

The next Saturday, Ben and I were on the water by ten. By early afternoon, we began to notice people standing up and waving us over. We were definitely on to something. The wind picked up as the day progressed and the shots became more exciting and dramatic. It also became more grueling. The more wind, the more chop and waves to crash through and the smaller and more fragile our little boat felt. Our legs and arms ached from the constant motion and the cold. But it was exhilarating.

We kept at it, and in only a couple of months, I had a new business. In addition to all the yacht portraits, our shots graced the pages and covers of local sailing magazines like *Bay and Delta Yachtsman* and *Latitude 38*. We covered races, greeted cruise ships, and documented the Tall Ship celebrations. We started working weekdays shooting special yacht portraits and covering the kiddy regattas at yacht clubs. I expanded the line of products to include coffee mugs, calendars, t-shirts, and greeting cards. I offered a line of custom-embroidered boating wear. And still we went out each weekend and photographed boats on the fly. In a few months, I was making a small profit, and working seven days a week again.

In July we got a full page article, with pictures, in the New York Times, and suddenly I was getting inquiries from people who wanted to know if they could buy in somehow: a franchise, a partnership, or even an outright purchase. It was heady stuff.

By October I had been out on San Francisco Bay almost daily for eight months. The Bay is a challenging place at any time, but pounding through it in an open thirty-foot boat in fair weather and foul can be downright nasty. I felt as battered as the boat. And with winter coming on, a couple of those buy-out offers were beginning to look attractive.

Visions of lounging on a white-sand beach, sporting a perpetual tan and walking barefoot in the warm tropical surf started to haunt me again. I played CD's of Caribbean music to help me endure the hours I spent at the computer, sorting pictures. I wore loud tropical shirts and switched my evening drink from whiskey to rum. I thought the palm tree hints I was dropping were pretty obvious so I was surprised one day to find, taped to the bathroom mirror, a page from the "Boats For Sale" section of the local sailing magazine, *Latitude 38*. Circled in a strangely familiar fire-engine red lipstick, was an advertisement for *Baby*, a barge...in France.

Chapter Three

"What, me worry?"

- Alfred E. Neuman

I suspected my darling wife right away. Taping things to the bathroom mirror was something she had taken to doing with some frequency lately. It started out as little Post-It notes on the refrigerator saying we were out of eggs or parsley. But somehow this had transitioned to such communiques as "Are we too old to adopt this Russian orphan?" or "Let's sell our home and go live on a barge in France."

This particular classified ad had the added impact of a photograph of *Baby*, a forty-five-foot Luxemotor barge, showing her nestled against a wooded shore on a very peaceful looking stretch of water, presumably near some vineyard or other. I don't know if it was the serenity of the scene or the fact that this thing did not have an outboard motor that attracted me, but I paused long enough to notice the phrase, "for more photos, go to *www.Babyforsale.com.*"

I spent the next two hours going through pictures of *Baby*, clicking on them for enlargements, and composing an email to her owner. Nothing too eager, of course, but something detached and professional, asking if there were any large holes in the hull. Next,

I tracked down the authors of a couple of books on the subject of barge travel in Europe and from them I learned that there were two fundamentally different approaches to shopping for a boat in France. I had been attracted to the idea of barging by the pictures of *Baby*, which was a converted former Dutch milk barge. I liked her rugged lines that spoke of long years of hard work on the water and a colorful, even romantic past. I also came across other classic examples of working barges that had been turned into private cruisers with names like Luxemotor, Tjalk, Clipper Aak, Ijssel Aak and Peniche. All these converted barges were unique with layouts and mechanical specifications that reflected the ideas, and the pocketbooks of their owners.

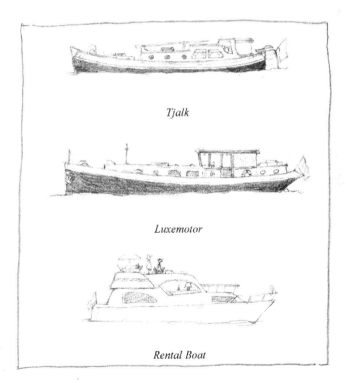

Tjalk

Luxemotor

Rental Boat

The opposite was true of the modern river cruisers, mostly built in Holland, that were pretty standard from boat to boat. They had lines typical of most power cruisers you could see cruising on salt water or fresh. All you really needed to know was the length and the year you were looking for to go shopping. I was definitely drawn to the perhaps less practical, but more intriguing converted barges. Armed with all this wisdom, I began to scour the websites of three barge brokers in the South of France. By the end of the day, the authors were sending me signed copies of their books and three boat brokers were compiling lists of available boats in my price range.

I had a price range.

I was still there that evening when Linda came home and found me deep in a Google search for maps of the major canal routes through France to the Mediterranean.

"You found it," she said.

"What? Oh, that ad taped to the mirror?"

"Uh-huh."

"Was that you?"

"So, what's a barge?"

"We're going to France in two weeks to find out." I clicked on a picture of *Baby* surrounded by swans. "That's called a Luxemotor. See the shape of the back end?"

"I can't go!" Her face dropped. "I've got a deal closing."

"Good. We'll need the money." I replied.

In that one afternoon I had chucked the palm-tree-beach-bum vision and hatched a new, much more civilized plan. It was elegantly simple. In the mid-summer and winter, we'd stay in California where I'd dash around the bay taking pictures of sailboats and Linda would sell lots of multi-million dollar houses. We'd spend the spring and fall on our barge in France, traveling the waterways of Gaul in comfort and gastronomic style at a leisurely three knots, in temperatures between 72 and 88 degrees Fahrenheit. If it were hot, we would meander north, navigating the locks to the shady hills of Burgundy. In the cooler months, we'd join the crowds lounging in the Med. When friends came to visit we would take them out to the little bistros we'd discovered, where the proprietors, who considered us like family, would laugh with us over the latest gossip in French, then offer us special bottles of wine and assiettes of delicate cheeses. Our happily married daughters would bring their husbands for brief stays aboard the boat and promise to have grandchildren soon so that they too could experience the richness of European culture. We'd cruise in stately comfort through picturesque little villages, renowned for their wines. We'd spend weeks exploring gentle rivers like the Rhone, the Saone, and the Seine. Paris! The Seine goes right through it! We could go to Paris!

Of course, normal people don't just decide one day to do something as potentially disastrous as buying an old, converted milk-barge six thousand miles from home. But sometimes, fantasy begins to look more like opportunity, if you're willing to entertain a little risk. So I put on my most adult face and sternly reminded Linda, "Now, I'm just going to look at these boats. Looking is only looking. Nobody says we have to buy anything."

"Right," she said. "Of course."

"Do you want your martini now?" I asked.

"No thanks. I brought home a bottle of wine." She batted her eyelashes. "It's French."

The time to leave for France was fast approaching and my optimistic fantasies were being intruded upon by ever-increasing dope-slaps of reality. Linda and I had agreed that we were not suddenly looking to say *au revoir* to our family and friends. We were not going to cut and run from our lives in California. My mother had done that when I was a kid. One day she'd announced that she'd had enough of picking up after five brawling kids, especially since she had really only wanted two in the first place, and the rest had all been dad's doing. She then moved to Mexico, only returning two weeks a year to renew her visa. It left us all feeling abandoned and generally pissed off. Linda and I were not about to do that to our two daughters. We had to make sure they understood that we were trying to expand the entire familys' horizons; our plans would always include them.

Linda took on the job of reassuring our girls with a phone call. "Hello? Hello? Pick up if you're there." (Pause). "Okay, well, it's your mother calling. I just wanted to let you know that your father and I have decided to start living our lives to the fullest.

Life's a banquet and we've decided to gorge ourselves. This means that we'll be dipping into our savings and probably spending most of your inheritance, but you shouldn't worry because – Oh, you're there."

"Well, yes," she continued. "You did have an inheritance, a small one, for a while I guess." (Another pause). "Yes dear, but we'll be needing it now." (She listens). "Well, the mortgage, food, clothing, a barge in France – France. Yes, dear, it's in Europe."

I could see that Linda had the situation well in hand so I turned my attention to someone very dear to us whose approval was equally critical to the whole project. She had come to live with us recently and had quickly become a key member of the family. I had to convince her that going to France would be a good idea and I knew French bread was the key. I began by toasting her a slice and feeding it to her in little warm bites. She wagged her tail and barked for more and I said, "There's more where that came from. Does Sarah wanna go to France, where they let dogs in the restaurants?" The technique seemed to be working but the true test would come if we did buy a boat and she actually had to fly all the way to France. Sarah was an Irish Setter and at 75 pounds, she was much too big to have a seat on the plane. She'd have to ride in a crate in the cargo hold. She didn't know about that part yet, but I figured I could get her to go along if I upped the ante with a little pate or brie.

The barge books I'd purchased online soon arrived and, although they were exciting, they offered glimpses into the serious nature of owning one of these large iron boats. The older barges, like *Baby*, were retired commercial vessels that had been converted to private use as houseboats or vacations cruisers. Each conversion was unique. Some were fully thought out, professional jobs with top of the line systems for power, water and navigation, and others had been done by well intentioned dreamers in old barns by the river.

The authors would recount their in-depth research into barge specifications, sizes, builders, engines, and systems of all sorts. They would discuss the barge handling classes they had attended and the numerous summer vacations they had spent on rental boats. They traveled through Holland, Belgium and France, searching for the perfect boat that met all their exacting criteria. And then once they'd found it, they would sent it to a boat yard to be torn entirely apart.

I thought I'd dispense with all that and proceed in my usual impulsive manner. I already knew the essential truth about the whole business: no boat I have ever owned, or have ever known anyone else to own, was trouble free. That's Rule Number One of boat ownership. One just accepts it going in. After purchasing a few boats in my life, I had gotten pretty good, I thought, at spotting tell tail signs of weakness, finding oil and fuel leaks, checking electrical connections and insulation, and separating the bells from the whistles. Once on board a potential purchase, I could give it a pretty thorough going over and spot most of the trouble signs. For my trip to France, I planned to take a flashlight, knife, screwdriver, small hammer, and other helpful tools. I told myself I would not be shy about taking up floorboards, testing valves, banging on pipes or probing dark, filthy holes in the bilges in my search for weakness or bargaining points. I'd insist on a professional survey, in English, if possible. But a rule's a rule.

While we're talking about rules, Rule Number Two in boat owning is that the cost of fixing anything increases in direct proportion to the degree of difficulty in reaching the problem. For example, something on the deck in plain sight is a degree of difficulty of One. A leak in a tank that is welded into a space underneath and behind the oak paneling in the main salon is a Ten. Anything on a boat in France when you live in San Francisco is a Fifteen. These add up to Rule Number Three: There is no rational reason to buy a boat. Unless you're a tugboat captain or you must fish for food, a boat is a toy. It is, at bottom, an emotional decision that you make when you clap eyes on *the* boat. The one that is just too beautiful to resist. Once that has happened, your sober determination not to make another damn foolish decision goes right out the window. In other words, in the grip of Rule Number Three, you forget Rules Number One and Two.

In early October, I boarded an Air France flight to Paris. I had my knife and hammer safely packed in the checked luggage and a large manila envelope of boat pictures and spec sheets on my lap. My mind kept flipping from excitement to anxiety, with brief stopovers in visions of warm afternoons moored along a canal by a vineyard in Burgundy. I've been around a few boats, I told myself. I'll just check these barges out and if they aren't right, I won't buy anything.

Then I smiled and looked out the window, oblivious to the raucous laughter coming from the gods who wrote Rule Number Three.

Chapter Four

*"If you are lucky enough to have lived in Paris as a young man,
then wherever you go for the rest of your life it stays with you,
for Paris is a moveable feast."*
- Ernest Hemingway

The sun was setting by the time I checked into my room at Chez Holiday Inn on Rue de Lyon in Paris. I was jet lagged and tired but desperate to stretch my legs, so I went down to the street to wander around. The glass doors at the Holiday Inn slid open and the city poured in. Contrary to just about every movie depiction of Paris, the true sounds of the city aren't accordions playing *La Vie en Rose*. Rather the broad tree-lined boulevards and quaint side streets reverberate with whining scooters, thundering motorcycles, small honking cars, tinkling bicycle bells, and bleating police claxons, all clog dancing over a background buzz of people talking a mile a minute. The pace is manic. Engines of all sizes impatiently rev at stop-lights while pedestrians, dressed in black with nine-foot-long scarves, leap off curbs with the assurance of trapeze artists who know they'll always be caught by their lover and greeted with a kiss on each cheek.

I made it twenty feet to the first sidewalk cafe and ordered an espresso. A waiter jogged by and took my order on the fly, then returned *tout suite* and slid the tiny cup and saucer under my nose. Then he dropped his little plastic change tray featuring an ad for Pastis, slipped the bill under it, and ran off like his apron was on fire. I love this place.

The sky had darkened to a deep topaz blue and it was getting cold by the time I found myself leaning on the stone parapet at Pont de Sully and looking down at the Seine. To my right was the Ile St. Louis and beyond that lay the Ile de la Cite and the flying buttresses of Notre Dame bathed in light from below. The Seine churned and split at the tip of Ille St. Louis and the amber streetlights reflected in the water created a necklace of waltzing stars around the island. My eyes followed the current as it rolled under my feet and on toward the glowing heart of the city. The bridge would take me across to Notre Dame, so I headed for it.

Stars were appearing in the sky above the city as I trudged toward the bronze plaque in front of Notre Dame that proclaimed it the official "Point Zero" of Paris. The wind from the north blew cold and raised a chop on the river that slapped against the stone quay. I wrapped my scarf tight around my neck and zipped my jacket under my chin as I walked along the riverbank that I had first explored thirty-five years before.

It was the late sixties and I had joined the wandering herds of starry-eyed college students who invaded Europe each summer, looking for adventure and hoping for romance. We clustered along the roads and highways at the outskirts of all the major cities with our thumbs out, clutching cardboard signs with, "Paris S.V.P." or "Istanbul" or "Spain" scrawled in pencil.

At the tender age of twenty, after hitch-hiking two days from Amsterdam, I had found myself standing on the Pont Neuf, looking down the Seine toward the Louvre. My art history professor had begun and ended each class by showing slides of works by artists like DaVinci, Michelangelo, David, and Vermeer. Now I realized that those masterpieces were hanging just a few blocks away. Catching the revolving beacon on the tip of the Eiffel Tower as it swept the sky, my eye followed its sweep until it pointed to the slender spire of St. Chapelle peeking above the Conciergerie at the center of the Ile de la Cite. I'd heard that it held stained glass windows from the 13th century that were said to be the most beautiful stained glass windows in the world. I looked across the river toward the Right Bank and imagined the meringue candy towers of Sacre Coeur at Montmartre, where artists hung out and showed their works for sale on the streets. I'll go there tomorrow, I thought.

I hoisted my pack and continued across Pont Neuf to Quai des Grands Augustins and turned left walking under the trees toward Notre Dame. Perched precariously on the rampart over the river, the book sellers' stands were locked up tight, like miniature boxcars along a river siding. All along the left bank, Paris seemed to glow in a rich, golden light. People were moving everywhere, parading past the brightly lit cafes and restaurants. Couples walked past and around me, talking, touching shoulders, holding hands.

Beautiful, neo-classical buildings lined the street, their elaborate wrought iron balconies dripping red and white geraniums. On the top floors, the mansard rooflines were interrupted by tall windows. Artists' lofts, I told myself.

This wasn't a city like any I'd known. It wasn't a haphazard sprawl of wood and brick, of concrete, steel and glass. I didn't see a gas station or a drive-in burger joint anywhere. As I looked, it came to me that Paris was built of stone, but it wasn't hard and cold. Masons and sculptors had softened it, curved and shaped it over centuries. They had decorated it with statues of lounging nudes, laughing and scowling gargoyles, prancing horses and graceful fountains. When the dust had settled, the Parisians had stepped in and added flowers, trees, lights, street musicians, used-book sellers, pastry shops, and beautiful women dressed in fashions that accentuated their charm. Then they installed sidewalk cafés every fifty feet so they could sit and admire their work and congratulate one another.

Together, over the centuries, Parisians had created a city that is a work of art. Not untouchable art to be placed on a wall or a pedestal, but art to be lived in, accessible to all who walked its streets. I'd finally found a place where art was essential. Here, everything from the lamp-posts to the Louvre, revealed an artist's heart. It was the first time I could believe that being an artist was worthwhile, and that caring about art, just for the joy it gave, was good enough.

Thirty-five years later, I now gazed at this same beauty, carefully maintained and protected from the worst impulses of the past four decades. I was struck by the thought that I was perhaps returning, not only to the place, but to the joy I had glimpsed as a twenty year old, with not much more than my health, a hundred and fifty bucks in travelers checks, and a lifetime ahead of me.

All this emotion was making me thirsty so, after a moment of silence, gazing up at the twin towers of Notre Dame, I reversed my course and headed for the Atellier Charonne just off the Place de la Bastille where I knew I could get a chilled glass of Chablis and maybe even hear a little Manouche jazz. As I was crossing the Place de la Bastille, I happened to look back toward the Seine and I noticed something odd. There were trees lining what looked like a park that stretched from the Place all the way to the river. I went over to take a look and I couldn't believe my eyes.

Laid out below me was a yacht harbor. It did indeed stretch all the way to the Seine, where a pair of lock doors stood guard over the exit to the river. It looked about 400 yards long and was lined with at least a hundred boats and barges of all sizes.
I had discovered the Arsenal, the Port de Plaisance de Paris. In English, that's the yacht harbor in the middle of town.

Every trip to Paris in the past had found me walking the riverbanks for hours at a time. I had gazed longingly at the barges moored along the riverside, peeked into their windows at night, and paced them off for size, but I'd never noticed the lock just above the Pont Sully. I never suspected that a whole community of floating barge and boat homes was just off the river in a lock-protected estuary, in the very heart of Paris. Damn! I thought. We could really do it. We could bring a barge up here from Burgundy. We could live in Paris.

The air was thick with a misty rain the next morning when I arrived in Dijon after the two-hour TGV bullet train from Paris. I had the names and addresses of three boat brokers on the Soane River in the little town of St. Jean de Losne, also known as The Barge Capitol of France. I'd been corresponding with them via email and was expected, so I hopped into a rental Peugeot and headed south. The Luxemotor Club, where *Baby* was waiting, was at the top of my list, followed by Bourgogne Marine and a place simply known as H2O. Since hatching the bright idea of buying a barge, Linda and I had not only done research on the internet, but had also had conversations with the authors of those books on barging, as well as with some friends of friends who had first-hand experience living on, cruising, and even running a bed and breakfast barge on the canals of Burgundy. We hadn't dug up much on the Luxemotor Club or Bourgogne Marine, but everybody seemed to have something to say about H2O. And these impressions were uniform enough to put me on my guard. H2O was the biggest operation in the area and had a lot of boats for sale, but their name was accompanied by warnings like "Do your homework," "Take pictures of everything," and "Be careful." Good advice for anyone about to wade into "boat broker world."

The first thing you see when you drive into St. Jean de Losne is the Port de Plaisance, which is dominated by H2O. Giant yellow flags emblazoned with the company's logo, were flying at the head of each pier. These brought back memories of the colorful plastic flags my father would string across the used car lot he owned when I was a kid. I remember the feeling of excitement as he and my grandfather would get out the boxes filled with what seemed like miles of red, white and blue plastic flags to string above the cars as if the circus had come to town. They'd even throw in a clown, and hot dogs for the kiddies while my grandfather walked around in coveralls, wiping his hands on a greasy rag and playing the role of The Honest Mechanic. In the middle of the car lot was the office with an old-fashioned, wraparound porch where the salesmen sat like hungry lions in two-toned shoes, waiting for the rabbits to poke their heads up. I recalled sitting there too, just eight years old, on the top step of that porch, with the cream of the C. W. Hammond and Sons, Fine Used Cars sales team, lounging behind me in a row of rocking chairs. There was Leg-Bone Louie, Raincoat Wilson, and an ex-jockey they called Kong, all smoking cigars and sizing up the customers wandering around, kicking tires and peering into the windows. Pretty soon, Raincoat's eyes would fix on some innocent young family and he'd lick his lips and say, "Gents, that nice little couple over there's got my money in their pockets. I'm gonna go get it," and he'd push up from the rocking chair, cock his fedora, walk down to the clown for a balloon, and then stroll over to make the kill.

As I parked the rented Peugeot on the dirt road in front of H2O's office, I looked around for any signs of clowns or rocking chairs. Finding none, I took a deep breath, climbed the rickety staircase to the door, and pushed my way in.

I had an appointment with Robert Bond, one of the owners of place. A few days before, I had emailed him from Sausalito to tell him when I'd be arriving. He replied that they would have the croissants and coffee hot and ready for my arrival. What I found was a small hairy dog playing dead in the middle of the floor. At a desk in the corner slouched a very large man, deep in concentration, a pencil clutched in his fist, his tongue darting in and out of his mouth.

My entrance had not been subtle, considering that the door had almost come off in my hands, but there was no greeting from man or beast. When someone breaks a door down, he usually gets noticed, but that was no watchdog asleep on the floor and the man at the desk was totally absorbed in the task of drawing small circles on a piece of paper.

He lifted his pencil and cocked his head to admire his artwork just as a mop of curly brown hair with a woman under it clomped up the stairs and puffed into the room. She noticed me right away and while hastily fastening the top two buttons on her blouse, asked who I was and what I wanted. I turned from the fellow at the desk, gave my name to the woman, and told her that I had an appointment with Bond to look at boats. To which she replied, "Monsieur Bond is not here. He is gone to Argentina."

"Argentina? He said he'd have croissants waiting. And coffee!"

"Yes, yes, Argentina." She looked out the window in the direction of Argentina.

"But I have an appointment with him. To look at boats!"

"Yes, well, perhaps Charles will help you? He is the partner with monsieur Bond."

In the course of my stateside investigations, I had learned that H2O was owned by partners, an Englishman and a German.

The descriptions of the two had been consistent: the Englishman was feckless and the German was, I'll just say, difficult. I had therefore planned to keep my dealings with the Englishman. But the feckless slacker, had fled the country, so I steeled myself for "difficult." I told the woman that I would be overjoyed to work with Charles and asked if he was available.

"Charles," she said, turning to the doodler, "can you show this gentleman some boats this afternoon?"

Charles rocked back in his chair, fixed his eyes on me and licked his lips. Just like Raincoat Wilson.

Chapter Five

*"The day after tomorrow is the third day
of the rest of your life."*

- George Carlin

"You want to see boats, huh?" Charles said, and draped one leg over the arm of his chair. "What kind of boats?"

"Barges."

"Barges?" he said. "Barges? I don't have to show you no stinking barges."

"Ha. That's good."

"The Americans seem to like it." He lit a cigarette. "The French don't get it at all."

"So can I see some?"

"How do I know you are not wasting my time?"

"Is that from a movie too?" I asked.

"No. It's a real question. I'm very busy here."

"I came here from San Francisco, in California?"

"Okay," he replied with a shrug then fished a piece of tobacco off the tip of his tongue. When he stood up he was at least 6'5", lean, with close-cropped jagged gray hair, squinting, marble-black eyes and tall man's stoop that gave him all the appeal of a giant vulture. I showed him the spec sheets on the boats that I had arranged to see with Bond. "I'd like to start with these," I said.

He took them in a hand the size of a skillet and scanned them from left to right, using his dagger-like nose as a pointer. "These three are here," he finally said. "This one is in Normandy, and this one is gone. The owner got drunk last night and took it up river. You don't want that one anyway." He sauntered over to a couple of sagging armchairs in the front of the office, fell into one and continued to stare at the remaining spec sheets.

I lowered myself into a cracked vinyl chair and picked at the stuffing while he rubbed his chin and made faces at the papers. Slowly we sank lower and lower into our slippery chairs, until I noticed that his knees had come level with his ears.

"Look," he finally said, "these three boats are just out in the harbor there. You can take the keys and go look at them yourself. I am going to lunch. Leave the keys downstairs in the store when you're done." This sounded good to me so I set off to look at boats. The dog hadn't moved.

The first boat on my list was a converted Dutch Tjalk that measured sixty-eight feet. Tjalks were originally designed as North Sea sailing vessels. They're flat bottomed, their bows are round and bulbous instead of sharp and pointy like most boats, and their rudders hang off the back like barn doors on a hinge. I found this one tied at the end of a pier just down from H2O's office, and climbed aboard. This was the first time I had actually set foot on one of these boats and I was surprised at how big it seemed. Standing at the helm at the rear, I was also struck by how much I couldn't see. With a boxlike steel cabin plopped on its deck, the boat had all the grace and glamour of a giant floating shoebox. Unlike the boats that I was accustomed to, which relied on their sleek lines to slip through the waves driven by only by the force of the wind, here was something that pushed its way through the water by brute force.

Inside, the cabin was devoid of furniture, built-in settees or bunks, so I had the impression that I'd walked into a vacant apartment. The paneling looked like it had been bought at a Home Depot fire sale and installed by my uncle Matt, who lost three fingers in five years to home improvement projects. The engine compartment was a dank hole from which emanated the acrid smell of stale oil, bilge, and perhaps a dead rodent or two. Poking into the darkness with my flashlight, I noted the neglected condition of the visible wiring, couplings, seals, and valves. This was no princess, but I took a few pictures to show to Linda, and then fled the poor wreck.

The next up was a Luxemotor of 62 feet by 13 feet. Like Tjalks, the Luxemotors are a Dutch design, but they bear no resemblance to each other. Luxemotors have a fine, sharp bow that drops straight into the water like the blade of an axe. The deck is high in the front and swoops down and up again in the rear to a raised pilothouse and behind that, a rounded fantail extends over the water. Sitting at the end of another of the company's piers, this boat looked much like an out of work oil tanker, with a massive steel superstructure sitting on top of the rather elegant black hull.

At least the cabin did have some furniture, including a broken canvas chair and a bright pink foam futon so crushed in the middle that it rocked on the floor like a smiling happy-face without the eyes. On the counter in the kitchen I found a couple of binders of information covering the boat and its systems, including meticulous records of services, installations and repairs, which showed that at least it had once had an owner who cared. I took a few pictures and left. About forty feet down the dock, I turned to look at her again and realized I was looking at about the ugliest boat I'd ever seen.

Somewhat more subdued than when I started, I went looking for the third and last boat offered by H2O. This one was listed as a 56 foot Dutch Tjalk, built in 1925 and loaded with "charm." From the outside it looked alright. In fact it had an almost graceful set of lines. Despite the piles of dead leaves and muddy badger footprints, I could tell that the paintwork was in pretty good shape. It had real brass portholes instead of aluminum windows from a motor home. Scattered around the deck and cabin were intricate oak carvings that were, in fact, charming. To get into this one, I had to unzip a thick canvas awning that enclosed the back of the boat. I now found myself standing in a real marine cockpit with teak grates on the floor and a well-used ship's wheel attached to an old-fashioned varnished binnacle. Hanging above all this was a brass bell with the boat's name, *Phaedra*, engraved around its base. Two large stained glass windows filled the bulkhead separating the cockpit from the main salon. To the left of the windows, a set of oak-paneled double doors and an elaborately carved oak hatch formed the entryway. An iron skeleton key turned smoothly in the brass lock and the doors swung open. As I stepped inside, I caught the familiar smell of varnished wood.

Phaedra's floors were solid polished teak and her walls and ceiling were mahogany. A built-in settee, upholstered in thick floral brocade, was flanked by a varnished mahogany bookcase, set off by a brass clock and barometer set. A key hung on a hook next to them, so I fit it to the clock and wound it. The clock started ticking. I walked through a tidy kitchen and into a large open area lined with built-in bunks and hanging closets. The end of this dormitory marked the forward end of the main cabin. A low passageway continued under the deck so, dropping to my hands and knees I crawled through and found myself in a fairly good-sized room that seemed to be a combination sleeping area and storeroom.

I spent about an hour poking around and could find nothing much to complain about except the sleeping arrangements. The bunks were well constructed and finished, but I knew that Linda would want separate sleeping cabins for when Nicole and Krista came over. But that, in the scheme of things would be a minor issue. The boat seemed to be remarkably sound structurally. The engine room was spotless, the hydraulic installations for the steering and bow thruster were surgically clean, and the bilges were bone dry. Hell, they were dusty. I sat down in the main salon to rest and collect my thoughts, the silence broken only by the steady tick-tick-tick of the old brass clock.

That sound took me back to the afternoons I would spend with my father down on the waterfront in Oakland. My dad loved to walk the docks and look for a fisherman or a deck hand who would give him permission to come aboard their boat and look around. "My boy here wants to see your ship, friend," he'd call up to some battered old character high above us mending nets. It wasn't me who wanted to see the ship, but I kept my mouth shut.

If he couldn't find someone to invite him aboard, he'd just say, "They won't mind." Then he'd grab my arm and in a flash we'd be up in the wheelhouse, with him explaining what all the dials and levers were for and how to steer by a compass. The first time I heard a brass ship's clock chiming out its bells, I was afraid because I thought we had set off some kind of alarm, but he said, "No, no, son. That's the time. Four bells. That means it's two o'clock. Four bells is two o'clock. Six bells is three. Eight bells is four and that's when they change the watch."

He used to talk about selling our house and buying an old fishing boat, maybe a purse seiner. Then he'd convert the fish hold into a floating home for us five kids and our mom, who of course would have to be heavily sedated. We'd go bumming up and down the coast, not fishing, just living, maybe hauling groceries to the islands up north. He'd eye the various ships and point out where he'd put in all the bedrooms we'd need. "Plenty of room," he'd say, crossing his arms and nodding his head. I'd cross my arms and nod my head too.

One night he got so excited he dug out his sextant from his days before the used car lot when he tramped the world in the merchant marine. He called me into the backyard and told me he was going to teach me how to navigate by it. He stood there, fiddling with it in the dark, looking through the little eye piece at the neighbors' houses and up at the moon. Then he said, "Too many damn trees and hills. No horizon. Can't get a proper fix like this." So we gave up and climbed up onto the roof and sat there all night, picking out constellations and stars. This kind of stuff ended when his used car lot burned up and my mother left and his world shrank down to figuring out how to feed his kids. He never did get his boat, but I still have the sextant.

The clock struck five bells. Two-thirty. I ran my hand along the brocade cushions and looked up at the sun coming through the stained glass windows. Well, she's no purse seiner, I thought. But she's a damn pretty little boat.

Chapter Six

*"Tell us what you've seen
in far away forgotten lands."*
- The Moody Blues

An hour later it had started raining and I was in my car, following landmarks and road signs out of St. Jean de Losne to a tiny village further up the Saone called St. Symphorian-sur-Saone, the home of Bourgogne Marine. I was on my way to see *Rose*, a fairly new, 60 foot, modern English replica of a Luxemotor. Her mechanical specs had passed muster but the photographs of the interior had given me pause because they suggested the entire thing had been painted the color of tomato soup.

It's only paint, I thought, as I pulled into the muddy boatyard on the edge of the canal and went looking for the proprietor, a Welshman named Roger Walster. *Phaedra* doesn't need paint, was the thought that popped unbidden into my mind.

Bourgogne Marine seemed to be an odd collection of barges crammed together in a small estuary backed up behind the lock that empties the Canal du Rhone au Rhine into the Saone. The rain and the flat, gray light through the bare trees gave the whole place a deserted and disowned look. The stones in the walls and buildings looked particularly hard and cold and the trees seemed to droop lower, mourning the rain instead of standing up to it. I was tired and cold and about to give up when I noticed the silhouette of a man standing on the deck of a 110 foot barge holding an umbrella.

"Bonjour. Oo-ay la Bourgogne Marine?" I yelled, hoping I'd said, "Where is Bourgogne Marine?"

"This is it," the man replied in English.

"Where?"

"Well, right here," he said, spreading his arms over the dripping parking lot of barges.

"Is Roger Walster around?"

"Yes."

"I came from California to see him," I said, wiping the rain from my eyes.

"You found him. I'll make some tea." He turned and disappeared into the barge's wheelhouse. I found a gangplank and climbed onto the deck and followed him into a beautifully finished wheelhouse of varnished oak panels. It was about ten feet square, with windows offering a 360-degree view of the canal, the forests, and an old stone water mill set astride a short creek that ran through the parking lot. The wheelhouse was outfitted with comfortable upholstered settees and chairs. A large polished wheel and impressive control panel made it clear that this was the bridge of a functioning ship. The warmth from a wood stove drew me closer. A small whippet dog, lying by the oak doors that led down to the main salon, got up and escorted me down the ladder into the boat.

Walster was about sixty, just under six feet and shared his body type with Shrek. He had all his hair and a heavy brow that folded over a nose that you often see attached to some fake Groucho glasses. His arms were thick and long and weighted down by a pair of heavy hands. He motioned for me to sit at the dining room table and then he set about arranging a collection of teas for my selection. I chose something green and we sat down to talk.

For more than an hour we sat there talking, drinking tea and petting the dog. He expounded on the width and height of the tunnel at the top of the Canal de Bourgogne, the depth of a certain stretch of the Canal de Midi, and the problem with France's plan to stop the big hotel barges from emptying their effluent directly into the canals.

It was getting dark when we finally came around to *Rose.* She was just down the way he said, smack in the middle of a raft of eight barges moored together at the head of the estuary. The rain was letting up, so, following the whippet, we jumped and climbed from boat to boat until we landed on her deck and let ourselves inside.

We were in a smaller version of Roger's wheelhouse, only without all the lovely details. From there, we stepped down into the main salon, which was clean but oh so tomato-y. A galley with knotty pine cabinets, looked useable, but the rest of the boat was a mess, with rooms too small for a bed next to closets too big for clothes and a toilet only a man could use. A companionway led forward into a huge space filled with anchor chain, an outboard motor, and a workbench. Roger was full of suggestions for moving walls and adding plumbing, but I wasn't listening. I was thinking of the tiny, almost insignificant little changes that could be done to that cute little Tjalk back at H2O to change the dormitory into two private staterooms, which then would make *Phaedra* a perfect boat.

It felt like a week since I had arrived in France to look at boats, but it was only two days. I had found a room in the only inn open at that time of year in St. Jean de Losne. The Auberge de la Marine was a cozy little hotel sitting across the Soane River at the foot of the old stone bridge. From the window of my tiny room, I could see the barges tied along the riverfront of the old town, just below the church. Madame Dominique, the chef in charge, insisted on feeding me like a long-lost son. Her cooking and a carafe of her house Burgundy, had me dead on my feet. I fought off sleep as long as I could because I wanted to sketch some ideas for changing the interior layout in *Phaedra*, but fatigue and jetlag, and just a tiny after dinner cognac, did me in. I was sound asleep by nine o'clock. At 2:47 a.m. I was wide-awake. By three I had my jacket zipped up and was out the door. It was just six in the evening in California, a perfect time to take a walk around a French village and maybe go down to the harbor to see if *Phaedra* was still there. Who knows? Someone might have bought her when I wasn't looking.

St. Jean de Losne was quiet during the day but it was almost surreally silent at three in the morning. I stopped in the middle of the bridge and looked across the river to the sleeping village and the boats and barges tied along the riverfront quay. To my left, a full-sized grain carrier was moored along the bank, empty. A faded gray stripe painted around its deck suggested a well-worn bit of vanity that almost seemed quaint on the scarred and dented ship. I noticed a small car sitting perched on the deck behind the pilothouse, the barge version of a super yacht's helicopter.

The road across the bridge continued straight through town to H2O harbor, but I turned right instead to walk the riverfront. From the road, a series of long stone steps, more like terraces, sloped down to the water where more barges were sleeping, two by two, like old married couples, their noses pointing into the current and their rudders tucked under their backsides as if for warmth. Heavy steel mooring cables drooped from their decks, carving graceful arches toward the thick iron rings, set into the curbstones at street level, some eight feet above. In the warm glow of the street-lamps, I could see that although their hulls were a somber and businesslike black, the barges' pilothouses and living quarters were painted in jelly bean colors: purple walls and chartreuse trim with yellow window sills, red cabin sides with white, gray and pink trim, and bold lettering in green and orange. Anchor windlasses, skiffs, bollards, vent pipes, and doorknobs were outlined and dolled up with pin striping, stars, and elaborate curlicues. I imagined some grizzled old barge hand with a #1 paintbrush in his fist growling, "Not now, Cap'n. Can't you see I'm right in the middle of my interlocking heart and hummingbird frieze?"

I left the lights of the quay at the first road I came to and headed into the village. The stone buildings lining the narrow, winding street were shuttered and dark. There were no streetlights, so I made my way by moonlight. The odd-shaped houses and shops seemed to lean in above me, so I moved to the middle of the street and walked carefully, afraid of twisting an ankle on the slippery cobble stones.

There was more silence than sound. A dog may have barked, but I don't remember it. There were no televisions behind the shutters or tires rolling on the pavement. There was only the rustle of my jacket and the occasional crunching pebble underfoot to alert the stray cats that a bleary-eyed stranger was prowling their village at this absurd hour.

It could have been any year. In this hour of shadows and darkness, the three hundred-year old buildings could have been just built, their shutters freshly painted and tiles newly laid. This could be Hemingway's France or it could beVictor Hugo's. Were those my footsteps echoing off the walls ahead, or were they those of Madame Bovary pursuing her lover? Just around the corner there might be knights in armor waiting on horses with fair maidens serving them flagons of wine. The iron ring embedded in a stone wall had been placed there to hold a flaming torch to light their way. Letting my gaze go wide, blurring details and blending shadows, I felt myself surrounded by the lives that had passed along these cobblestones, under the patterned roof tiles and through the ancient wooden doors now so gouged and battered that they hung from their hand-forged iron hinges by only a lacework of gnarled black oak. To open one would be like breaking a seal on time.

The road opened onto a small square rimmed with benches, trees, and shops, and there, parked up on a narrow curbstone was a small silver Citroen. A car, I thought. Not a knight in armor, but no matter. It's a French car and I'm in France, and just over there's the canal. And that canal leads to Paris.

Chapter Seven

"Dance with the one who brung ya."

- Texas Little

I woke up later that morning with my back against the headboard and my face on the nightstand. I looked at the sketches in my notepad from the night before and saw that I had actually made some limited progress in solving *Phaedra's* only real drawback. The problem was to create two private sleeping compartments where there currently was one big open room. I figured that by putting a new wall athwart ship in the middle of the dormitory, I could split it into two compartments. Then with a second wall, running fore and aft along the right side, I could seal them both off and create a narrow, but useable, hallway for access to both. Add two doors and *voila*, two private staterooms. Linda would love it.

Conceptually, it was pretty simple, but there was still reality to deal with. At this point, I had no actual measurements, no dimensions, and no scale to know if I had room for master king-size beds and a sauna, or a pair of child sized bunk-beds. This called for another visit to *Phaedra,* armed with a tape measure.

But wait. This whole venture had been sparked by an ad for a boat which I hadn't even seen yet. Linda and I had told all our friends that we were going to France to look at barges, then to prove it, we showed them pictures of *Baby*. It was "*Baby* this," and "*Baby* that," on the canals of France. Linda had sent me six thousand miles on a mission to see *Baby*. The other boats were supposed to be filler to add a bit of maturity to the project. *Baby* was still waiting for me at a place called The Luxemotor Club. There I was supposed to find her, declare my love, throw money at her owner and then we'd all go cruising happily ever after. Promising myself that I'd do this thing like an adult, I went downstairs for one of Madame Dominique's hearty petit dejeuners and then called the number I had for a certain Jean Luc, who would take me to *Baby*. He gave me directions to his own converted barge moored in the industrial end of the Canal de Bourgogne, from which he ran his business of fixing, remodeling, running, and occasionally selling barges.

Waiting for me as the Peugeot splashed to a stop in a pothole at the edge of a bustling boatyard was an unmistakable Frenchman with wild dark hair and an impressive set of yellow teeth clamped down on a hand-rolled cigarette. "Jean Luc?" I asked, climbing out of the car.

"Yes, yes. Welcome to France," he said, sounding just like Maurice Chevalier. "You 'ave come to see the *Baby*, yes? She is here, but she is a little sad at this moment," he said gravely.

We made our way across his boat, through a tangle of extension cords, bicycle parts, and assorted machinery to a short ladder that led down to the boat that had launched me on this adventure. *Baby*, moored next to Jean Luc's boat, looked like a poor little orphan. Her colors were right: black hull, red cabin, but they were not quite as bright as they had seemed in my imagination. I recognized the wheelhouse at the aft end of the deck, but somewhere along the line, the sweet romance of her lines had faded. Cords and cables cluttered her decks alongside buckets, boards, boxes, and bicycles whose flat tires and rusted spokes showed evidence of being long forgotten.

Jean Luc jumped down to her deck, produced a key, and opened a hatch that led to the main salon. "Go ahead and look around. I will make us some coffee. She is nice, eh?" Then he disappeared back to his boat and left me peering into the gloom.

Staring down at *Baby's* junky deck, I felt like I was a reluctant groom looking out across a sea of beaming faces, and now, coming down the aisle in her mother's white gown, with the veil, I see my fiancé and high school sweetheart who I've just realized scares the heck out of me. Then suddenly, the door to the church crashes open and Julia Roberts bursts in and yells, "Stop!!" All at once I know: That's the one I love!

By the time Jean Luc had reappeared with the coffee, I knew that my next step in this adventure would be to go back to *Phaedra*, measure everything in sight, and start drawing up plans for a couple of private staterooms. Jean Luc, showing tremendous grace and French civility, leant me his tape measure.

By late afternoon the following day, I was prepared to have a chat with Charles at H2O. Clutching my notebook crammed with sketches, I clumped up the rickety stairs, shoved the door open, and stepped across the dog. Charles was leaning back in his chair at an angle almost parallel to the floor, with his legs splayed out across his desk. He saw me through his eyebrows, grunted, and returned his attention to his fingernails. I walked over to the vinyl sitting area and laid out my drawings on the coffee table and commenced to shuffling them going "hmmm," to myself.

For a while, the only sounds were the snoring of the dog and the shuffling of paper. Eventually, a match struck and I caught the first heavy whiff of Gauloise smoke. "Well?" Charles offered, through a swirling blue cloud. "All this measuring. I wonder what this says?"

"Well, I'm not sure if it will work, or what it will cost, but I have some ideas about a few changes to that little Tjalk," I said. "And if they're possible, I might make you an offer. Want to see?"

Slowly, very slowly, he dragged his legs off his desk and groaned to his feet. He lumbered over and stood above the table, dropping ashes across my drawings. "Hmm, this is interesting. A lot of work here but it might be possible. Who will do this work?"

"I don't know for sure. Jean Luc is supposed to be pretty good at stuff like this. Do you guys do interior work?" I asked in my most off-hand way.

"We do the best work like this," he said, with a small show of energy. "I will call Philippe. He is my nephew, and the chief of the atelier. He will have a look at this," and he punched a number into a cell phone. "So, you want to buy this little *Phaedra*, eh?"

"I might, but it has to fit into my budget."

"Philippe will know. It is cold outside, eh? You want brandy?" Charles bared his teeth in what might have been a smile. I wondered if he filed them or if they were naturally pointed like that.

The brandy shot was about ready for a refill when Philippe and a wall of frigid air crashed through the door together. For a second he just stood there, filling the doorway like the obelisk in the movie *2001*, a cloud of twigs and leaves swirling around his feet. He was even taller than Charles, at least six foot seven. In his early thirties, he was good looking, with blue eyes, and dark hair, solidly built, and dressed in tattered layers of flannel and fleece. He looked like he shared a tailor with Frankenstein. In two strides he was at the table, then he sat down and started pawing through the drawings. There was a lot of head nodding, chin rubbing and finger pointing, accompanied by long streams of German and French.

Two minutes later we were down at the boat and I was explaining to the two Germans how I intended to squeeze two bedrooms and a bath into a space that they filled just by breathing. They crept along behind me, folded over almost double with their arms flapping behind them, seeing nothing much more than the floor. I had figured on this, though, and in a brilliant piece of forethought, had borrowed a roll of masking tape from Madame Dominique. As they stood there with their heads hanging down like a pair of Clydesdales, I laid out my new walls and doors in tape on the floor under their noses, so to speak. Pretty soon, they were getting it. "Ah, I zee," Philippe said. "This is the wall, and the new toilet, it goes here?" and he pointed at a masking tape "X" on the floor.

"Exactly. Toilet paper holder goes here and a shelf for towels just behind." I chose items that would be added close to the ground so they could see them.

"We must put a hole in the hull here for the intake and another for the exhaust," Philippe said.

"Well, I figured we'd do that when we haul it out for the survey," I said. "That is, if I decide to buy it."

"It is getting cold, no?" Charles grunted and rubbed his knees. "I think brandy now. We'll talk, eh?"

"Sure. Let's talk," I said and waited while the two backed out, one at a time, to the main salon where there was enough room for them to turn around.

Back at the brandy bottle, we dialed in a few more details like positions for lights, plugs, switches and cupboards, and then they mumbled to each other in German for a spell. Finally,

Philippe suggested that he would work up a complete estimate for the project and have it for me in a week. "Great," I said. "I'm going up to Paris tomorrow to meet my wife. If your estimate is in the ballpark, I'll bring her down to see the boat. If she likes it, we'll make an offer."

Charles had that look a vulture gets when it hears tires squealing on a country road.

Chapter Eight

"Danger, Will Robinson, Danger."

- Robot B-9, Lost in Space

I met Linda at the Gare de Lyon as she stepped off of the Air France bus from Charles de Gaul. She was at the end of her endurance but gathered enough of a second wind to pepper me with questions. "What happened to *Baby*? Oh, *Phaedra* sounds lovely. Does it really have stained glass windows? In a boat? Sarah says hi and she sends you a lick. What do we do next with *Phaedra*? When do I get to see her? Oh, there's my bag. God, I need coffee."

We had rented a sunny little apartment off Avenue de Segur for two weeks. It had a view of the Eiffel Tower, and a fax machine. I called Charles immediately and gave him the number and told him I'd be checking it regularly. Paris was cold and windy but dry, so Linda and I were able to drink gallons of cognac-laced coffee in outdoor cafes between long strolls through the Louvre and brisk marches up and down the Seine. We went to the Marais for falafels and the Luxembourg gardens for crepes. I took her to the Port de Plaisance and watched the lights sparkle in her eyes as she imagined herself living on the water, in the heart of Paris.

On the fifth day, we arrived back at our apartment and found Philippe's estimate sitting in the fax machine tray. To us, the boat was worth its asking price, but only after all the work was done. So, I subtracted Philippe's estimate for the work from the original asking price of the boat, and sent that number to Charles as my offer for the whole thing. I added a note saying that if he could get his seller to agree on the price, I'd bring Linda down and if she fell in love with *Phaedra*, he'd have a deal. Two days later we were on our way to St. Jean de Losne.

We found *Phaedra*, tied exactly where I left her at the bottom of the ramp on Pontoon B. She was still streaked with black shmutz where piles of leaves had decomposed into a moldy goo, and there were fresh muddy tracks indicating that the badger family was healthy and active. As we made our way through a cold clammy river mist, I looked at Linda. Her eyebrows were revealing. They were all bunched up over her nose.

"Come aboard," I said, and climbed aboard. I shoved a pile of rotting leaves to one side and offered her a hand. I unzipped the awning that enclosed the cockpit and climbed inside. Linda followed and her expression softened as she took in the varnished oak and mahogany. She turned and saw the ornately carved binnacle with the patina'd brass inlays and the ancient black oak ship's wheel. She reached out to touch the two stained glass windows and and her shoulders settled down a bit. Just to the left of the windows stood the pair of paneled oak doors that led into the cabin. I gave the doorknob a gentle turn and they swung open. I stepped aside and let Linda lead the way inside.

The teak floor creaked as we stepped down into the cabin. Linda stood for a few moments and then noticed the barometer and clock, still ticking, on the wall above the small bookcase. I watched her eyes as they took in the richly upholstered settee and the wine rack and then I stood back as she moved forward into the galley with its small stainless steel sink, three-burner stove, refrigerator, and carved oak cabinets with bottle-glass inlaid doors. She took a deep breath and the familiar smell of varnished wood made her smile. "It's a boat," she said.

I led her forward to the big open sleeping area and showed her the tape still on the floor outlining where we'd put new walls to make the bedrooms. She raised her hand and framed the doorway in the air. She could see it. We made our way back to the main salon and I set about ripping up floorboards to show her how nice the bilge was. Linda began to explain how a nice dinner for six could be whipped up in the cozy little kitchen and how she'd set the table with the pretty dishes that she would find in a quaint little flea market in some nearby village.

"So does that mean you want to buy a barge in France and hang out on it five or six months a year?" I asked, laying a floorboard aside.

"No. Let's wait 'til we're seventy."

"Is that a yes?"

Chapter Nine

"Boy, those French: They have a different
word for everything!"

- Steve Martin

"How's it going? Got the bunks torn out yet? Oh, I see...Okay, well, let me know if there's anything I can do." I was back home in Sausalito, chewing the erasers off pencils. We had done the deal and were now the proud owners of a barge in France, one that was being stripped and gutted in a boatyard full of French workers who would either employ exquisite, old-world craftsmanship every step of the way or slap it together with duct tape and thumbtacks and then hide it all with paint. All I could do was call France every half hour to check on their progress. Linda was no help. "Why don't you quit bugging them?" she said when I hung up the phone.

"I'm not bugging them. I'm encouraging them."

"You're bugging me then. Go outside and play."

"There's no one to play with, and it's too early to drink," I said.

"Why don't you learn French?"

"Huh?"

"Quick, say, 'Help, I'm sinking,' in French."

"Can't."

"See? Might come in handy." Then she went off to her office to water her plants and wait for someone to walk in and buy a house.

She had a point. I decided to master the French language. Linda had engaged in the fantasy of becoming fluent in French quite frequently over the years and had accumulated quite a supply of French flash cards, cassettes, and even an eight-track tape of French phrases, all stored in the backs of drawers and under the beds. I resolved to start with the flash cards, settling for the mastery of no less than one hundred new words per day. At the same time, I would listen to nothing but French phrases on cassette tapes during waking hours and then converse in these phrases with anyone I happened upon, particularly Linda.

This, as it turns out, is a less than ideal way to learn French. There are few things as boring as memorizing flash cards. The most interesting thing about the cards is their name. Once that excitement has passed, there is nothing remotely flashy about them. After the first day of flashing, I scaled back my minimum requirement to twenty-five new words a day. I skipped the second day but conscientiously left my stack of twenty-five flashcards prominently on the kitchen counter so as not to overlook them first thing the next morning. A couple of days later, the stack had found its way into the drawer where the keys to the paint shed and coupons for drapery cleaning were kept.

The cassette tapes were more promising. Or they would have been if I had a working cassette player. The technology had obviously progressed since my dear wife had last determined to become bilingual and we had become a CD-only household. A new approach was thus called for. I got on the Internet and did a search for French tutors in the area. A surprising number of people these days had become French tutors it seems. They were not as numerous as Spanish or Chinese tutors, but they were quite well represented. I sent email inquiries to three whose posted offerings seemed to fit my requirements, which boiled down to this: they should charge no more than twenty-five dollars per hour.

The first two were eliminated due to schedule conflicts and an overabundance of what some might be tempted to call "French Attitude." The third tutor, however, seemed delightful. Raised in Paris she was a recent UCLA graduate with a degree in business finance. In line with her major, she had helped to finance her leisure activities while in college by tutoring her professors and had developed a very professional approach to the whole thing. Her schedule was open and the price was right. She even had books and a curriculum figured out. I agreed to meet her the next morning at her apartment for a language assessment and aptitude evaluation.

That evening, I told Linda that I had decided to take my commitment to learning French to the next level. "I've given up on the flashcards, dear," I told her. "But I might still need them if my tutor, assigns them as homework or something."

"Your tutor?"

"Didn't I mention that I had hired a French tutor?"

"No."

"Well, I think I have. I'm going over to her place tomorrow morning to meet her and take an aptitude test."

"Her place? Who is this tutor?"

"Oh, just someone who advertised on Craigslist. She teaches college students and she's going to assess my aptitude and plan my curriculum."

"What's she cost?"

"Twenty-five bucks an hour."

"And she's a college professor? That's pretty cheap."

"Well, she's not exactly a professor. She taught while she was in college. She's out now."

"How old is this tutor, who just got out of college and who I presume is French and whose place you are going to for your assessment?"

"I'm not sure. She sounds old on the phone though."

"What's her name?"

"Lisa."

"What time are we supposed to be there?"

"We? You're coming too?"

"Oh yes."

Lisa's apartment was in an industrial part of San Francisco and she was waiting for us with the door open. Linda kept her composure as the stunning brunette with eyelashes you could tie knots in emerged to give her kisses on both cheeks. We walked down the hall and into the kitchen/dining room where croissants were warming, espresso was brewing, and Charles Aznavour was crooning on the stereo. "I'm so, so happy to meet you both!" Lisa cooed. "I am so excited that you are going to France. You are going to love eet. Oh my god, your earrings, they are *magnifique!*" she said, as she reached over and touched Linda's dangling rhinestones.

I've often thought that my wife would have made a damn fine prosecuting attorney. She can pick you up, spin you around, and turn you inside out before the sugar dissolves in your coffee. By the time I was able to speak, Linda had learned all the particulars: Boyfriend? How long? Serious? How old is he? How much older? What's he do? Ever married? Your degree is in…? Parents? Planning to stay in San Francisco? Any girlfriends hanging around the apartment who are in any way similar to you? I sat and drank coffee and ate the croissants until the inquisition was over and our hour was up. As we walked back to the car, Linda turned and said, "You could have told me she was so drop dead beautiful."

"How could I know that? Besides, she's twenty-three and French," I said. "Of course she's beautiful."

We arranged to study with Lisa two hours a day, three days a week. As a rank beginner I needed this concentrated approach and Linda, well, she had a new determination to learn. Lisa never failed to have croissants warming in the oven when we arrived. We would sit at the kitchen table and she would offer us a selection of espresso roasts that her father sent from Paris. She would then serve the espresso with little chocolates on the side, the way the French do, bless 'em, while I buttered the warm pastries. And once the caffeine, sugar and carbs kicked in, the conversation would begin to flow.

Progress was slow at first but over the next few months, I did begin to learn some French. I learned the present tense of a few verbs, some adjectives and a few simple phrases, which I could retain until called upon to use them. At which point, Lisa would look at me with a confused expression and say, "What?"

It was clear that my accent was the problem. An American trying to learn a French word by seeing it in a book or on a flash card may think he is pronouncing that word correctly because he is making the sounds indicated by the letters in front of him. He will practice the word, learn its meaning and then eagerly use it in a sentence to a French person, quite possibly in Paris, only to have the French person look at him as if he just asked for ice in his Chablis. This can be discouraging.

In most cases, it is not the French person's fault. A perfect example of this confusion happened to me about two weeks into my lessons with Lisa. I was in a French restaurant in San Francisco with my cartoonist friend, Phil Frank. We'd been friends for twenty-five years, ever since the day I had appeared on his doorstep, begging for advice about how to get my comic strip into newspapers. He had two daily comic strips going at once, one that ran exclusively in the San Francisco Chronicle and another that was nationally syndicated, and those were in addition to single panel gags running in magazines all over the country. Phil was a couple of years older than I, with a full head of dark hair, a bushy mustache, and a giggling laugh that would break out suddenly, pushing his shoulders up around his ears.

That day, we had dropped off some of his cartoons at the Chronicle and were walking back to the car when I spied a nice little French café and suggested we stop for lunch. Phil wasn't the lunching type as a rule, but I had been working on him to come to France with me when the boat was finished, and since one of his fears about going was that neither of us spoke the language, I thought a little demonstration of my linguistic skills would be encouraging.

Having worked hard on the present tense of the verbs "to be" and "to want" I felt a tiny bit courageous. I had learned from my flash cards that the word for hungry was "faim" so I rehearsed the sentence, "*Je suis faim*," a few times for Phil. "Juu swee fem," I said to him. "That means, I am hungry."

"If you say that to him, I'm leaving," Phil said.

"Let's have the chicken," I said. "Chicken is poo-lay."

"Do they have anything stronger than wine here?"

"Wine's best," I said and signaled for the waiter.

The waiter arrived, gave us the day's specials, and awaited our order. "Juu swee fem," I pronounced. "Juu tem mon petite poo-lay," I said and looked up at the waiter. A profound silence greeted my effort.

Now, I was making an effort to speak his guy's language, and he could have made a little effort to figure out what I really meant. But when speaking French, you do one little thing wrong and you can end up so far off the mark that, if you're lucky, you'll merely come off as a harmless lunatic.

See, it was clear from my book and my flash cards that the French word for hungry is *faim*. But somehow I missed the part where the French don't pronounce the "m," so, I pronounced it. It came out sounding like *femme*, which, wouldn't you know, is the French word for woman. I had just said to the waiter, "I am a woman."

He could have ignored that and got on with the order, but I babbled on. I had thought that I was saying, "I would love a piece of chicken." What I actually said was, "I love you, my little chicken." This is how misunderstandings begin.

A misunderstanding with a waiter in San Francisco is one thing. Informing a welder in a shipyard in France that I am a woman and he is my little chicken is something entirely different. With this in mind, I redoubled my efforts with the tedious flash cards, paid more attention to Lisa, and bought a computer program that promised to have me speaking French in a matter of hours. I'd soon find out if they worked.

Chapter Ten

"Go Boldly Forth"
- Henry David Thoreau
"Maybe, after Lunch"
- Captain Bob

"You have your ticket and passport?" Linda asked me after we'd already left the house. It was the middle of March and Linda was driving me to the airport bus where I'd meet Phil and together, we'd catch our flight to Paris. I'd convinced him, despite my language skills, to come with me for a fun-filled week in St. Jean de Losne. He'd offer support as I made sure that all repairs had been done to spec, got *Phaedra* outfitted for summer cruising and learned to drive her. I also needed his baggage allowance. As for him, I think his cartoonist's nose for a punch-line was twitching.

Phil and his wife, Sue, were already waiting at the bus shelter. She was fussing at him like he was a kindergartner going off to his first day at school. "Do you have your ticket, Phil?"

"Yes, Sue, it's right here."

"Don't keep your return ticket with your going ticket. You might confuse them and lose it." Sue took the envelope with the tickets and put his "going" ticket in his jacket pocket and the other one she zipped into his carry-on bag.

"Do you know which airline you're going on?" she asked.

"Yes, Sue, Air France. It's easy to remember because we're going to France."

"What time's your flight?"

"One fifty."

"You should be all right then. Don't make any jokes about bombs, Phil."

"No, Sue. I won't."

"Where are you staying when you get to Paris? You're just staying one night in Paris, right?" Sue nodded as she spoke.

"Well, no. We decided to stay the whole week in Paris. Cris has some friend from his gym who's over there." He turned to me. "What's her name?"

"What?" Sue and Linda said in unison.

"He's lying," I said. "Oh, look. Here comes the bus."

The morning sunlight flooded the room when I pushed back the curtains in *Phaedra's* main salon. The ambers and gold's of the brocaded couch glowed beneath floating crystals of dust as red, green, and yellow angels, cast by the stained glass windows, swayed slowly along the mahogany walls of the boat. It had taken Phil and me two long days of travel to get to *Phaedra*, lying cold and dark in the murky waters of the boatyard at St. Jean de Losne. I had rushed aboard so I could check out the new interior that still smelled of fresh wood and varnish. The dormitory was gone and two staterooms and a bathroom now stood in its place. The new walls were painted bright white and the mahogany doors and trim glowed under fresh coats of varnish. The floors were bare plywood and the new built-in bunks had no mattresses, but a quick search turned up a couple of the foam pads and original linens from the old beds, so we claimed our staterooms and slept for ten hours straight.

I could hear Phil, still snoring in his stateroom, as I looked around at my new home in France. It was lovely, this room, with its mahogany bookcases, brass lamps and lace curtains. For the first time I truly believed that Linda and I had done the right thing. There had been doubts, lots of them over the past five months, but standing there on that first morning, I felt warm and content. My chest relaxed and I breathed deeply and easily for the first time in months. The doubts and fears were fading away.

Oh, I knew there would be challenges ahead, lots of them. Learning a new language at my age was not going to be easy, and my early efforts had not been promising. Linda and I would be away from our home, family, and friends for months at a time – far from familiar terrain, treading new ground. In addition, this boat represented a big part of our nest egg and it was floating, precariously, six thousand miles away from home, surrounded by French boat mechanics, electricians and plumbers all smiling and licking their chops. There were plenty of risks, but together Linda and I had decided to stick our necks out one more time and try something just a little crazy, while we still had it in us. Maybe I was being naïve, but right then, I felt that our first steps on this journey had been good ones. I was convinced that we couldn't have found a better boat. *Phaedra* had spirit, and a voice, and at that moment, I thought I heard her saying, "I'll take you to Paris but first, get me out of this damn boatyard."

The next voice I heard was my own, saying, "I need coffee." So I stepped into the galley and in no time I had produced a pretty decent pot of pressed French roasted coffee. Through it all, Phil had not stirred from his stateroom at the front of the boat so I took my cup out onto the cockpit to greet my first morning on my own boat in France.

I pushed open the doors and, rather quickly, some of the magic fled and reality slid in behind.

We were moored in the greasy butt-end of the Canal de Bourgogne, in front of H2O atelier. All avenues of escape to open water were blocked by other barges and boats in varying states of decay or repair. Across the basin was a big barge maintenance yard, owned by Joel Blanquart. Up the way was another barge refit and dredging outfit called The Luxemotor Club, owned by my friend Jean-Luc. On the muddy bank just next to me was a perfect jumble of old engine parts, bicycles, anchors, cables, drums of oily waste, and dying weeds. The sounds in my ears weren't the birds chirping in the vineyards, but rather the rumbling of motors powering compressors and forklifts, punctuated by the piercing screech of electric grinders tearing metal. As I took in the scene, I could feel the dubious eyes of the French waterfront workers upon me.

Just then the doors from the cabin were thrown open and, as if to an imaginary drum roll, out stepped Phil in his signature black silk leopard print pajamas. He had a cup of coffee in one hand and in the other, a small, battery-powered milk whisking gadget made of pink plastic that looked a lot like a very dangerous little sex toy. He pointed it toward the sky, revved it up a couple of times for effect and then said, "Would you like your milk foamy?"

The only sound from the boatyard was that of power tools hitting the ground.

While Phil changed into more sensible clothes, I looked around and decided it was time to start planning our escape from the boatyard and our move over to H2O yacht harbor. This represented a voyage of at least four hundred yards and included traversing our first lock, not an insignificant undertaking for two guys who had yet to figure out how to even start the engine. But that looked to me like the easy part. Between us and the open water ahead, were three 120-foot steel barges in partial stages of destruction or despair. Tied directly behind *Phaedra* was a listing fiberglass number named *Wannabee* that appeared to have become one with the sludge. Two more rusting cargo barges were nestled up next to her. A similar wall of steel loomed in front of us. Short of being airlifted, I didn't know how we would get free without playing hours of Rubic's Cube with 100-ton barges.

Seeing Philippe drive by on a forklift, I ran to flag him down. "Good morning, Philippe," I yelled. "How soon do you think we can move the boat back over to the harbor?"

"It makes no difference. You go when you want to go," he yelled back from his perch atop his forklift.

I looked over at the rusting junkyard of giant barges and said, "Tomorrow?"

"This is fine. We will move you at ten o'clock." He then revved his engine and sped off looking for something heavy to pick up.

Excellent, I thought. I went to tell Phil who was just getting comfortable with his sketchpad and his cup of coffee, with foamy milk. "We're moving tomorrow morning at ten."

"The boat?" he said. "From here? How?"

"I don't know, but Philippe said he'd move us at ten."

"Where are we going?" he asked, ever the practical one.

"Into the boat harbor. Right there." I pointed toward the big parking lot for boats just under the bridge.

"Wow, all the way over there, huh?"

"Hey, we have to go through that lock to get there."

"On second thought, maybe we just oughta stay here. It's not so bad, really."

"Phil, we're going. It's our maiden voyage. You go get provisions, I'm going to find Captain Bob."

"Provisions?"

I had met Captain Bob in November, hanging around the oil heater at H2O chandlery. He was a retired U.S. Navy Captain who lived on his boat with his wife Peggy and their chubby daschund, Twinkles. Whenever I'd go into the shop, there he'd be, warming his hands by the heater and offering advice and opinions on any subject broached in a language he could understand. Standing about five foot seven, he was in his early sixties, he wore a faded baseball hat pulled down low, shading a lumpy, bulbous nose at the end of which rested a pair of wire-rimmed half glasses in their own permanent rut. He had big jug ears that stood straight out from his head and a bushy grey Fu-Manchu mustache. He was constantly on the lookout for peanut butter, which he swore couldn't be bought in France. He prided himself on having compiled over fifty pages of "tips" on St. Jean de Losne alone. Which is pretty amazing when you consider there really was nothing in St. Jean de Losne that actually warranted a "tip."

Since I had never driven a barge before, I thought it might be wise to see if he'd be willing to help us bring *Phaedra* into the harbor. I tracked him down on his boat, *Chapeau*, over on Pontoon

B and banged on the hull. A hatch popped open and he stuck his round little head out. "Hey, you're back," he said.

"Got in last night. We stayed on the boat. It's over at the boat yard ," I said.

"I know. I took it over there last winter. Ready to come back?"

"That's why I'm bothering you. I think we're going to need a little help bringing her around. Never actually driven a barge before."

"Sure. No problem," he chirped. "When do we go?"

"Tomorrow morning," I said, adding, "with the tide." Which was stupid because there is no tide on the canal.

"There is no tide on the canal."

"I know. Just kidding," I said. "About 10 o'clock?"

"See ya then," he said. Then he added, "Can I bring Twinkles? He loves boat rides."

"No problem. See you tomorrow morning. Thanks." Back at the boat, I found Phil making a list of provisions for the trip. "It's all set. Captain Bob'll be here at ten o'clock to get the engine started. It *should* start," I added.

"It does run, doesn't it?" Phil asked.

"Sure."

"You ever seen it run?" he asked.

"No, why?" I said and went to find the corkscrew.

At ten-thirty the next morning we were ready. The temperature was just above freezing and a smart breeze was blowing from the north to keep it interesting. We were a half hour behind schedule already and still sitting here behind a barrier reef of derelict hulks when Philippe strolled up munching on a baguette.

"Hey Philippe, we're all set," I said. "Just waiting for Captain Bob. I don't know what's happened to him."

"It is not a problem. The time is changed. We will go after lunch," he said. "There is a strike at the lock, but only until lunchtime."

"A strike? The lock keepers are on strike?"

"No, the railway workers, I think. But the lock keepers are sympathetic. So they are on strike until lunchtime. There is a boat coming up through the lock this afternoon. He will come through first, then you go down after."

Adopting a French attitude toward life had been near the top of my to-do list, so faced with the overwhelming inertia of the trade unions of France, Phil and I decided there was nothing to do but have more coffee and start thinking about lunch. We wandered off toward Madame Dominique's auberge to get started on three or four courses of the local fare.

Just as we were mopping up the last of the sauce with the last of the bread and shaking the last drops out of a carafe of the local wine, I looked out the window and saw a 120 foot Luxemotor barge, painted a faded red, come tooling down the river and start to make the turn toward the lock entrance. "That must be the boat that's coming in," I said. "We better get back."

Captain Bob arrived at *Phaedra* just minutes after we did. He was fully equipped with life harness, foul weather gear, walkie-talkie, and Twinkles, who had his own life vest, complete with a whistle. He also brought along Jean-Paul who ran the chandlery for H2O and had loads of experience running boats up and down the river. Jean-Paul appeared to be somewhere between a worn and ill forty-five years of age and a youthful seventy. His head was covered from chin to crown with crudely cropped, nicotine-tinged, pewter hair that framed a hatchet-edged nose and bulging red rimmed eyes. He spoke excellent English in a gravelly voice and was never without a cigarette.

He and Bob had driven this boat before so in no time they had all the proper switches thrown, valves opened and the engine cranking over. In the meantime, two of Philippe's dockworkers had untied all the outside barges at once and, while Phil and I stood there as useless as kittens, they began dragging them away in one huge raft. Miraculously, clear water opened up beside us.

With the engine revving and thick clouds of smoke billowing forth, Captain Bob took the controls and cried, "Let's go!"

Phil and I ran forward to untie the bow and push off. The breeze was holding us against the shore, but everyone pitched in and slowly we were shoved clear. By this time we seem to have attracted a large crowd of interested observers on the shore and on boats, wagering, no doubt, on how much damage we'd do before we were safely tied up again. Captain Bob did some fiddling with *Phaedra's* bow thruster. (This is a propeller installed at the front of the boat that pushes it left or right and is my favorite mechanical thing on board.) Bouncing and bumping our way free of the barges ahead and behind, we began to swing toward open water. Not a small amount of paint was exchanged along the way, but no one seemed concerned, except me.

And then, suddenly, we were free! *Phaedra* churned up a small wake as she emerged from the wreckage of the atelier and we floated proudly into the estuary. There we stopped. Our captain ordered us to stand by as he maneuvered us alongside a rusting hulk no more than thirty feet from where we started. At his signal, we tossed our lines onto the other boat to hold us while we waited for the big barge out on the river to come up through the lock.

"This may take some time. *Regardez*," Jean-Paul said and nodded toward the river below the lock.

The red barge was indeed nearing the lock, but it seemed to be coming at it sideways. As I watched, it slowly swung around to the right and then plowed straight into the riverbank, about forty feet from the lock entrance. "Is it supposed to do that?" I asked Jean-Paul.

"No, he has run into the bank. He missed the lock." Jean-Paul was chuckling.

"Does this happen often?" I asked, thinking ahead to my first crack at squeezing *Phaedra* into a lock.

"No, no." He pursed his lips sternly. "I think this captain, he is hurrying too much. He has a lot to learn." Then he shook his head and rolled a spare cigarette.

As we watched, black smoke belched from the red barge's stern and the boat slowly backed away from the bank. She swung her bow around to make another dash for the lock. More smoke emerged as her engine rumbled and growled and a small wave appeared at her bow. She started forward again, this time gaining speed and heading directly toward the stone wall on the other side. The barge's captain jammed it into reverse and gave it full throttle, but too late. With brown water boiling and churning around the back of the boat, she majestically crunched her bow into the chipped and paint-scarred stone wall. A low boom echoed across the estuary as the poor boat half bounced, half dragged herself free and immediately started swinging wildly in the opposite direction.

I was spellbound by this performance but I was even more amazed by the complete indifference shown by three little old ladies who were sitting on a bench under an umbrella on the barge's deck, knitting. I heard Phil say to himself, "Man, old French women can knit through anything."

The bruised and humbled red boat drifted in front of the lock entrance, idling, seemingly collecting her wits and shaking the cobwebs from her head between rounds. Then, as if a bell had rung, a cloud of smoke shot from her stern, and again she moved forward aiming her bow toward the center of the lock. But this time her back end kicked around to a cockeyed angle that spelled failure once again for the boat's captain, and entertainment for the growing audience on the banks. Dark water erupted from under her stern and more black smoke engulfed her pilothouse as the captain furiously threw the boat into reverse. The stern swung around the other way until it was pulling the big boat back toward the river. Gears shifted again, the engine roared, water thrashed and boiled and she moved forward, heading directly toward another collision with the bank, only this time on the opposite side. The old ladies sat unperturbed as her bow disappeared into the overhanging bushes and crunched to a halt.

A very long and painful hour passed before the hapless captain of the red barge finally found himself perfectly aligned and poised to enter the lock. Backwards. At that point, I think I would have just driven off never to return. But this captain was made of stronger stuff. He swallowed his pride, put it into reverse and backed his battered ship in.

It took twenty minutes for the lock to fill and the Luxemotor to rise up to our level on the canal. As the doors began to open, I took a look around and tried to figure our next move. The estuary we were loitering in was maybe 300 yards long and sixty yards wide but it was narrowed considerably by the boatyards and barge maintenance companies that lined the shore. With a 120 foot bumper car about to back through our crowded little estuary, I was beginning to feel like a delicate Dresden tea cup watching a hundred-ton bull about to walk into the shop.

I looked back to our pilothouse to see if Captain Bob and Jean-Paul were showing any signs of panic but they seemed remarkably calm. Bob was sipping from a cup of coffee and Jean-Paul was rolling a cigarette. I turned to Phil and said, "I hope that guy can steer that thing better going backwards than he did going forward."

"Don't most ships handle better in reverse?"

"We'll see. But, if it looks like he's going to ram us, you don't have to throw your body in the way to protect *Phaedra*," I said and laid a hand on his shoulder.

"Actually, I was thinking of going ashore and standing behind that tree over there."

"Here he comes!" shouted Captain Bob. "Look alive up there."

Phil and I ran around the deck trying to look alive as what looked like a giant red supertanker slowly poked her rear end into the estuary. Almost half a football field of battered steel emerged from the lock and just kept on coming, her deck crew of little old ladies looking like Madame LaFarge and her friends, settling in to see what happens next around the village guillotine.

"Untie us and be ready to shove off as soon as she's past," yelled Captain Bob. Phil and I each took charge of a dock line, ready to slip free when he gave us the word. All eyes were on that mountain of red steel moving down the estuary. But she wasn't moving down the center of the estuary. The wind had caught her bow and slowly she was pivoting around so that her front end was heading directly for an abandoned barge that was tied just ahead of *Phaedra*. If her captain didn't get her under control in the next ten seconds, she'd crash right into it. *Phaedra* would be next.

Turns out ten seconds wasn't enough time. The sound of crashing iron and steel reverberated across the basin as the red goliath dragged and bounced her bow along the length of the wreck. Moments before impact with us, a man stepped out of the red boat's pilothouse carrying a big blue rubber fender in his arms, intending, I assumed, to place it between the hulls to cushion the inevitable blow. His sense of urgency, however, seemed no greater than that of the elderly knitters on the foredeck and his blue fender remained cradled in his arms.

We were trapped. We couldn't maneuver out of this spot and there was no way to avoid being slammed into. Still the rubber bumper idea looked like a good one. Phil and I each grabbed one of *Phaedra's* fenders off the deck and prepared to slip them between our hull and the seven-foot wall of red steel that was bearing down on us.

A gust of black exhaust hit us first. Then the churning water boiling around her rudder as the strange backward wake rolled across the twenty feet of water between us. Like a moving iron boxcar, the gigantic fantail slid by, casting a grey shadow over us as the space narrowed.

In seconds the massive barge was on us. I could reach across now and touch cold, grainy steel as it rolled past. My eyes were darting back and forth as I gauged the exact spot where that monster would first hit us so that I could place my rubber fender to take the hit. I'd only get one chance. The gap narrowed to less than a foot, just enough room to slip our fenders in. I swung mine over the side to set it. Just then a voice called out, "Hey, are you Cris?"

"Huh?" I looked up and a grinding crash shuddered my boat.

"You're the guys from San Francisco." It was the crewman on the red boat smiling down at me, still holding his useless big blue fender still in his arms. "I'm Barry," he continued, above the rumbling crash of iron. "I'm from Memphis. Is that your boat? It's nice."

I was pushing frantically against the moving wall of rusting steel. "Say, Barry, could you put your blue fender in there? You know, kinda cut down on the damage here?"

"Good idea." he said. "Hey, how long you been over here?"

"Barry? The fender?"

"Oh, yeah." He wet his lips and slowly lowered his fender into the gap that Phil and I had opened up.

Just then Jean-Paul ran up to tell us that Bob was going to try to use *Phaedra's* bow thruster to push both boats out into the estuary. Our instructions were to put in place as many fenders as possible to minimize the damage, so Phil and I and our new friend Barry pushed and crammed rubber bumpers into any space we could open up. I heard the bow thruster come on and saw the water kick out the side as both boats started slowly to swing into the channel.

"Wow, is that your bow thruster doing that?" Barry asked, looking down from his deck. "I keep telling my wife we should get a bow thruster, but she says you don't need one if you know what you're doing. She wants a washer and dryer. We plan to start our own barge bed and breakfast thing, you know, soon's we get a few things fixed here, like a new washer/dryer." At that point, I wasn't paying any more attention to Barry except to think, Oh my god! They're going to be loose on the canals in that destroyer!

Phaedra's bow thruster was going strong and pushing both barges into the estuary. When there was enough room, Bob quickly reversed the thrust and we were pushed free. Then he put her in gear and, pushing her own little bow wave, *Phaedra* charged toward the lock. I heard applause coming from the shore.

Barry and his red disaster were left safely in our wake, banging their way up the Canal de Bourgogne so I went back to the wheel to watch Captain Bob maneuver us into the lock. The antics of Barry and his red boat from hell had made me realize that this was something that would take some learning. Moving calmly and deliberately, Bob aimed *Phaedra* slightly into the wind and just a little high on the lock entrance. At the last minute, he slowed her so the wind pushed us down and lined us up perfectly, then he hit the throttle again and we slid sweetly in and stopped in the center of the lock. We drifted gently to the edge where Phil and Jean-Paul stepped off the boat and wrapped their lines around the steel bollards set in the stone tying us off. In Captain Bob's hands it looked as simple as putting on socks.

The final leg of our maiden voyage was smooth and peaceful. We floated down in the lock, the doors opened and we eased into the harbor and tied up on Pontoon B. Bob even let me steer part of the way. After he and Jean-Paul left, Phil and I shut everything down and opened a bottle of wine. Phil poured himself a glass then looked at me and said, "You know you're crazy."

"Yes, but I'm committed."

"You oughta be committed," he said into his glass.

"You'll see, Phil. I learned a lot today."

"Yeah, like why there are so many boats for sale around here."

Chapter Eleven

*"How can you expect to govern a country that
has two hundred and forty-six kinds of cheese."*

- Charles de Gaulle

The next day, we took *Phaedra* out on the river for a
training session under Jean-Paul's guidance. It was a short cruise. I
went straight, I turned left, turned right, I stopped, backed up and,
on the way back, I rammed the fuel dock. Phil was having a blast
watching me. As Jean-Paul danced nervously from toe to toe,
dying to grab the wheel, Phil giggled and sketched on the pad he
always had with him.

He'd sketch no matter what was going on around him. In
the middle of a conversation he'd pull out some crumpled piece of
paper covered with tiny writing and cartoon characters. He'd
quickly add a scrawl, smile to himself, then tuck it back away. In
the evening we'd open a bottle of wine and he'd pull out all those
scraps and the two of us would start cracking up, remembering
simple things, like two burly French truck drivers, sucking
lollipops at an outdoor cafe or a large round woman pushing a cart
down a supermarket aisle with a half a baguette sticking out of her
mouth like a giant cigar.

Phil found humor everywhere. Cartooning was in his bones and blood, and he was very good at it. The beauty of his work was that even though he was a tireless perfectionist, his pay off came in smiles and laughter. I'd show up at his house in Sausalito and he'd come out of his studio with an armload of sketches. "Tell me what you think of these, look," he'd say. Then he'd lay the cartoons out on the dining room table and, no matter what my mood when I came in, I'd end up laughing. It was a gift he had, one that made him happy only when it could be shared.

I had once had that gift too, but simply sharing it hadn't been enough for me. The payoff in laughter hadn't paid the rent, so I had let my art go twenty years ago. Now, all these years later, Phil was still sketching and giggling, and I was still searching. Watching him with his sketchpad, happy as a kid, I realized how much I missed being an artist. I had brought my laptop, my cell phone and even a compass to France, but it had never occurred to me to pack my set of oil paints or a drawing pad or even a couple ink pens.

Thursday morning, Phil and I decided it was time to get some serious outfitting and provisioning done. We needed basic kitchen tools, like a toaster oven, frying pan and proper coffee pot and we also needed guy tools, like screwdrivers and wrenches and a hammer. We had a big shopping list in hand so we wanted to get an early start, but leaving the boat during daylight hours was a complicated affair. *Phaedra* was about halfway down the dock, which meant that we had to run a gauntlet of at least thirty boats to get to the parking lot. Most of those boats contained at least one person who had to know where we were going and why were were going there, and would then offer their personal opinions, insights and suggestions on why we should wait and do it tomorrow.

The first obstacle was *Chapeau*, moored no more than four feet from *Phaedra*, with Bob and his wife, Peggy, on guard. Captain Bob fancied himself the unofficial dock master and liked to keep an eye on the happenings and goings-on in the harbor. Peggy was the president and chief social organizer of The River Rats, a group of harbor inhabitants, mostly retired Brits, who gathered for shopping and laundry trips and evening entertainments like bowling, bingo, and the ever popular Game Night. They had their fingers on the pulse of the harbor.

Phil and I made it two feet down the dock when Bob's head popped out of his hatch. "Good morning," he said, then yelled to Peggy, inside the boat, "It's Cris and Phil."

Peggy's head squeezed out next to Bob's and they perched there, looking like two puppies in a box. "Good morning," she said. "Where ya' going?"

"Going to buy a broom and stuff."

"What for?"

"Well, to sweep things up."

"Why? Did ya spill something?"

"No, but…"

"Well, don't go to the Geant market. They're cheaper at Mr. Bricolage," Bob advised. "They were on sale yesterday." Mr. Bricolage was Bob's favorite place. In his book of tips, he had it down for everything from "Best Place for Deals on Space Heaters" to "Best Vending Machine Coffee." He also declared it the "Best Restaurant Outside of Paris" for the buffet chicken dish that came with dumplings.

"No, Bob, that was last week," Peggy corrected him. "Why don't you offer him one of our brooms, Bob? We have that extra one that Annie, on *Compass Rose*, gave us."

Phil was reaching for his pen and sketchpad.

"I gave that one to John and Sue on *Aryana*, Peggy," Bob said and nodded toward the next boat down. "Remember? We traded it for the chipmunk salt shaker you liked."

"Oh, yeah." Peggy smiled. "It's so special." She turned to me, "You want to come in and see it? Bob made me a special shelf for it."

"Love to, but we've gotta…"

I was interrupted by John on *Aryana*, who had just come onto his deck with his morning tea. "Cheers Bob. Cheers Peggy. What's doin?"

"Cris and Phil are going off to buy a broom," Peggy cried excitedly.

"Oh? Hey, Dan, on *Spirit*, said they're on sale at Geant," John said.

"That's just the push brooms, John," Peggy corrected him.

Just then, John's wife, Sue, popped up. "Is someone going to Geant?"

All the way down the dock I could see people emerging from their boats and getting comfortable as they waited their turn to keep us from doing whatever it was we had in mind to do that day. I grabbed Phil by the arm and we started jogging, all the while nodding and shouting merrily, "Hi! Nice day. Gotta go. Oh, hi.."

We pulled into the parking lot of Mr. Bricolage at about 11:30. Captain Bob was right: this was a first class, big-box hardware store. There were pallets of lawn fertilizer stacked in the parking lot next to small garden buildings, and personal tractors lined up by the front doors and displays of gas grills and barbeques framing the entrance. It was like a giant Home Depot with pop muzak.

We found the housewares department first and went straight for the toaster ovens. The best croissants in the world are, of course, to be found in France. But I had decided that to make the best croissants even better, they had to be warmed up in a toaster oven. Although Mr. Bricolage proved that France was well represented in this department, we finally chose a sturdy little German model because it had only two knobs. Into the cart it went.

We needed spatulas, knives, pans, dishes--the works. We quickly filled one cart and grabbed another one as we headed for the hardware and tools section. We found a hammer that looked efficient and a complete set of sockets and wrenches. Next I hit the drill aisle while Phil got a toolbox to put all this stuff in. We met back in the power tool section to examine saber saws and power sanders. We scooped up rolls of tape and wire, pliers and wire cutters, a matt knife, garbage bags and mixing bowls, and were heading for the electrical department when the lights in the store blinked on and off a couple of times.

We paused for a second, wondering what that was all about, but quickly concluded that it was some French power glitch and went on shopping. We were examining extension cords when, out of the corner of my eye, I saw a young man in a blue Mr. Bricolage shirt come running toward us, frantically gesturing and crying loudly, "*Allez, allez! Le magasin est ferme.*"

He was waving his arms so desperately that we grabbed our overflowing carts and trundled after him as he raced toward the front of the store. There we were confronted by three more blue-shirted young men and one large, heavily pierced young woman, all looking decidedly annoyed. I looked around and noticed that we were the only customers in the place and that the tractors, small buildings grills and barbeques from the parking lot were now inside the store next to the exits. Suddenly I understood.

Phil and I had committed an unimaginable transgression. We had violated the Sanctity of Lunch. It was noon, and these good people were supposed to be sitting down to their cigarettes and *jambon parsielle*. We were *merde*. I started to apologize and tried to empty our carts onto the young lady's conveyor belt to check out, but it was too late for that. There would be no check-out for us. It was lunchtime. We must leave. Now. We were barely across the threshold when the metal doors crashed to the ground behind us. We were left standing there, staring at two acres of parking lot, completely empty, except for one small rental Peugeot. Ours.

We decided to use our extra time to take care of a few other errands. We had a lot to learn. We wanted to buy stamps and post cards. There was a post office in a little village we had passed through, but when we got there, it was closed for lunch. Across the street was a pharmacy and next to that, a magazine shop, both were closed, for lunch. We needed gas, but the gas station was closed for lunch. We gave up and went to the market to get something for lunch but it too was closed, for lunch. The boulangerie? Closed. France was closed and was not to be disturbed. The French were eating lunch.

We gave up. We went to lunch. There was a little place by the side of the road that was painted the color of Pepto-Bismol and emblazoned with the name "Auberge Cheval Blanc." The parking lot was packed, which Phil took as a good sign.

The place was full of truckers and road crews, identified by their leather faces and the Day-Glo reflector tape on their trousers. The air was blue with smoke and the walls shook with heavy voices, clinking crockery, and bursts of laughter. Plastic tablecloths were covered with jumbled plates, baskets of bread, ashtrays, coffee cups, and carafes of wine. We stood there for a second taking it in before a husky woman with a cigarette dangling from her mouth rushed up and herded us into a back room. She pushed us down at a table for two and rushed off. Moments later, she was back with a chalkboard that she propped on the table. Then she made it clear that she was out of everything, except something called *Joue de Porc Braisee au Bourgogne*, which she wrote on her order pad. We both bobbed our heads like pigeons and she sped off, yelling towards the kitchen.

"What are we having?" Phil wanted to know.

"I'm not sure, but maybe pig cheeks." Ten minutes later the lady was back with two carafes of the local red and a plate of pates and little pickles.

And so began one of those memorable meals one sometimes finds along the roadside in France. There were two kinds of pate, one a creamy *foie de volaille* laced with pistachios, and the other, a coarse rabbit terrine with small peppercorns that popped when you bit into one. The crusty bread had a soft, almost sweet, airy center and the wine, well, it was just house wine but it was a local house wine, and we were in Burgundy.

After a suitable period of rest to prepare ourselves for the main course, the *patronne* brought out two small, covered, iron pots, and set them before us. With all the flourish she could muster and holding her cigarette well out of the way, she raised both lids simultaneously, said, *"Voila!"* and then scurried off. Each pot held six tiny new potatoes resting in a burgundy sauce so rich and thick that it rose up and over the small chunks of braised meat like a baby's down blanket. *Joue de Porc Braisee au Bourgogne* was indeed pig cheeks, and oh boy, what cheeks they were. I leaned close to take in the delicate aroma of mushrooms and wine then took a first bite. The meat was so tender it barely needed chewing. I took a sip of wine and then paused for a moment to appreciate what had just happened on my tongue.

As I looked around the room at the truckers and construction workers I thought of my working lunches back home. I remembered sitting at my desk in San Francisco, eating a salad out of a plastic carry-out container, drowned in dressing squeezed from a metallic envelope, all the while sending emails to corporate explaining to them how I'd try to make more money for them next month. Here, stores kicked paying customers out at the stroke of twelve so the staff didn't miss a minute of their two-hour lunch. All over France, patisseries, boulangeries, boucheries, hair salons, insurance offices, real estate offices, gas stations, banks, hardware stores, even churches were closed for a two-hour lunch. How did they get anything done? But, on the other hand, with lunches like this, what else could any human do but stop and enjoy it.

Phil was cleaning his pot with the last crust of bread when our dear waitress came by and asked us if we'd like our cheese now. I turned to Phil, "You have room for cheese?"

"Oh yes, and more of the vin rouge, *s'il vous plait*," Phil said, using all his French at one go. She gave him a wink, and walked off.

"Have you noticed," I asked, "that no one here seems to be in much of a hurry about anything except lunch? Sometimes I feel like I'm stepping on the backs of people's shoes around here."

"Yeah, but I thought this whole boat thing was all about slowing down, cutting the stress, feeding the ducks. Eating the ducks." He answered.

"It is. But I still have to get things done. Linda will be here soon and I've gotta drive that boat and her to Paris."

"You know, it takes seven weeks to get there from here."

"Really?"

"Captain Bob told me."

"Christ, we don't have seven weeks!"

"You've got years, guy. Take it in little bites. See what's up the river. Paris will still be there. What's your hurry?"

"We're getting old, man."

"You're not old."

"I don't mean decrepit. But we're getting to that point where anything can happen, at any time. You know, you're talking to a guy one day, great plans, and the next thing you know, poof! Gone. Healthy as a horse, then finished. Totally random."

"So, you think stressing out about getting to Paris in record time is going to improve your odds of not dying?"

"Kinda. Maybe. Well, probably not."

"Anyway, don't you think you oughta learn to drive that thing down here in the country before you go cruising into the middle of Paris."

"You may have a point."

"Take your time," Phil said. "Enjoy the trip, just in case, you know, you don't make it all the way to the end." He looked at me almost as if he knew something he wasn't telling me.

Chapter Twelve

"What barnyard animal gets a sunburn?"

- Trivial Pursuit

For many people, the idea of living in France conjures up visions of starting each day with a trip to the quaint, friendly little local boulangerie on the corner for a nice, buttery, freshly baked croissant to go with your morning coffee. My lessons at Lisa's apartment in San Francisco hadn't taught me much French but they had turned me into a croissant junkie.

So after Phil left, I settled into a morning habit that demonstrated just how far a true addict will go for his fix. I would trudge, bleary-eyed and hunched against the biting morning wind, down the narrow main street of St. Jean de Losne, past the ancient stone façades and shuttered balconies and up a little side street just before the church, to the village's brightly lit bakery. And there I would pause. The windows were always filled with shining trays of gaily-colored cakes and tarts. Tantalizing miniature golden quiches, sat in rows above flaky cinnamon twists and *pain au chocolat.* Beyond, in the warm interior, the glass display case was packed with golden, buttery croissants, puffy brioches, apple and cherry turnovers, and sweet cheese pastries. Behind the counter, standing in racks, were crusty baguettes and loaves with names like *Amourette, Patrissee,* and *Pain du Terroir,* all hot and fresh from the oven.

Artisan Boulangerie

As I stood there, gazing upon this scene of sensual delights, I would be overcome with a feeling of imminent doom. Since arriving in St. Jean de Losne, I had come every morning to this little family-owned boulangerie presided over by *Madame La Pattissier* herself, and had asked her for the same thing: one croissant and one baguette. Did her eyes brighten with recognition when she saw me? Did she smile warmly and say, *"Bonjour, Monsieur Cris. Comment ca va?"* and then reach for her most perfectly formed croissant? Did she call to her husband in the back to bring out the cart of loaves he'd just pulled hot from the oven?

Non! Every morning she looked at me as if I had just run over her cat. The problem was that croissants and baguettes have a sex, a gender, and at that hour of the morning, I could never remember which was which. Normally, I don't concern myself with the gender of pastry, but in this shop it was critical, because I wanted just one baguette and one croissant. There was a female way to say one, which was <u>une</u>. And there was a male way to say it, <u>un</u>. If the gender of the number didn't match the gender of the pastry, in this patisserie you were dead meat. As I struggled to remember my gender agreements, my mouth would go dry and sweat would start to trickle down my back.

If it were later in the day, perhaps *une* versus *un* wouldn't have been such a challenge, but without coffee, I was lost. Plus, the Madame was a nasty piece of work. Facing her each morning with her dough-punching fists planted on her hips, would make my mind go completely blank. But my need for a croissant was overpowering, so I stepped inside.

"Monsieur!" the nightmare barked and jutted out her top chin.

Instantly I forgot the sexual identity of croissants and baguettes. Visual cues suggested that a baguette had to be male. *"Un baguette et une croissant, s'il vous plait,"* I blurted out hopefully, holding up one finger. Instantly it was apparent that I'd got it wrong.

The dragon behind the counter shifted her weight and rolled her eyes. *"Quoi?"*

Oh, Christ. Maybe croissants were male too. *"Un baguette et un croissant? S'il vous plait?"* I begged.

"Quoi?" She was beyond guessing what I might mean even though I've got one finger in the air and the other pointing at the tray of croissants. *"Monsieur?"* she said again impatiently.

"Une baguette et un croissant?" I cried, out of options.

"Oui," she said and pulled out the tray of croissants.

Baguettes are female? That can't be right. Then I noticed that she had grabbed three croissants in her fist and was crushing them into a tiny bag.

"Madame? S'il vous plait," I said meekly. *"Un croissant, s'il vous plait,"* and held up one finger.

This threw her completely off. *"Quoi?"* she stopped with one mangled croissant not quite in the bag.

"One croissant." I said in English and then I held up one finger.

Now, I was in new territory. I was using hand signals. I wanted just one croissant, so I held up one finger. But, in France, when you hold up the index finger, it's either to make a point, or to wag it under someone's nose while saying, *"Non, non, non."* To signal that you want one of something, you hold up your thumb. In America, of course, holding up one thumb means, "Atta boy!" or "Can I have a ride in your car?" or "Up yours!"

I stuck up my thumb. At last, we were communicating.

Back at the boat, I had just popped my rather bruised croissant into the toaster oven when I heard the unmistakable sound of someone tramping across my deck. There was a knock on the door and Jean-Paul's cigarette appeared in the companionway. "Is this still without the power?" he asked.

The night before, all the battery power had gone out in the boat. It wasn't a big deal since the batteries only powered the cabin lights when I wasn't hooked up to shore power. But in this case, I was quite comfortably plugged into the dock, so I had light to read by, refrigeration for the white wine, and my beloved toaster oven for my morning croissant. I'd survive. However, I'd mentioned the problem to Bob, who'd quickly told Jean-Paul, who was devastated by the news and immediately put in a call to the company's electrician, Pierre, at the home of his mistress.

Jean-Paul had bad news. *"Alors, monsieur* Cris, I have call Pierre at his Juliet house, but he has turn off his phone. But maybe I can find something to fix. Maybe a fuse is burn?"

"I checked the only ones I could find and they all seemed okay," I said. "But, I need coffee. Want some coffee?"

"No, no, I will just look for more fuses." I poured some water into the kettle and lit the gas while Jean-Paul opened a small hatch built into the woodwork under the table in the cockpit. He quickly shimmied in up to his waist.

"I think I have find something here." His voice came from under the seat cushions. "I just need a torch. Do you have such a torch?"

"Some place," I said. "I'll have to find it."

"I can't get out," Jean-Paul added.

"What?" I said.

"I am stuck, I think."

"Do you want the torch, or do you want out?"

"Out, please."

I grabbed his legs and began to pull just as Captain Bob showed up.

"What'cha got there?" he asked.

"A Frenchman," I said. "Would you like some coffee?"

"Had mine, thanks. "Hey, Peggy wants to know if you're coming to the River Rats' Quiz Night."

"What kind of quiz?" I asked.

"I don't know but it's really, really fun." He was beaming. "Last time we played Trivial Pursuit and Peggy and I won a bottle of wine."

"Sounds good, count me in."

"I'll tell Peggy," he said. "It's not always Trivial Pursuit, but if it is, you can be on our team."

"It is time to pull me out now please," Jean-Paul piped up.

"What's burning?" Captain Bob asked, sniffing the air.

"Oh damn, my croissant!"

The featured game for Quiz Night was indeed Trivial Pursuit, but not like I had ever played it before. There were five tables, each with four or five people, and each table was a team. Questions were read out by the Official Reader at the head table. Also at the head table were the Official Card Picker and The Referee, whose job it was to settle disputes and punish cheaters.

And there was a lot of cheating going on. People would get up to go to the bathroom and as they walked by, they'd peer over shoulders to cop answers. They had answers from previous games written on cigarette packs that they'd pass around as if we believed they were passing cigarettes. I caught one Australian in the bathroom paging through a pocket encyclopedia. There was nothing very subtle or clever about it all and the guilty were always getting caught. When confronted, they would deny like crazy while their accusers puffed and fumed and stuffed wads of potato chips into their mouths for solace.

The Aussies were probably the biggest con artists per capita, but the Brits took the cake by sheer volume. The French quit early and just sat around drinking wine, so it didn't matter if they cheated. There were only three of us Americans, and none of us cheated, so we lost, but Peggy left a plate of spaghetti on a bench and a British woman from Pontoon A sat on it, which served her right because her team won and they were the biggest cheaters of them all.

Linda and Sarah came into Paris two days later. Poor Sarah and her travel crate weren't allowed on the train to Dijon, so I drove up to Charles de Gaul on Sunday night to meet them at the plane, then the next morning we all drove down together. The A6 is a beautifully maintained motorway that rolls through the thick forests of Fontainbleau and across the River Loing at Nevers. From there the vistas opened up as we made our way toward the rolling hills of northern Burgundy where Linda would point out small, red-roofed villages and farms nestled among the trees in the fields. Vast green pastures spread out before us, sectioned off by ancient stone walls and hedges, that marked the changing colors of the alfalfa, wheat and rape seed fields. Wild forests came to a halt in straight, but haphazard lines marking the boundries for grazing herds of the famous white Charolais cattle. Above it all, the sky was so incredibly clear that I would swear I could see the Alps.

We stayed on the A6 past the junction to Dijon so that we could catch a glimpse of the storybook castle of Chateauneuf, perched on a hilltop overlooking the summit of the Canal de Bourgogne at Vandenesse. Within minutes we were cresting the low mountains that protect the Cote d'Or, heading down toward Beaune nestled at its base. The vines were just starting to show buds, giving the hills an almost dusty green complexion that would be exploding in the weeks to come.

At Beaune we left the motorway and took the back way along the Saone River. Grazing horses, apple and pear orchards, and estuaries alive with swans closed in around us as we neared our floating home in St. Jean de Losne. Linda was bursting with anticipation. My descriptions of *Phaedra's* new interior had done nothing to calm her down.

The car was still moving when Linda opened the door and took off down Pontoon B. By the time Sarah and I caught up with her, she was already inside testing the opening and closing ability of the stateroom doors. She was dancing around touching everything and going, "Oooh, that's nice," and, "We could hang a picture here." Then she went into the galley and moved everything from where I had it to someplace new, so I completely lost track of the corkscrew.

The next morning, I went to the patisserie and really tripped up the old bat by changing my order to a non-gender specific two croissants instead of one. By the time she finally got out of bed, Linda had fresh brewed coffee and a hot croissant waiting for her.

I was pouring her second cup of coffee when she turned to me and said, "So, when do we leave for Paris?"

"Ah, I've been meaning to talk to you about that. I've done a little research and it seems that it takes about seven weeks to get there from here. If all goes well."

"Seven weeks? We don't have seven weeks. We're due back in Sausalito the first of June."

"Dear, we have years," I said, channeling Phil. "I thought we'd do some short cruises around here first, get the hang of it. Then, in the fall, maybe start heading north."

"But we *will* get to Paris eventually, right?"

"I promise."

"Okay, then, is Strasbourg on the way?"

"Strasbourg? You want to go to Strasbourg?"

"If it's on the way."

"I guess it could be. We can get some charts... Might take some time..."

"Honey, we've got years." Now *she* was channeling Phil.

Chapter Thirteen

"Get a bicycle. You will not regret it, if you live."

- Mark Twain

Linda loved being in France. If anything went wrong, she'd just say, "Yeah, but we're in France." It didn't fix the plumbing or breathe life into a dead battery, but she'd usually smile when she said it, so for a moment at least, who cared? This attitude made her hard to resist and she quickly became part of the social life on the dock. She actually enjoyed talking her way through the gauntlet of Pontoon B every morning. And she was really excited to discover that if she missed any gossip on the pontoon, she'd be sure to hear it on Tuesday and Thursday mornings when everyone disappeared into their boats at 9:00 a.m. and tuned their VHS radios to channel 19 to hear some British woman, going by the handle of "River Gal," presiding over a free-for-all talkfest between anyone who had a radio and knew how to use the 'talk' button.

Linda would listen intently as River Gal announced things like, "Sue and John, off *Maria*, on Pontoon A, lost a red and white striped towel in the dryers yesterday," or "Captain Bob says that the Casino supermarket in Tournus has the best price for canned tuna - only thirty cents a tin." She actually took notes.

Linda had been in France two days when she came running down the dock, leaped aboard the boat and said, "Bikes! We need bikes." She'd been out walking Sarah and had seen a small group of people cycling along the river and thought they looked so French, with their baskets full of bread and wine. "We need bikes!"

We went immediately to Captain Bob, who of course had a tip on the subject of buying bicycles. He knew of a second-hand store, a *brocante*, in the next village that was known to have a used bike or two in the back barn. The place was rarely open, but the River Rats had spotters everywhere and the moment that junk man came out of his house and put the "*Ouvert*" sign on his front gate, River Gal would have it on the net.

The first step in buying a used bike in France is to pull out your English/French dictionary and learn the word for bicycle, which turns out to be *bicyclette* if it's a female or *velo* if it's a male. Of course, if you want to just call it a bike, it's *becane* if it's a female, or still *velo* if it's a male, unless of course by 'bike,' you mean motorcycle, in which case it's a *becane* or a *moto*, both of which are female because there are no male motorcycles. It's enough to make you want to take the bus.

Armed with our pocket edition dictionary and repeating phrases such as "I/we would like to buy a male/female bicycle" and "Can I/we take him/her/it for a test ride?" Linda and I boldly set off on foot to buy some wheels. To get to the next village of St.

Usage, we walked past the lock, through Joel Banquart's shipyard and to the place at the end of the pound where the Canal de Bourgogne left St. Jean and headed north in a straight line to Dijon. The plain trees and maples shading the towpath receded in the distance in perfect lines of perspective, the canal a straight mirror of water, fading in the mist. Linda took my hand and said, "I still can't believe we're doing this."

"I think it's a good idea. We need bikes."

"Not that, dummy. This." And she pointed up the canal.

St. Usage was a tiny place and we were soon standing at the gate of an old stone house with an off-kilter tile roof, peeling shutters and a barn emblazoned with a hand painted sign that said "Brocante." We both love antique stores and flea markets, and our mouths were watering at the prospect of rummaging through a dusty old French junk shop, particularly one with a rusting bug-eye Citroen parked in front and a cast iron fountain in the shape of a dancing goat leaning against the wall.

We were still standing on the street taking it all in when the woman of the house emerged from her doorway and started making her way toward the gate.

She was a sturdy *grand-mere* with her grey hair clawed back into a bun. She wore a faded housedress under a full floral printed apron that at some point would have been called frilly. As we watched, she shuffled over to the gate, grabbed the *'Ouvert'* sign and turned it to *'Ferme.'* Then she began dragging the gate closed behind her.

I looked at my watch. It was 11:55! She was closing up for lunch, a lunch that could last for days. This called for some quick thinking. Linda ran up to her and cried, *"Velo! Velo! S'il vous plait. Velo?"*

The old woman ground to a halt and chewed her gums for a few moments while she looked at Linda from under her eyebrows. Then she said in cockney English, "You probably mean *bicyclette*, dearie. Unless you're looking for a bike for him." And she nodded at me. Half an hour later, we were the happy owners of a pair of gently used, gender appropriate bikes, one blue and one black, and a wire egg basket in the shape of a chicken. We were now fully equipped to cycle the countryside and lost no time in doing so.

It was April, and the trees that had only been wraithlike shadows throughout the winter and early spring were suddenly shimmering with color, as if they had been lightly sprayed with millions of tiny budding leaves. Beyond the river, radiant yellow mustard fields formed crazy quilt patterns alongside newly green pastures sprinkled with dandelions and swirling waves of white and blue wild flowers. Fruit trees--cherry, apple, pear, and quince-- peeked over crumbling stone walls, trailing clouds of fat pink and white blossoms to attract the bees. I couldn't help wondering what it would be like to tackle it in oil paints and get it on canvas.

It's a seductive thing, to spend days at a time moving to a no more demanding imperative that one's own body clock. On the boat, we had no television, radio, email or Internet. Our cell phones were turned off. Once a week, we could walk to the tourist office in town to check our email, and the magazine shop near the boulangerie sold the *International Herald Tribune*. Other than that, we had no media input to agitate our minds and fray our nerves. Our anxiety level was sinking and our sense of calm was palpable. We were settling into a routine in the harbor that Sarah saw no reason to change, but we humans had some decisions to make.

Linda's jet lag was fading and we were ready to start living the dream that had brought us to France. Floating serenely along a canal past vineyards and pastures, sipping wine and nibbling on local cheeses was the point of our journey after all, not lazing around Pontoon B. We agree'd that a mad dash to Paris would be far too stressful so we decided to plot an out-and-back cruise that we could easily do in six weeks. All we needed was a destination and some tips on how to get there, so we went looking for the oracle of St. Jean de Losne, Captain Bob.

We found him and Jean-Paul standing around the space heater in H2O store, deep in conversation with a Dutchman on the dire consequences of being caught in France with illegal red diesel fuel in your tanks instead of the regulation white variety. These conversations don't have clear beginnings and endings. You had to merge into them like jumping rope. I waited while they talked about surprise boardings by the gendarmes, spot diesel inspections and big, big fines. When it reached the point where they were all just shaking their heads and shuffling their feet at the injustice of it all, I said, "That sucks. Hey, we're thinking of taking the boat out for a week or two. Any ideas where we should go?"

They looked at each other and the Dutchman smiled broadly and said, "Dole is nice."

Jean-Paul walked over to a display rack of charts and maps, grabbed one and spread it on the counter. "*Oui, oui*, this Dole, it is very beautiful. *Regarde*," he said, then pointed his cigarette at a spot on the chart. Dole was just nine locks up the Canal du Rhone au Rhin, which had its first lock onto the Saone only two and a half miles up river from where we were standing.

Bob handed me a Michelin guide open to a photograph of the city taken from the river. It showed barges and river cruisers moored by a lawn at the foot of a beautiful Renaissance style town. Rising from the center of the town was an immense, white 16th century church and bell tower. The book said Dole was founded in the 11th century and had been a major center of commerce and learning and the medieval capitol of the Comte region until Louis IX, in a fit of pique because he couldn't possess it, burned it to the ground in 1479. It went back and forth in bloody battles between the Dukes of Burgundy and the Hapsburgs until it was finally conquered by Louis XIV and awarded to France in 1678.

The church in the photograph was the Collegiate Church of Notre Dame, built in the 16th century in an early Renaissance style and supposedly containing remarkable interior decoration in wood, polychrome marble and stained glass. The guide listed lots of delicious sounding restaurants, cheese shops, and three open market days a week.

This was exactly what we were looking for. Our first trip together on *Phaedra* would be a real voyage of discovery to a magical city where we could moor in the shadow of a church called Notre Dame. Dole was only a day or two away but beyond that, we could continue along the canal for days or weeks before turning back for home, all of it through new territory. As we looked at the chart we saw villages and towns with descriptions of churches, castles and chateaux all the way through the Jura into Alsace. Some of the town names were familiar, like Besancon and

Colmar, but there were dozens more with Roman ruins or ancient abbeys, waiting for us to discover.

All we had to do was get *Phaedra* up the river in one piece. Jean-Paul had taken me out a couple more times and guided me through some docking and steering maneuvers and I was beginning to get the hang of it, but I hadn't done a lock on my own yet. The advice I got from everyone on Pontoon B was to just go really, *really* slow. Which was fine and I was good at going really slow. But when it came to the first lock off the Saone onto the Canal du Rhone au Rhin, everyone said, "Just make sure you're going really fast or the river will crash you onto the rocks." Apparently, the first lock I would attempt completely on my own was known far and wide as a tough one. It came off the river at a 90-degree angle and the current of the river there tended to sweep barges down onto the stone abutments and lock doors. So I would have to go in fast, then once inside the lock, hit reverse, floor it like hell and hope to stop before hitting the doors at the other end of the lock. If we survived that, we'd have a straightforward run along the Canal du Rhone au Rhin, all the way to Dole.

So, back at the boat, I sat down with my new chart and began studying it as if I were planning a solo voyage around Cape Horn. I was used to charts that showed tides, currents, depths, and prevailing winds. I needed to know if there were any shoals, hidden rocks, or submerged hazards that could rip *Phaedra's* bottom out or cripple her rudder. I looked for the compass-rose showing magnetic north so that I could plot my headings and turning points along the way. I wanted to know of any lights, buoys or markers that would indicate channels or harbor openings. My new chart had none of those things. It was basically two parallel lines, filled with light blue, signifying water, broken by occasional "V's," indicating locks, and numbers, indicating the distances between them. Instead of hazards or shoals, there were icons for patisseries, boucheries, and restaurants along the way. *Vive la France!*

While I was plotting our course, Linda called one of her oldest and best friends who lived just outside London. Gillian and Linda had bonded twenty years before at a wedding reception over vodka, champagne, and a very bad dance band. Since then, no major event had happened to either of them without racking up either hundreds of dollars in phone bills or trans-Atlantic flights. No maiden voyage on *Phaedra* was possible for Linda without Gill, her new husband Nick, and their eight-year-old daughter, Daisy. Daisy, as it happens, was packed and ready, awaiting Linda's call.

Three days later, and two days before Easter, our crackerjack British crew emerged from the train in the dusty and largely deserted train station at St. Jean de Losne. The first one off the train was Daisy, who charged Linda like a one-girl Light Brigade, her baby blue jacket flapping like a cape and brandishing a Barbie in each hand. While Sarah pranced around barking, Linda scooped Daisy up and spun her around and they both screamed enough to wake up the crows. Gill emerged next. A statuesque brunette, she wielded a spicy English wit wrapped in an accent that sounded just like Marry Poppins. She ran over and joined Linda and Daisy in their group hug while I moved forward to help Nick, the designated pack animal. He stood about six-foot-four, rail thin with striking blue eyes and jet-black hair. He had gotten himself wedged in the train door amid a pile of suitcases, backpacks, Barbie paraphernalia and two guitars, and was in danger of being carried off to the next stop if he didn't get free right quick. I pried a guitar loose, which broke the logjam, and, moments later, we were all piled into a taxi on our way to the harbor.

Linda had been cooking all day and the aroma of *coq au vin* greeted us as we all piled in. Nick almost knocked himself out on the doorframe when he stepped into the boat, and had to lie down, while Daisy and Gill got the full tour, with Linda proudly leading the way. She had fixed up a room for Daisy complete with a Pokeman duvet for the bed, which Daisy declared to be "simply smashing."

Whiskey and some aspirin quelled the throbbing in Nick's head and soon we were tucking in to plates of Linda's divine creation, some really good Burgundy and special tarts and cakes from the patisserie for pudding (which is British for dessert.). After dinner, Nick got one of the guitars out and did a little strumming and picking while we talked over the plan for the next day. I was about to give my captain's speech about safety at sea, when Gill interrupted me.

"Oh, Nicky knows all about ships and things, don't you, love?" At which he got a distinctly sheepish look. "His father was the captain of the *Q.E. II*."

"The *Q.E. II*?" I said. "Did you ever go on it?"

"Yes, actually, one or two times."

"So, how's *Phaedra* compare to the *Queen*?"

He rubbed his head and said, "Better headroom for a start."

"You think the headroom's bad? Wait until you try to stretch out in your bunk."

Chapter Fourteen

"She'll never hold, Captain!"
-Scotty, Chief Engineer,
Starship Enterprise

We were finally doing it. We were on our own boat, cruising under our own power up the Saone River, heading for a canal, just like we had planned. I don't want to say I was terrified, very nervous would be a better description. As we set off, I gripped the wheel and listened for noises indicating that the engine was about to blow up or the propeller had fallen off. Gill and Nick were good crew, asking where they should stand or what to hold on to. Daisy was sending me into fits of panic by running around the boat and dangling over the side hoping to see a fish. Linda finally corralled her and sat with her up front and counted ducks. All this in the first five minutes.

Our first stop was the fuel barge, just outside the harbor, where we topped up the tanks. Amazingly I managed to do this without ramming the dock or losing any crew. From there, we pushed off and headed up river, looking for the doors leading to the first lock of the Canal du Rhone au Rhin.

The Saone was wide and flowing easily against us. There was a light mist floating on the river in the bright springtime sun. Like a cottony rainbow, it swirled and fled before us as we passed under the stone bridge, the water splashing and echoing against the arch that seemed almost too low for us to pass. At the southern end of the bridge I saw the Auberge de la Marine where I had first stayed. I wondered if Madame Dominique might be looking out her window and recognize us on our first trip out. I waved just in case.

As we emerged from the shadow of the bridge, Linda touched my arm and pointed back at the sun reflecting off the medieval church at St. Jean de Losne, looking more brilliant than I ever remembered it to be. With clear river ahead, I pushed the throttle down and listened as the rumble of the engine rose a full octave to where it sounded comfortable, and the water gurgling down the side took on a shade more urgency. The speed felt good, so I leveled it off and pretty soon St. Jean de Losne fell astern and we were into more open country. Wheat fields and green pastures, sectioned off by impenetrable briar hedges and crumbling stone walls, spread out from the banks of the river until they were stopped by dense forests or manicured gardens surrounding storybook chateaux. A small group of horses that had stopped their breakfast to watch us pass were quickly given names by Daisy: Sasha, Buttercup, Prince, and Eleanor.

We were looking for a small village just before the entrance to the canal. St. Symphorien was just a couple of buildings on the road and a few homes backed up against the river, but when we saw it, we knew the lock would be just ahead. Once through that lock, we would have taken our first baby step onto a canal system that had been in operation in France since 1642. It had been conceived and had prospered as a purely commercial enterprise, providing a water-born highway system that when linked with the country's major rivers, allowed the transit of goods all over the country, from the English channel to the Mediterranean and into Germany, Belgium and Holland. There are over four thousand miles of canals in France alone.

The navigable rivers and canals of France

The locks were the key to the whole thing. By using the power of the water to literally float fully laden barges in steps over mountains and around rapids, commerce could suddenly flow throughout the country at record speeds. The basic principles of the lock system haven't changed since Leonardo DaVinci refined the Chinese concept in 1490. It's quite simple really. A barge floats in one end of a box and the doors close behind it. The box is flooded and the barge rises with the water. When it's full, the doors at the other end open, and the barge sails on its way, having just gained altitude. Our first lock of the day would lift us nine and a half feet from the Soane River onto the Canal du Rhone au Rhin. By the time we reached Dole, we would have risen a whopping sixty-four feet.

What has evolved however, is a certain uniformity of size of the locks. In 1879, the French Minister of Public Works, one Charles Louis de Saulces de Freycinet, determined that a single standard size needed to be established for the canals and the locks so that builders would know with confidence that their barges would be able to travel freely throughout the system. He came up with the Freycinet Standard that survives today. So now, the vast majority of the locks on the canals in France are 148.5 feet long and 16.5 feet wide. Not surprisingly, most of the major commercial barges built since then were 16 feet wide and127 feet long (leaving just enough room for the doors to open inward at the upstream end). I've seen some of these things going through the locks and there is barely enough room to put your foot between the wall of the lock and the side of the barge. Not that you'd want to.

To us, the most important measurement of the Freycinet standard is the width, 16.5 feet. We had to fit through it. *Phaedra* is 11.5 feet wide. If I could maneuver her from the river smack into the middle of the lock, I'd have two feet of clearance on either side. With *Phaedra* weighing in at twenty-three tons, two feet didn't seem like much.

Linda and Daisy were the first to see the lock looming on the right as we slowly progressed up the river. There was heavy foliage along the bank and tall trees shaded a path that ran beside the water. The greenery was suddenly broken by a weather streaked stone wall, that rose from the water and embraced a pair of giant dark steel-framed doors. It looked much like the maintenance port on an Imperial Death Star. The doors were closed but we could just make out the form of a man, presumably the lock keeper, perched on a catwalk on top of one of the doors. He saw us and carefully began to pick his way toward an ancient mechanism planted in the ground at the side of the lock.

Since the doors were closed, we continued past the lock for about a hundred yards, then turned the boat to circle past again. As *Phaedra* came across the flow of the river, I could feel her being drawn down and realized why Bob had called this a tough lock. To get into it, I'd have to calculate the drift of the river across the mouth of the lock, aim the boat above the doors and accelerate toward the wall. If I did it right, I'd be driving toward the stone wall while the river pushed me down toward the lock opening. Just at the last minute, everything would line up, I'd floor it, and we'd slip in unharmed. If I did it wrong, I'd accelerate into something very, very solid. I had two feet to play with.

There are no brakes on a boat. If things started to go bad, I would have to try to slow *Phaedra* down by putting it in neutral or reverse. This, of course, would throw the boat pretty much out of control and then the best I could hope for would be that the river would sweep me past the stone walls and into the foliage and trees on the river bank. As I contemplated the outcome, I circled again and on the third time around, the doors had opened.

I decided to make my approach from down river. Going against the current would give me a little more control than being swept along by it. My intrepid crew gathered around the steering station for a little pep talk and some standard docking instructions. I explained that I'd be trying to get in there without hitting the walls or the doors and, if it looked like we were gonna crash, they should brace themselves and hold on. I also reminded them not to get between the boat and the walls. At twenty-six tons, it'll squash you like a bug. Nodding in understanding, Nick went up to the bow while Gill took Daisy into the cabin to play with her Barbies. Linda and Sarah stayed with me so that she could tell the story later.

We came slowly up the river until the opening to the lock was just about even with the back of the boat, where I was standing at the helm. This put the bow about 50 feet past the opening. I spun the wheel hard to the right, which kicked the stern out into the river and began to bring us broadside to its current. The current hit the bow and began to sweep us around. I pushed the accelerator hard and *Phaedra* drove forward toward the upstream wall. Nick was standing at the bow to let me know how close I was getting. He looked back at me and made a face resembling Eduard Munch's *"The Scream,"* then dove for cover behind the anchor windlass.

We were heading straight for the stone wall upstream from the open doors. I was certain we were going to plow right into it, when suddenly I remembered I had a bow thruster. At the last second, I pushed the joystick for the little thruster and the bow jumped to the right. I hit the accelerator and we drove through the doors into the lock. I kept the power on and the helm hard over until the stern was out of the pull of the river and then I straightened out and hit reverse, hard...Piece of cake.

And then, *Phaedra* was in, without a scratch. We floated serenely to a stop in the middle of the lock, under the bemused gaze of the man standing on the ledge, nine feet above us. He lit a cigarette and waited for someone to throw him a rope. Linda and Nick were a bit stunned to find themselves unharmed and the boat in one piece, so it took them a moment to remember that there were further steps involved, but eventually Nick grabbed a mooring line and tossed it up. The lock keeper wrapped it around a bollard and dropped it back down, then went to close the lock doors behind us.

Linda, having closely studied her Barging in France books, scrambled up the slippery iron ladder that was set into the stone wall with her dock line clenched firmly in her teeth. She found the nearest bollard and tied us off. Placed at regular intervals along the edge of the lock, steel bollards ensure that your boat won't get smashed to bits when the lock keeper starts flooding the lock. The turbulence that this can create can toss a boat around like a tennis shoe in a dryer and it's impossible to hold without a good stout bollard for support. With all our lines secure and snug, the lock valves opened, water poured in and *Phaedra* started to rise.

Tied along the banks of the canal were dozens of brightly colored barges from all over Europe. People who were working on their boats, trimming their flower boxes, hanging out laundry, walking along the canal, or just chatting with friends, stopped to watch *Phaedra* as she slowly presented herself to the Canal du Rhone au Rhine for the first time. A few people strolled over to chat. Others just smiled and went back about their business. It all seemed so calm and normal to be floating on a canal in France in our own boat with our friends. The serenity of the scene almost made me forget the magnificence of the moment.

But Linda is not one to take these things calmly. She felt an overwhelming sense of greatness welling up in her and she had to do something extraordinary to mark the occasion. She decided to tip the lock keeper.

Abandoning her rope, she dashed into the cabin to find her purse and emerged moments later with a five euro note in her hand. Then she ran off to tip the lock keeper. She caught up with her target, who was standing by the lock house and, after expounding exuberantly in words and gestures of an international nature, she pressed the five spot into his hand. He looked at it with some amazement and in French, graciously told her that he really couldn't accept it, but thank you very much. Then he turned to leave. Linda's joy was not so easily thwarted as this, so she caught up to him and insisted that he take it. Again he demurred, but the third time, her persistence paid off and he gave in. Thanking her profusely, he pocketed the money, then walked over to a nice looking woman sitting on a bicycle with a small child perched in a seat on the back. He picked up his bike and the three of them continued on their morning ride into San Symphorien sur Saone, with no idea why that crazy woman had forced him to take five euros.

The real lock keeper watched this drama while leaning on his control panel, marveling no doubt at the extravagance of the Americans.

The rest of our voyage on to Dole was the sort of adventure that Indiana Jones would have slept right through. It was a one-day run and the boat performed beautifully. The weather was perfect, the locks were easy, and the company was warm and happy. At the second lock, La Tuilerie, we passed a stone mill that still grinds flour by water power. The pastures and fields opened up around us. Linda pointed out a cream colored 18th century chateau with tall slate roofs and soaring turrets nestled in a stand of trees across a field where a small herd of horses grazed. The little village of Abergement-la-Ronce was reputed to have a baker renowned for his bread, so we stopped and drove stakes in the ground to tie off while Gill and Nick walked into the village and got a couple of his famous *Pain de Fountain* for our lunch. Cruising along at a speed not much faster than a determined walk, we passed through small villages and along pastures carpeted with cowslips and dandelions where horses and ponies grazed and watched us pass. The locks closed at 12:30, so we pulled to the side of the canal under a tree and had a proper French lunch of fresh bread, quiche, salad, cheese, and cookies for pudding. Afterward, Linda and Gill put the bikes onto the towpath and rode on ahead to alert the lock keepers that Nick and Daisy and I were on our way.

Each cruise has its moment of panic and ours to Dole had one too. A little before lunch, Nick came out of the cabin with a look of concern and announced that there was water flowing over the floor in the forward stateroom. I stifled a scream and dashed forward to see if we were indeed sinking. When I got there, I found a substantial puddle forming on the floor around the new toilet and sink. Dollar signs started dancing in my head, alongside visions of us all sitting on the side of the canal gazing upon *Phaedra's* radio antenna, the only visible part of her still above water.

After admonishing all to remain calm, I went to work frantically tearing out floorboards and wall panels to get at the leak before we all drowned. I quickly found it. No point in going into too much detail here, so to make it simple, the people at H2O who installed the sink had used the wrong size hose for the drain. Instead of finding the correct size they had simply put a clamp on it and tried to squeeze it into shape. The leak wasn't any danger to the boat, just a mess to clean up. It did, however, give an indication of things to come.

We left the canal just below Dole where the lock ushered us onto the beautiful, gently flowing River Doubs. From this point on, we'd be following a course alternating between canal and river. Our first cruise on the Doubs was a short one, lasting for only fifteen hundred yards before we reached the lock of Jardin-Philippe, our final lock of the day. Beneath the magnificent Notre-Dame basilica rising high above a cascading array of tile-roofed stone houses from the Middle Ages, we found pontoon moorings along a grassy park.

Phaedra's bow thruster swung us easily across the canal and we nudged up against the pontoon as gently as an autumn leaf landing on the grass. Nick jumped off the boat with his mooring line and tied us securely to the dock. We were home for the night. Our first need was electricity to heat the water for showers, so I grabbed the shore power cord and trotted off to find something to plug it into. I trotted for a while and well before I found a plug, I ran out of cord. This is the second reason you have to have a bike on a boat: to ride to the nearest hardware store to buy more extension cords. I found a Mr. Bricolage about two miles away and bought about 150 feet of cord. I was back at the boat in time to enjoy a glass of wine and the appreciative glow of two beautiful ladies who were going to have hot showers that night.

Our first day of cruising was drawing to a perfect end. While Linda and Daisy clattered around in the galley wearing pink rabbit ears and coloring Easter eggs, and Nick sat tuning his guitar, I settled on the deck and rested my feet. As I sat there, tossing bread to a couple of friendly swans, and sipping a chilled Burgundy and munching on bits of an aged Comte cheese and fresh walnuts, the picture that had started it all, of *Baby* moored along a canal in France, came to my mind. I realized that we were living that picture now.

Sitting on the bow looking back at *Phaedra* resting peacefully at her mooring in this wonderful city in France, I was amazed at how at peace I felt. Maybe I should have been worried. I was still technically unemployed, we'd just blown a huge hole in our life savings and I had no real idea what would happen tomorrow. But none of that bothered me. I wasn't worried. I was astonished. When Linda taped that picture to the bathroom mirror, she wasn't just saying, "Let's take a vacation." She was suggesting that we upend our lives and take a risk, loosen our seatbelts and hang our heads out the window for a while and see if it's really more fun out there. And we did it. That was astonishing.

Notre Dame at Dole, from the boat

The next morning was Easter and we woke up to two inches of snow. Linda and Gill snuck out and hid eggs all around the lawn and bushes in the park next to the boat, followed closely by Daisy who had them all in her basket before they even knew she was there. Then all three flopped down and made snow angels while Nick took pictures. Next came the snowball fight and the snowman after which we all went back inside for a bracing English breakfast of fried slice, bangers, eggs, tomatoes, and crumpets, prepared by the Brits.

After breakfast we went to explore the town. The snow was an unexpected surprise that turned an already lovely little city into something from a fairy tale. Daisy led the way, looking for unicorns. The Michelin Guide had given us the highlights of the city, but it didn't prepare us for its narrow, winding 15th and 16th century cobblestone streets climbing the hill from the port. Stone houses with their own turrets and coats-of-arms over their doorways lined the little side streets clustered around the church of Notre Dame. Half-timbered buildings leaned at odd and comic angles over our heads as the melting snow rained down from shuttered windowsills and sagging wooden planter boxes. The bells from the basilica rang once, then two more times at a measured, rather somber pace before suddenly erupting with a wild cacophony of bell ringing that flew through the town, cutting loose a glorious noise for what seemed like five or ten minutes. Easter mass was about to start.

We walked on past ground floor shops, cafes and restaurants, all shut tight but holding promise for the next day which was market day at the square in front of the church. Gill and Daisy had promised to make us all a special tart full of fresh fruit if they could find them. Linda had some serious cheese shopping to do. She was hoping to find some of the famous morbier cheese that the Jura was famous for. At a square halfway up the hill we discovered an outdoor café that was open so we called a halt and sat in the hazy sun and warmed ourselves with coffee and hot chocolates. A moment later, the waitress brought a bowl of water and a cookie for Sarah. It was at least an hour before we were ready to move again, slowly at first but then picking up speed as our stomachs began reminding us that it was getting near lunchtime.

The next two days passed quickly and too soon their long weekend was nearing its end. It came time for Gill, Daisy and Nick to get back to England. We said goodbye to them at the train station in Dole, with Daisy crying and Linda trying hard not to. We were sad to see them go, but later, at a café on the square, sadness turned to exhilaration when we realized that for the first time, Linda and I were actually completely on our own with our boat, our dog and our very limited language skills. There was no Phil, or H2O, or River Rats, no friends for support, encouragement or emergency rescue. Linda turned to me and said, "Well, dear, here we are. What do you want to do now?"

"Eat."

"No. Shall we go back to St. Jean or keep going up the canal? See what's up there?"

"If we go back, we can be back with the River Rats in a day."

"Sitting safely in the harbor watching our butts grow."

"Exactly. Or, we could head up the river like Colonel Fawcett of the Amazon. We could go out for maybe four weeks, then turn around and push back in two and be back in time to make the plane home."

"I love it," she said. "Let's go."

By mid-morning the next day, we had untied, unplugged, and headed off into new territory. Our books and charts had said that the Rhone au Rhin was pleasant up to Dole, but when it blended with the River Doubs it became spectacular. They didn't lie. Leaving the pond at Dole, the first lock was just a couple hundred yards off. Going through this lock, we were lifted into a tunnel-like canopy of plane trees that were reflected in the glass-still water ahead of us. On the right were green pastures where horses grazed in front of a rose colored chateau trimmed with white stone and nestled into the green hills beyond. On our left, vine-covered stone walls broken by ornate wrought iron gates and topped with crumbling red tiles, bordered the stately homes along the canal.

We moved very slowly and took our time those first weeks on our own. We'd stop every day for lunch somewhere along the bank or find a small park or lawn in a village where we could drive our stakes in for a while. Each morning I'd get on the bike and set off to find the nearest patisserie to get our morning croissants and bread for the day. We'd explore the little villages or small towns where we stopped for the night and occasionally find a restaurant or auberge that was worth sticking around another day for. Some days it just felt good to hike around the area or read all afternoon, so we'd linger where we were.

We spent a lot of time on the River Doubs. The flow of the river is controlled by periodic dams or weirs, so most of the time, it moves at a gentle pace. Boats can't go over the weirs, of course, so they're funneled off the river into the canal. The canal will mosey along, sometimes right through the middle of a village or under an arched bridge of ancient stone and brick, until it comes to the lock. Once through the lock, we're back onto the river again. It's a really pleasant mix of narrow, manicured canal environments and wide, lazy, sometimes wild but always beautiful river.

We had nowhere to be and weeks to get there, so we perfected the art of meandering. Our only scheduling concern was that we actually did have plane tickets to go back to the U.S. and the boat would have to be safely put away in St. Jean de Losne when we did. So, after about four weeks we calculated that it was time to turn around for our dash straight back to our home port. At a little village, called Aveney, which is only about six miles from the walled city of Besancon, we reluctantly decided it was time to turn around.

Checking my chart, I realized that we had covered about forty miles beyond Dole and gone through twenty locks on our journey into the wild, with only one noticeable bounce off a wall, back at lock number three. We found a spot near the bridge at Aveney that looked wide enough for a U-turn and spun *Phaedra* around. The next morning, in an intimate sunrise ceremony, we planted a small American flag in the ground at our farthest point and claimed all the land around for America, then we began our steady charge back to Dole.

We felt like seasoned old river hands going back. We found familiar moorings and knew where to look for the locks, snags and weirs on our route. Villages, although familiar, still looked new and exciting as we approached from the opposite direction. Although it was early in the season, we encountered a few rental boats making their way through the locks and we patiently watched the newcomers learning the ropes. We met a few of these folks, moored for the night along the way, but most nights we had the river to ourselves.

Finally back in Dole, we found our old pontoon vacant so we slid back in again. The dock master greeted us like old friends as we got out our enhanced shore power cord and settled in for the night. Linda and I were in the Café des Artistes that night, relaxing after dinner when our waiter appeared to offer us a digestif. Just the thing, I thought. I'll have a spot of whiskey.

Gerald, our waiter, had proudly informed us that he was a veteran of service on cruise ships and confidently spoke French, English, Spanish, Dutch and German, so we could dispense with our broken French and do our business completely in English. This we had done with some success through dinner and Linda was able to avoid having veal brains twice in one day.

"I'd like a Jameson's Irish Whiskey, please, with just two ice cubes," I said.

"Jameson's," Gerald confirmed. "Two or four centiliters?" He asked, referring to the size of my tipple.

"Four centiliters, please, with just two ice cubes." It's important to not put too many ice cubes in whiskey so I generally specify how many to use.

"Ice cubes?" Gerald asked, confused.

"Ice cubes. Ice?" I tried to think of a hand gesture for ice.

"Ice? Glace?"

I was beginning to suspect that Gerald wasn't quite fluent in English after all. "No. Um, ice. Cubes. Of ice? Like snow only bigger."

"Oh, glace!"

"Glace. Yeah. Okay." Now we're gettin' somewhere. "Two." I held up two fingers.

His eyes lit up. "Two glasses of Jameson's," he said jotting down the order.

"No, no. One glass of Jameson's with two glace. Four centiliters." We're almost there, I thought.

"Okay," Gerald said. "So, two Jameson's with four glasses."

"No! One Jameson's. One glass. Four centiliters with two ice cubes." I could tell that Linda was about to jump in to help at this point, but I could handle this.

"Ice cube? *Qu'est-ce que ice cubes?*" Gerald asked.

He's asking me what are ice cubes?! Where's he been? Slowly now, I said, "Glaaaace."

"Oh. Glace." Finally, he got it!

"Yes. Glace is ice, right?"

"Si, si. Right away." And he disappeared with his newly learned English vocabulary. I was left wondering if he might be Spanish.

Ten minutes later Gerald brought me two glasses of Jameson's and a bowl of ice cream. I drank the whiskey and gave the ice cream to Linda. "Here, dear. I ordered this for you. Um, what are you doing?"

"I'm praying that *Phaedra* never springs a leak and you have to call someone for help."

Chapter Fifteen

"The Dodge Caravan has seventeen cup holders.
That's 2.43 per passenger."

- Bill Bryson, *I'm A*

Stranger Here Myself

Four days later Linda and I, with Sarah in steerage, were on an Air France flight back to San Francisco. *Phaedra* was back in her home slip in St. Jean de Losne with Captain Bob and Peggy keeping their ever-watchful eyes on her. Our semi-retirement plans were taking shape. We'd return to the boat in September but for now, to-do lists were already forming in our heads. The summer sailing season on San Francisco Bay was in full swing and I figured I'd better be out there taking pictures. Meanwhile, the town of Sausalito was waiting for Linda to cover it in "Home for Sale" signs. We dove right in. There were bills to pay.

There was also culture shock. After two-plus months in the French countryside I was amazed by the American phenomenon of the SUV. The roads were filled with lumbering convoys of these leather-lined armored personnel carriers as they protected their owners from all the dangers of a trip to the supermarket. These "Trail-Rated" cup-holder-packing monsters probably never faced anything more challenging than the afternoon stampede to pick up Tiffany from ballet class, yet they were the hottest selling thing in America since the Whopper. Hell, even I owned one.

And the food! Tasteless muffins the size of your head, croissants made from Wonder Bread and pork chops two inches thick were the norm. Fresh bread? Not likely, unless you found a health food store that charged four dollars for a loaf of whole wheat, nut, berry, sprouted grain with raisins bread. Wine? Napa and Sonoma, an hour away, provided wines at two, three and four times the price of Premier Cru's from Burgundy. Forget about the cheese.

For days I floated in a fog. The TV was on every night and the computer was sitting there, brimming with Spam and junk-mail. The newspaper, radio, television, and Internet made sure that I was up to the minute on the latest horror, danger, outrage and threat. Politicians insulted my intelligence and gangsters insulted everything else. I was an outsider, the oddball driving at the speed limit on the freeway. I felt like I was sitting in the audience, a mere spectator at a tragic play that I had been acting in all my life.

It didn't last. Slowly, but inexorably, I was reabsorbed. Sailboats packed the Bay filled with people with money to burn, so I called Ben, and we went shooting. It felt good to be doing something that had a routine and a payoff, but before long I began to remember how grueling it was to be tearing around out there, crashing through five-foot swells like I was twenty-two years old again. One day, as we were hauling the boat back onto the trailer at the end of a particularly nasty day of shooting, Ben looked over at me and said, "You look like shit."

It was probably my aching back, or maybe my wobbly knees or the way I grimaced whenever I cranked the wheel to the left. "I feel like it," I said. "I'm tired. Energy's just about all used up."

"Your aura's all screwed up. You need your chi released," Ben said. "It cured me."

"My chi?"

"You gotta release it and let it flow, man."

"How do I do that?" I asked, and laid down on the ground.

"Acupuncture. Frees your chi like that." He snapped his fingers. "Smooth's your aura. Gets your body energy cookin'."

"Cookin' sounds good."

"I know a guy who's good. Name's Dr. Chin. He's in the City." He gave me the phone number.

Four days later, I found myself staring up at the offices of Dr. Chin, above the Radio Shack store on Clement in San Francisco. A small doorway between storefronts led up a steep set of stairs into what had once been a two bedroom flat and was now a thriving Acupuncture and Eastern Medicine Clinic, specializing in the care and coddling of auras.

I gave the receptionist my name and told her I was there to see the doctor about my chi. She gave me about ten pages of forms to fill out, then took my credit card and docked it for ninety-five bucks.

I don't live in a bubble. I'd heard of acupuncture and know it involves lots of needles but I had never gotten this close to it before. So although on the outside I was all tranquility and peace (very smooth aura) a little western edginess was inside playing games with my chi.

Half an hour later an extremely mellow young lady named Breeze appeared and summoned me, in hushed tones, to follow her. We walked on tiptoes down the hall to my private room, which was in reality an old bedroom that had been divided by a couple of pieces of plywood. My half had just enough space for me to stand next to a single pallet, upon which was a thin mattress covered by paper. Breeze handed me a sheet and told me to disrobe and make myself comfortable. My treatment would soon begin.

Taking great care not to pre-puncture myself on splinters from the makeshift partition, I did as I was told. After another half hour of waiting, boredom set in. I had already explored everything in my makeshift cubicle and was not a little disturbed at finding a large number of bandage gauze and Mars Bars wrappers on a shelf at the foot of the bed. But the real challenge to my aura was a piped-in endless loop of The Captain and Tennile songs done in Chinese, featuring such favorites as "Muskrat Love" and "Love Will Keep Us Together," which would have driven Confucius to slap little children around.

I became more anxious to see Dr. Chin. As if I had willed it, the door to my partitioned cubicle finally opened and a man walked in carrying a tray of strange and assorted implements.

He was a large man, wearing a tight black t-shirt stretched across a prominent belly and emblazoned with the name of some metal rock band. Heavily tattooed with a shaved head and decorated with what I would call opulent body piercing, he announced, "I'm Jake. First, I'm going to massage your organs, then I'll cup you."

That's when my cell phone rang. "I need to get that," I said, and grabbed for my pants.

The call was from a man who was interested in buying my yacht photography business. The previous summer, the write-up in the *Times* had sparked a fair amount of interest from prospective partners and buyers, but I hadn't been prepared to entertain them seriously at the time and eventually they had died out. But this call, coming just as Jake was getting ready to cup me, caught my interest. In ten minutes I was hurrying to the corner Starbucks to call him back. I was about to order a coffee when my phone rang again. I answered it. "Hi. I was just going to call you back…What? Who?…Yes, this is he…Oh no. When? Is he hurt?"

Room 214 at the V.A. hospital had four beds. Covered windows at one end let in a diffused, grey-green light that made shadows of everything and seemed heavy enough to muffle sound. Curtains were drawn around the bed in the back, revealing only the pale blue pant legs and rubber soled shoes of a nurse moving carefully and silently around it. A fluorescent bulb above another bed highlighted the caved-in contours of the pale, bewildered face of a man that turned toward me when I walked in then turned back again to stare at the ceiling. Bed 214A, the first on the right, held a shrunken old man with a scraped forehead and a bandaged lip. His eyes were wide and anxious, red rimmed but otherwise without color; even the pupils, dilated in shock, were fogged and milky. Tears had dried in salty streaks that trickled into his hair. A flimsy plastic ID bracelet circled his wrist next to a pair of rubber tubes running up his arm. His hands clutched and fiddled with the sheet pulled across his chest. I noticed that the fingernails were yellowed and longer than they should have been. I recognized his hands. They once taught me how to place my fingers along the laces of a football so I could throw a spiral.

I couldn't breathe. I had to sit down.

My father, Chauncey Wilbert, was eighty-three and lived alone in a small studio apartment at Walnut Creek Manor, an apartment complex for seniors with a pool and a small workshop for hobbyists. His place was crammed to the window sills with lawn mower parts, dishes, laundry, broken toasters, carburetors in need of rebuilding, tool boxes, plastic flowers, books he could no longer see to read, a stationary bike, and flying above it all, a nine-foot kayak hanging from the ceiling. My father was almost blind, mostly deaf, lame in one leg and one arm, had a bad stomach, one miserable kidney, no prostate, and was supposed to take sixteen different pills at odd intervals every day. With all that, he still worked three or four days a week as a handyman and gardener for the lonely and adoring widows in his complex. Many of whom would leave him valentines of chicken casseroles or plates of brownies on his front porch, which he would often step in because he couldn't see them. Lately he'd developed a tendency to do things like flood his apartment, forget to eat, and run stoplights in his car. After crashing into a small Toyota, I had taken his keys away. Later I had to go back and take the distributor cap from the engine after I found out he had hotwired the car then lost it at the local Safeway.

He wasn't at all happy with the way the aging process was treating him. "Don't ever get old," he'd say every chance he got. But he still had his sense of humor and pride in his ability to remain independent. Because of the pain in his knees and back, it was taking him longer to walk to the store these days and he'd often have to sit and rest on a curb or a wall along the way. But even so, his pride wouldn't allow him to use a cane or a walker.

My siblings and I would bring over bags of food and he'd scold us for getting the chicken breasts when the legs were so much cheaper.

We had tried to get him to move into an assisted living facility after he'd flooded his apartment for the third time, but he'd have none of it. He knew his neighborhood, his neighbors and exactly how many steps it took to get from his bed to his fridge, the mailbox, or his front door. In spite of his physical pain and frustration over his ever-shrinking world, he still had his mind. He was weak and frail, and he and I couldn't play catch with a football anymore, but we could talk about it, and he remembered.

That morning, on the sidewalk in front of Walnut Creek Manor, he tripped on a curb and fell. He banged up his knees, split his lip, and knocked himself out. When he came to in the hospital, his mind stayed behind on the curb.

"Dad?" I said. "Are you all right?"

"We didn't mean it. It was an accident," he breathed.

"What accident? You fell, dad."

"It rolled over. I wasn't driving."

"He thinks he was in a car accident in Richmond," said the nurse. "He thinks it's forty years ago."

"What does this mean?"

"It's too early to tell," she said, but she wouldn't look at me.

For two more weeks he languished in the hospital. He had a slight concussion, no broken bones and no internal injuries. But he'd never walk again, or be able to dress, eat or clean himself. Sometimes he'd recognize me or Linda or my sister or brother. Other times he'd say he did, but then ask us who we were. One day, I was on my way to meet my sister, Kitty, and the doctor at the hospital when I passed the activities center and looked in. It was about the size of three rooms joined together and decorated with colorful pictures of happy families with kids and dogs, playing in a park. Hearts and flowers cut out of pink and yellow construction paper were taped around the walls and on the windows. A boom box played tunes from World War II. A woman dressed in hospital greens stood in the middle of a circle of eight elderly people tucked into wheelchairs. She was tossing red balloons at them. The activity was to try to bat them back, keep them in the air.

I watched my father in his chair as a balloon came floating toward him. His eyes picked it up about three feet away and he gazed at it for a second then fixed it with a look of firm determination. His jaw set, his right hand made a fist, and he lifted it in short jerks from his lap. Then he cocked it in front of his chest. That balloon didn't know what hit it. It shot up and away, then slowed and floated over to land at the feet of an old lady across the circle who didn't notice it at all.

For a second I was proud of him for doing so well. As if I were watching my infant son, already able to hit a balloon. Then I remembered where I was and my stomach clenched, my eyes welled up and *I* wanted to hit something, anything, just hit something as hard as I could, find the jailer, take his keys and set my old man free.

But there was no jailer and there sure as hell weren't any keys. The walls and doors were cinder block and sturdy oak and the first punch hurt my hand so much that the next one was just a slap. There was no third. I brushed past the orderly and continued on to the meeting with the doctor.

The doctor was nice enough but also too busy to give us much more than the facts. He confirmed that Chauncey was basically gone and he gave us a week to get him out of his hospital. We had anticipated this and already had a full-care facility lined up that would take him in right away. It was only a few miles from his old place and rejoiced in the name Villa San Miguel. It smelled of Pine-Sol and the floors were polished to a mirror gloss, the halls resounding with the sounds of squeaking rubber-soled shoes. He would share a room with another man and have his own closet and bedside table. He'd be wheeled into the dining room for meals, and he'd have activities once or twice a day. There were people to help him in and out of his wheelchair, feed him, shave him, bathe him, and help him perform his other toilet requirements. We were encouraged to put family pictures and photos up in his corner and one of him in the hall by the door, over his name plate; Chauncey Lives Here.

He went straight there after the hospital. He never saw his apartment again. We cleaned it out. Most of his stuff went into the Walnut Creek Manor dumpster but we kept a few of the personal things. Kitty and I found paintings and drawings that we had done when we were kids that he had saved, so we rescued them. My brother, Jim, found some letters he had sent him, some poems and a box of photographs of him, his wife, and his sons. There were odd things like a small collection of broken pocketknives, and tie-clips from trucking agencies that I couldn't throw away. I added them to my own box of junk that I was cultivating for my future grandson to find. I found a picture of my grandmother, his graduation photo from Kings Point, and his seaman's papers, which I kept. I also kept his toolbox. It was full of worn out tools that he had used since he was fifteen and had to quit high school to go to work for his father in the car business.

We took him to his new home on a Thursday afternoon. Kitty and Linda and I tried to make it sound like a special outing and lots of fun and excitement for him. "Dad, guess what? You don't have to go back to that crummy old apartment any more. We got you into a really nice place. It's really clean," I said as we wheeled him out to the Villa San Miguel van.

"You're going to really like it, dad. It's got lots of..." Kitty couldn't go on.

"I'm not going home?"

"You're going to a new place. It's better, dad. We're going in the van." I climbed in with him and closed the door. Linda and

Kitty followed in their cars. We checked him in that afternoon. So far in my life, leaving him there that first day was the hardest thing I've ever had to do.

On the way home, Linda was looking out the window and said, "I'm so sad right now. I don't think I can stand it. Do you remember the first time you took me to meet your dad? He was in the hospital then too."

"Uh-huh, he had a kidney removed."

"When was that, thirty years ago?"

"Did you know that after that, his one kidney that he had left started packing up with calcium deposits and stopped working, so they told him he had to go on dialysis. Said he'd die if he didn't."

"I think I remember."

"He said, screw it then, I'll die. He didn't want to do dialysis three, four times a week. Lying there with tubes flushing him out for hours every day, sick the rest of the time. He figured since he was going to die anyway, no use taking all those pills anymore, so he threw them away too."

"God, the pills. What, like, sixteen, twenty a day, wasn't it?"

"Something like that, more I think. Anyway, he threw them away and the next day he started feeling better. Turns out the pills were working against each other and killing his kidney. He tells the doctors to go to hell and he ends up getting better."

Linda said, "He said the hell with it? I'd rather die?"

"He thought a life like that wasn't worth living, hooked up to a dialysis pump. Imagine what he'd say about Villa San Miguel if he were making his own decisions now."

"I know what he'd say. Same thing you'd say."

"Uh-huh. I'm telling you right now, if it comes to it, rather than put me in a place like that, just kill me."

"How exactly?"

"Sex. Kill me with sex."

"We tried that. You survived."

"I'm older now - and another thing, while I still can, I've made some decisions. I love doing art, so I'm going to sell the boat business to that guy who called and I'm going back to painting, and I'm taking you to Paris on that barge."

"Okay. Then I'll kill you with sex."

"You're welcome to try."

We went back to Villa San Miguel the next day and found Chauncey in bed in his room. We brought him a whole new wardrobe of warm-up clothes and a new pair of slippers, all of it with "C. Hammond" scrawled on the labels. We also brought some pictures of Nicole and Krista when they were little to put near his bed, and a clock with large numbers. We were trying to get him talking and pull some memories up when some sprightly old guy came spinning into the room in a wheelchair. He was smiling and full of energy. "Hey, how you doin'?" he said and twirled his chair in a tight 360. "You family?"

"He's my father," I said. "He just moved in here yesterday."

"I know. We been gettin' to know each other. I live cross the hall." He turned to my dad. "Hey Chauncey. How you doin' today? Remember me? You remember me. We were talking yesterday." My dad looked at him blankly. "You know me. Don't pretend you don't remember me."

"He doesn't seem to remember you," Linda said.

"Sure he does. Hey Chauncey. What's my name? What's my name?" More blank looks from my dad. "What's my name? Come on. Tell me. What's my name?"

Slowly my dad turned to me and said, "That guy's so far gone he doesn't even know his own name."

The happy new owner of Paparazzi H2O was an energetic young man, a refugee from the dot com blowout. He loved to sail, had seen us working on the Bay, and figured it would be a great business and lots of fun. There wasn't a lot of money involved in the deal but it represented freedom and a new start for both of us, so we went at it with a will and by August, he was ready to take over.

Meanwhile, strange things had been churning in Linda's mind. Her real estate business was moving sedately along but her mind kept wandering back to the boat in France. One evening, while we were enjoying a glass of wine she said, "Maybe we oughta sell this house."

"Really? Are you serious?" I said.

"I don't know. I'm just thinking that maybe this isn't the house for us. After being on *Phaedra*, it just seems huge. *Phaedra* is so small and compact, everything is right there. It's so simple. I look around at all this space, and all the money it costs us, and I can't help thinking it's all a little silly."

"You always said you never wanted to leave this house. Of course, you said that about the studio too, until you saw this place."

"Suppose we moved back to the studio. We could afford it much more easily and we loved living there."

"I don't know if I'm ready for that yet. A year ago, when I got laid off, it's one of the first things that came to my mind, but it seemed like a panic move, so I guess I resisted even mentioning it."

"I know. That's why I didn't mention it then either. But we're not panicking now, and I think it's something we should think about."

"Right. Think about it." I took a sip of wine and remembered back when we first walked into that house with the real estate agent. Linda ran all through it like she was a little girl at a pony show. I just stood by the front door saying to myself, I don't think we can swing this. Then she came down stairs and walked up to me and said, "Let's go. I don't want it."

"What's wrong with it?' I asked.

"It's too big, and I'm not worthy." Seriously, that's what she said, not worthy.

Of course I took the bait. "You are too worthy." Then I turned to the agent, "We'll take it." By the skin of our teeth, we took it. At first we felt like we were camping in the place. We had just enough furniture for one bedroom and a couch for the living room. But our daughters loved it. For the first time, they could come up and visit without having to sleep on the floor in the kitchen. They even brought friends and had BBQ's and parties. Back in the little art studio, when we had more than two friends over for dinner, the dining area was so small that people at the north end of the table had to go out the front door, down the driveway and come in the back door in order to use the bathroom. Now we had three bathrooms. It was the devil keeping them all stocked with current magazines.

Downsizing back to the little studio would make a lot of sense and fit much more comfortably into this new chapter of our lives. But something inside of me was resisting the idea. Maybe it was just one complexity too many.

Driving an hour and a half to and from Villa San Miguel twice a week was wearing me out. Coming back was the worst. The images and sounds would haunt me: his scraped chin and neck from a hurried, rough shave; his mouth open like a baby's, waiting for the next spoonful, wiping it off his chin; a woman ranting across the room. Then, leaving him there, slumped in his chair, lined up with the rest, waiting for the sunlight to move across the room. "Goodbye, dad. See ya in a couple days. Be good." I'd open all the car windows to get the smell of Pine Sol out of my nostrils. But the drive gave me time to think.

I wondered if Chauncey's life had been a happy one. He always seemed to be looking for something. He wanted to live on a fishing boat, buy a ranch, build an adobe house, patent a speed-reading machine. Once, when he was young and just out of the merchant marine, he answered an ad in a newspaper from a man seeking a partner in a gold mine in British Honduras. He spent his savings for half ownership then trekked on horseback into the jungle and found the place, a hole in a mountain above a river with a drunk sleeping in a hammock at its entrance. He came home and went back to work in his dad's used car business. Digging ditches through the yard, fixing plumbing, pouring concrete--these are the things he did in his free time. I never knew him to go to a movie or a ballgame. As he grew older, his greatest joy seemed to be to go to the park and watch little kids play on the swings and jungle gyms. He loved the way that they never walked anywhere. They always skipped or hopped or ran.

Those drives back from Villa San Miguel gave me time to examine my life and ask myself dangerous questions like, "What makes me happy? Would I know it if I tripped over it? How many hours a day do I spend on autopilot? What's more important, things or time? What is happiness?" The last time I really pondered that question, the answer appeared under my picture in my high school yearbook. I think I said something like, "Happiness is a keg party at Kamikaze's house." And I really meant it. Since then, however, happiness had been a motorcycle, a couple of apartments near campus, quite a few young ladies, a wife, two daughters, Irish whiskey in general, a painting coming out just right, several dogs and puppies, a sailing trip in the Caribbean. Happiness, it seemed, was a moving target. Would its next incarnation be piloting a canal barge through France? Painting landscapes of the hills and vineyards? Or would it simply be living a life with enough time to do those things if I choose?

Chapter Sixteen

"Murder is always a mistake. One should never do anything
that one cannot talk about after dinner."
- Oscar Wilde

By late August, my father's condition had slipped into a sort of wakeful, animated coma, albeit a safe and comfortable one. Sanity required that I get back to the boat and lose myself in a painting or two. Linda and Sarah would follow in four weeks, which gave me enough time on board alone to turn the place into a totally uninhabitable artist's studio, and then clean it up before they arrived. I had pulled together my old brushes, pallet knives, and paint-smeared tubes of color in a battered old plein air paint box that Phil donated to the cause, taped it all shut and hauled it aboard Air France flight 0083 for Paris, a solitary artist setting off to paint his masterpiece.

It was warm in France and the waterways were crowded with rental boats and hotel barges. In St. Jean de Losne, the River Rats were still planted in their deck chairs, ready to spread the latest news. And there was news: a suspicious death had taken place on Pontoon A. This I heard between the time I got my bags out of the trunk of the taxi and dragged them down the pontoon to the boat. Captain Bob was on his tiptoes with excitement and

Peggy was stuttering to show me almost ten pages of evidence that she had gathered, which she claimed solved the crime, a double murder.

Back in June, about two weeks before Linda and I had left France and returned to Sausalito, a strange boat had arrived in the harbor and moored at the end of Pontoon A. It was a sailboat, about twenty-eight feet long, and it was all black. The hull was black, the decks were black and so was the cabin. The wooden handrails and hatches were painted black. The lifelines, railings, winches, and rigging turnbuckles were covered in black tape. The small raft on the deck, the outboard motor, the oars and water casks were all painted black. The windows were blacked out from the inside and there was a black bicycle on the deck. The padlock was painted black. It was a black boat.

Peggy said that the owner was an American and claimed to have worked as a psychiatrist at the White House. He didn't like visitors. He was known in whispers as "the guy on the black boat."

At that time, the H2O harbor had a guardian swan named "Tough Guy," who charged out of the bulrushes to attack any boats that came in from the river. He had a sleek feathered wife and every year they produced a crop of baby swans. In the spring the whole family would cruise around the harbor looking for food. The mother would lead the babies from boat to boat and knock on the hulls with her beak, demanding handouts while Tough Guy stood watch. The pair would start each season with four or five babies and by the time they were too big to be picked off by the pike and the badgers, there would usually be two left. But about a week before I returned, the last two surviving chicks suddenly disappeared. Foul play was suspected.

People didn't automatically suspect the guy on the black boat. He kept such a low profile that people just kinda forgot he was there. But about three days after the disappearance, a rental boat came into the harbor and Captain Bob went out to greet them at the "By-the-Night" slips on Pontoon A. After he'd helped them tie up and given them a few of his tips about life in St. Jean de Losne, he happened to glance down the pontoon toward the black boat and he noticed something that wasn't black. He went for a closer look. Feathers!

On the pontoon and all over the slip next to the boat were swan feathers, hundreds of them. Clearly someone had plucked a swan. The evidence against the guy on the black boat was circumstantial, but damning. Captain Bob, having been for a short time a policeman somewhere in Florida, took on the investigation. He and Peggy staked out the black boat for a whole afternoon and an evening until almost eight o'clock, but the guy on the black boat never showed up, or perhaps he was inside all day, but they never saw him.

The next morning on the River Rat radio net, River Gal got everyone whipped up to go to see Charles at the H2O office and demand that the black boat be run out of the harbor. Charles, leaning comfortably back in his swivel chair and finishing up the last of what looked to some people like a triple-decker swan sandwich, promised immediate action. Sometime that night, the black boat vanished, never to be seen again in Burgundy.

That weekend, the River Rats held a celebratory barbeque in front of the store. Charles came and brought a pair of the biggest chicken legs anyone had ever seen.

By the time I arrived the excitement was dying down and things were becoming peaceful again, but all was not paradise on *Phaedra*. I had blasted aboard and in a jet lagged and exhausted fog, had set about fitting myself back into the cozy embrace of the boat. So it wasn't until the second night, when a mosquito mounted an air attack on my blood supply, that I tried to close the door to my stateroom. It wouldn't close. The next morning I took a close look at all the new woodwork that H2O had installed when they had reconfigured the interior. Back in April when Phil and I had picked up the boat, I had been pleased to see my designs actually in place. Although the varnish had been done by a blind, drunk, one-armed sociopath and needed to be redone, the basic construction had looked good. But I was wrong. All the beautiful mahogany woodwork that I had been so impressed with four months before -- the doors, trim work, a small bookcase and all the framing -- was coming apart. The beautiful post and tenon doors were warped. The doorframes were twisted and two of them were so deformed that they were actually starting to split. It was obvious that green, wet wood had been used to do all the cabinetry.

I went up to the H2O office to have a word with Charles on the subject. I found him sprawled in his chair, paring his fingernails with a pair of wire cutters. I slid into the broken-down seat across from him and started drumming my fingers on his desk. He snapped a fingernail off and it pinged against his coffee mug.

"Charles," I started off. " I've got a bit of a problem that I think you'll want to hear about."

"I am not so sure I want to hear of your problem," he said to his thumb.

"It's about all that nice woodwork and cabinetry you guys did on my boat?" I put a foot up on his desk.

"You should talk to Philippe then," he said. "He is on vacation."

"I will, but you're his boss. No?"

"I am his boss, sometimes. He is young."

"Yes, but you're his uncle too."

"What is this problem?" Charles put down his wire cutters.

"It's all coming apart," I said. "They used green wood. It's warped and splitting."

"This sometimes happens," he said and swept his feet to the floor. "The people who supply us with the wood. They don't always give us the most choice pieces."

"Really?" I said.

"If we were a bigger company, like the window frame factory in Dijon, we would get the best pieces." He leaned forward and crossed his arms on the desk.

"I don't care," I said.

"What?" He looked surprised.

"Not my problem," I said. "That's between you and your supplier." I moved a leg over the arm of my chair. "I paid you for a job that should last at least twenty years, not four months."

"It was very hot this summer. Wood will warp when it's hot like this," he said.

"Not dry wood," I said. "You're gonna have to redo it all."

"You should talk to Philippe when he gets back from his vacation." He leaned back and returned his feet to the top of his desk.

As I left the office and climbed down the shuddering staircase, the magnitude of the storm this could turn into began to take form in my imagination. Lawsuits! I'd have no hope. Threats, arguments, intimidation, sabotage, revenge, flames, blood, and more feathers flying all loomed on the horizon. I went back to the boat and tried to find things to do to distract me from this disaster. I got a tape measure and checked how far out of whack the bathroom door was from its frame. Four inches.

When I could forget about my looming legal battle/knife fight with H2O, I found myself caught between the peaceful serenity of life in the harbor and the chafing irritation of being surrounded on all sides by a community of people without much to do except pop their heads in my boat and say, "Bob says you're a painter. Can we watch?" I needed to get away, so I decided I would try to take a little cruise on my own.

Taking the boat out by myself seemed not an entirely unreasonable thing to do, if all went well. Linda and I had done forty-four locks on our trip last spring and there wasn't any great trick to it. I spent hours going through each step in my mind, from leaving the slip to moving through locks and tying up along the bank of a canal. I had faith in the power of visualization and my bow thruster.

The next morning I was ready to go. As the engine warmed up I unplugged the shore power cord and brought in my dock lines. My plan was to go down the Saone River about thirty miles to the entrance of the Canal de Centre, just above the town of Chalon-sur-Saone. With only two locks on the river to contend with, plus the large one at the mouth of the canal, I was hoping to make it onto the Centre by nightfall. I'd heard that it was a quiet canal, without much tourist traffic. It would take two or three more days to reach the wine village of Santenay where I could plant my stakes and try to do some paintings of the vineyards and the town.

Both Captain Bob and Jean-Paul did mention one obstacle along the way that was preying on my mind. The lock which marks the entrance to the Canal du Centre was thirty-five feet deep. The deepest lock Linda and I had done on the Canal du Rhone au Rhin was only nine feet. Just by its sheer size, and the force of the water it would take to fill it, this lock could be a challenge to handle alone.

Nevertheless, I was determined to go. I got *Phaedra* out of the slip, using the bow thruster to cut a sharp 90 degree turn. I missed my neighbor's rudder with more than two inches to spare, then proceeded out of the harbor at the speed of a leisurely dog paddle. I looked both ways and behind me, and scanned ahead with binoculars. I throttled up, slowed down, steered just a touch to the right, but then back just a bit to the left. I checked the chart for indications of hidden hazards and peered into the water going by, looking for large rocks or sunken automobiles. I chewed the hell out of my lip and realized that I had to pee.

I stood there, gripping the wheel and staring at the river opening up ahead and asked myself, "What the hell were you thinking?" I suddenly wanted to turn around and slink back into the harbor, but I knew that, on my own, I'd never get the boat back into the slip. I was committed to a solo trip down the river, up the Canal de Centre, and back. At least get it onto the canal, I told myself, it's only six feet deep. If it sinks, you can stand on the roof until help arrives.

The Saone is one of the major navigable rivers in France. It is a major component of the inland water route to or from the Mediterranean. Three canals, the Centre, Canal de Bourgogne and the Canal de la Marne, branch off the Saone and eventually lead to the Seine and Paris. To the south, the Saone joins with the Rhone at Lyon and flows to the Mediterranean Sea. It's a gentle river for the most part, falling only about 150 feet over its 231 miles from Corre in the east to Lyon. Commercial craft and pleasure boats have been plying its waters since the time of the Romans and it flows through almost exclusively rural parts of Burgundy. I was surrounded by farms and grazing land as I made my way down toward the first big lock just above a the small town of Seurre.

This lock was built on a much larger scale than the ones I had encountered on the Rhone au Rhin. Built for more heavy commercial traffic, these river locks can hold six full-sized commercial barges as opposed to the one-at-a-time Freycinet standard locks. I entered it under the watchful eyes of a pair of *eclusiers* seated in a glassed-in observation platform looking a lot like an air traffic control tower. Being their only customer at the time, *Phaedra* felt very small inside this mighty lock as the big doors swung closed behind me. I had over two football fields of water to roam around in as the flood-gates opened and we descended.

Once out of the lock I approached Seurre. Sheltered behind a small islet, Seurre is a delightful little town with a protected harbor that is a popular stopping point for commercial and holiday boaters. The stone houses along its waterfront go back to the 17th century, with one rather battered facade sporting a sign that proclaimed, *Bar De L'Esperance*, The Bar of Hope. I was tempted to drop in but the most convenient mooring was taken by a *peniche* (commercial barge) that looked like it was taking on cargo so I pushed on.

Beyond Seurre, the scenery became lush and lovely again. Stands of horse chestnut trees come right down to the water providing shade and shelter for families of ducks, circling and diving around dozens of rugged little fishing punts tied to stakes along the shore. Through breaks in the trees, the vistas stretch for miles to the dim hills of the Cote de Beaune, covered with even rows of vines marching up the slopes and down the ravines.

About twelve miles further I passed the junction with the River Doubs. This is the same river that Linda and I had traveled on when we were exploring above Dole in the spring. Just a short way up the Doubs was the small port of Verdun-sur-le-Doubs. My chart claimed that this was a Roman port established in the 1st century and that it was renown for it's local fish stew, called *Pochouse*. I made a note to stop there on the way back.

It was after five o'clock when I saw the three large yellow warning markers indicating that I was nearing the entrance to the

Canal du Centre. Even with the markers, I almost missed the dark, overgrown approach to the first lock, which had been ominously described by Captain Bob and Jean-Paul as "hellish." The mile-long passage off the river narrowed and the light grew dim as I crept past rusting hulks of barges, tied in front of dilapidated industrial buildings emitting loud groans and clanging noises amid bursts of steam and smoke. I felt like Martin Sheen in *Apocalypse Now*, driving his boat toward Colonel Kurtz and into the heart of darkness.

In the gloom ahead, I could barely make out a small boat that appeared to be tied just before the lock doors. The deep shadows cast by the dense forest played tricks with the light and I couldn't tell for certain if the doors were open or closed. The approach was narrow, with no room to maneuver, so I slowed *Phaedra* and held back, watching the little boat ahead. Once she moved into the lock, I'd know the doors were indeed open and I would follow her in.

This lock was like nothing I'd seen before. Massive concrete walls forty feet high surrounded the doors. Stained black and gray with creeping ferns and weeds clinging like spiders to weeping fissures and cracks, it reminded me of the wall on Skull Island. As I drifted closer, I saw to the right, a green light shining near the opening, meaning it was safe to enter, but the doors still looked closed so I hung back.

About thirty yards from the thing, I finally realized what I was looking at. The lock was indeed open, and the little boat was already inside, tied to a floating bollard in the wall. What threw me off was that there was no light down where he was at the bottom of the cavern. Everything was the same dank, gloomy charcoal grey that revealed no shapes or angles. But as I got closer, I could just see, toward the top of the wall, a few slanting rays of the afternoon sun hitting the edge of the vault, four stories up.

Realizing that I was holding things up, I pushed forward and slid into the lock just behind and beside the waiting boat. Every sound was magnified and echoed in the vast chamber as I caught a breath of the moist, moldy air. Water poured through the cracks in the concrete walls and the iron doors, high up at the top of the wall before me. The water I'd pushed in at *Phaedra's* bow churned and protested as it piled against the suddenly confining walls of the lock and then shouldered its way back out again.

My bow overlapped the boat ahead of me so I ran forward to tie off against a floating bollard in the wall to keep clear of her. Once that was done, I came back to the wheel and held on to a line I'd draped over a bollard off my stern. Suddenly a thunderous rumbling and screeching filled the chamber as tons of iron and cement descended from above. This lock was too deep for doors that swung on hinges. It had one massive door that lowered from the bridge above and slid in grooves down either side like some slow-moving, grinding guillotine.

Phaedra's rudder was just feet from this monster's path so I ran to the bow and dragged her forward using the line I had tied around the bollard. Then I went back to the stern and watched in awe as this rumbling monstrosity splashed into the murky water just four feet from me. At once I was pitched into an eerie, subterranean darkness, like being at the bottom of a well. Moments later the water started pouring into the chamber, 1,681,043 gallons of it.

It didn't come roaring in from the top like a giant waterfall. Instead it came from underneath and from the sides, boiling and thrashing, tossing *Phaedra* in all directions. She was bucking against her mooring lines and then crashing back into the sides of the lock. Her rudder was in danger of crashing into the concrete slab so I put the engine in gear and drove forward against her ropes. At the same time I was using the bow thruster to keep her away from the wall on our left, and then reversing it to soften the blow when she rammed, or was rammed by, the boat next to me, which was smaller than *Phaedra* and pitching even more wildly.

The skipper of the little boat was standing on his stern wielding a long wooden boat pole, trying to keep us apart. He had one end wedged against the front of my boat and was being tossed around on the other end like the unlucky hunter who sinks the first spear into a woolly mammoth. The bollards we were tied to were welded to square steel boxes that floated along tracks recessed into the walls, designed to rise along with the water. The tracks were slimy and slippery, but the crashing water and pull of the boats would cause the boxes to jam on their ascent until the water level almost covered them. Then with a screech they'd break loose and shoot up, like breaching whales, adding their own chaos to the ride.

This madness continued for about half the distance to the top of the lock and then began to calm down until it became positively serene. I was able tie off my lines and walk forward to survey whatever damage had been inflicted to our two boats. It looked like *Phaedra* had given as much as she took. His boat hook had carved a few designs in my paint and my anchor had bright white spots of paint on it from his swim platform. We both just shrugged, mouthed a *"c'est pas grave,"* and then I ducked below for a couple medicinal shots of cognac.

The whole ride up took no more than twenty minutes. The water continued to rise to just a few inches from the edge of the lock then settled, calm, peaceful and shimmering with the reflection of the afternoon sun. I untied my lines and *Phaedra* floated, perfectly still for the last few moments before the lock doors opened onto the Canal de Centre.

After the grand River Saone, the canal looked calm and tame and intimate. Tall shade trees stood in rows along each bank, their branches arching overhead to form a cool, vaulted tunnel reflected in the water ahead. A carpet of freshly mowed grass framed the towpath on my right as it wound its way toward the next lock. I put *Phaedra* in gear and began the next leg of my journey.

The first village I came to was Fragnes, where I tied up for the evening in front of a grassy park that offered free water and electric hook-ups. The boat that had accompanied me in the lock from hell was there also, so instead of wandering around the town, I took them a bottle of wine to make sure there were no hard feelings over the chipped paint on both our boats. Captain Georges and his wife, Brigitte, were in fine spirits and chipped in a bottle of their own, plus some olives, nuts, and thinly sliced wild boar salami. By the time the wine was gone, the sun had set and a challenging day was drawing to an end. Brigitte turned to me after draining her glass and said, "What is your job, Cris, in California?"

I looked up the canal and noticed the way the light breeze ruffled the water and made the reflections of the trees dance and twist. Their long shadows stretching across the canal seemed to be filled with subtle warm colors. "I'm a painter," I said.

The next day, seven locks up the canal just outside the village of Santenay, I found a shady mooring spot in front of a trimmed lawn by a stand of live oak trees. I pulled over and set my stakes then shut the engine down and silence filled the scene. Toward the center of the lawn freshly watered beds of pink and white geraniums and petunias surrounded an ancient iron well. From the trees edging the little park, someone had hung baskets overflowing with red, pink, white, and purple flowers. Through the trees, the yellow and black roof tiles decorating the spire of the church in the village below reflected the low rays of the setting sun. That evening, tiny white lights lit the way along a narrow path through the trees and down to the road leading into the village.

Santenay is a small village at the southern end of the Cote d'Or which gets it's name from the rich golden color of the vines at harvest time. Some of the best wines in the world come from this tiny region in France that is only about thirty miles long. The quality of the wines here is exquisite but so is the variety. From the white wines of Meursault or Montrachet to the reds of Romanee-Conte or Volnay, they are known the world over to set the gold standard.

From my mooring spot along the canal, I would ride my bike into the village each morning for bread and croissants. Twice a week, there were open-air markets in the village square where venders came from all over to set up their stalls. Cheeses of the region, from great rounds of Comte to palm-sized croutons of chevre, were displayed whole under glass and in bite-sized bits offered for tasting at the tip of a knife. Vegetables and fruit from local farms lay in great colorful displays, their vendors singing their praises and haggling prices; making deals you just couldn't refuse. Santenay was exactly what I had hoped to find.

Boats would pass by each day, mostly small rentals on their way to or from the hire base up the canal at St. Leger. Two or three times a week one of the massive hotel barges would squeeze past on their way down to Chalon-sur-Soane, or up to their home base at St. Leger. Converted from out-of-work 120-foot commercial barges they were the QE2's of the canals. They were usually preceded by small gangs of Americans on bicycles, working off the twenty-four-hour-a-day feedings they were enjoying on board. Passing within inches of our moored boats, these floating hotels pushed so much water ahead of them that they actually left a "hole" in the water when they passed. *Phaedra* would be sucked out into the canal as the water rushed in behind to fill it. When word came that one was on the way, all of us moored to the bank would check our lines and drive our mooring spikes a few blows deeper into the ground.

My days at Santenay took on an easy routine. Each morning I'd set up my easel alongside the canal and get to work on a painting. Mid-morning and mid-afternoon were the best times to paint. The long shadows cast while the sun was lower in the sky helped define the scene and add contrast to the light. I'd break for a lunch of cheese, fruit and bread, then take a short hike into the village before either continuing painting in the afternoon or taking on chores and projects on the boat. By six or seven o'clock it was time to do honor to the local wine while letting my eyes rest by staring across the valley to the changing colors of the vineyards above the town. In the evening I'd either go into the café in town or cook up something from the fridge for dinner. Read or walk after dinner then a spot of cognac and a look at the stars before bed. I slept like a baby.

But the truth is, my debut as a plein air painter in France was turning into a dismal failure. Almost as soon as my easel would be set up, a small crowd of bicyclists, skaters, and strollers would gather to watch and I'd become terribly self-conscious. They'd quietly stand behind me and observe as I covered my canvas with clouds that looked like wads of dirty cotton, trees and bushes that were little more than jumbled glops of green paint below a patch that had to be sky because it was painted sky blue. They would stand there in silence for a few minutes, then grunt or sniff, and continue on their way, no doubt remembering Thumper's advice to Bambi, "If you can't say something nice, don't say nothing at all."

But slowly and with only a few nighttime runs to the dumpster to dispose of ruined attempts, some of the old technique, skills, and even vision, began to come back. I started to slow down enough that I could see all the many shades of color in the scene and then recognize where they were lacking on the canvas. I remembered that I could add a touch of Zinc White to my Cerulean Blue and the sky would lighten softly as it fled toward the horizon. Titanium White for the reflective side of the clouds made them jump out. Adding Paynes Gray to the Viridian would bring down the green in intensity and cool it for shadows, where the red tint of Burnt Sienna would darken and brown it, keeping it warm. A surprising amount of Indian Yellow was present in the reflected light from trees. I never used black. Black is the absence of color, and there was always color in there somewhere.

One day, about a week and a half into it, I was down below making a sandwich when I heard someone knocking on the boat. I came up to find Earl and Cathleen from Colorado, sunburned and smiling on the lawn. They were on holiday aboard one of the hotel barges plying the Canal du Centre and while walking off a big breakfast they had spotted a couple paintings I had left drying on the deck. They wanted to know if they were for sale. I told them that although it would break my heart to part with one, I'd consider it, for three hundred euros.

After they left, cradling their new painting as if it were a baby or a pampered Pekinese, I sat there with my sandwich thinking, Shit-fire, I just sold a painting! Maybe I should have asked for more. Linda called that evening and I think I was pretty cool about it. "Guess what. I sold a painting."

"Get out! Really? How much?"

"Money's not the point, dear. Three hundred euros, but I could have gotten more."

"That's good. How much is that in real dollars?" She's the accountant.

"Doesn't matter. I'm spending euros over here and it's enough for the fuel and all my food for weeks, including wine. If I don't start the motor."

"How many paintings do you have left?"

"One."

"Get to work. Sarah and I will be there in a week and a half. We'll have an art show. I'll do the refreshments."

For the rest of the week, I made a point of putting my paintings out on the deck to dry. I sold one more before it was time to pull up my stakes and head back to St. Jean de Losne to meet my girls. On my way back up the Saone I took the short side trip up the Doubs to Verdun-sur-les-Doubes for an overnight rest and to try their famous *Pouhouse*, a fish stew with wine and onions that is considered a local specialty. As I was tidying up my lines and shutting everything down, a rental boat pulled in behind me and asked for a spot of help tying up. I recognized them as Americans and, as things tend to go, we ended up having a glass of wine together on *Phaedra*. To accomplish this, however, my guests had to navigate my easel, canvases, makeshift stool and other artist paraphernalia. As they were looking around for a clean place to sit, I grabbed a couple paintings and said, "I'll be right with you. I just need to set these out to dry."

Chapter Seventeen

"Hurdy gurdy, hurdy gurdy, hurdy gurdy, gurdy, gurdy…(repeat)"

- Donovan

When the girls arrived a week later, Linda was none too pleased when she saw that I had transformed the interior of the boat into a working artist's loft, not to mention the sorry state of the woodwork in *Phaedra*. She immediately went to work putting the boat back into a habitable condition and I set off at a trot to track down Philippe and find out just how big of a fight we would have on our hands getting it all redone. Sarah picked up his scent at the H2O office and followed his still warm trail over to the atelier on the canal basin. We just missed him there, but heard that he was headed back to the store and maybe on to a diesel supply place out by the river. There was no sign of him at the store, and the diesel supply place was closed for lunch when we got there, so the search was suspended for the day.

Two more days of "Where's Waldo?" all over St. Jean de Losne turned up no one who had seen Philippe recently, which was a bit suspicious given the fact that he was hard to miss, being the only 6'7" German in the village. Finally, I decided to hunt like the Navajo do. When I was a kid, my father had told me that Navajos hunted bear not by going looking for one but by sitting under a tree or bush next to a beehive, where they eventually turn up. This can take a while, so my dad advised that when hunting bear, take a book. And that's what I did. I took a folding chair from the boat, a sandwich, a beer and a book and camped out at the foot of the stairs in front of the office waiting for Philippe to show up.

The first day, I had no luck, but I did notice that Bouba, Phillipe's right hand man, who was rumored to be mostly illiterate, seemed to be carrying lots of paperwork and files in and out of the office. On the second day I was joined by John, an Aussie off a river tug that was tied next to us on Pontoon B. He was also looking for Philippe, regarding some alleged double billing on some work done to his fuel injectors. On the third day, two Brits and another Aussie brought their chairs and beer. We were all sitting in a circle singing "We Shall Overcome" when Philippe finally gave up and came out of hiding.

Although I was first on the list of problems to deal with, we were all crowded around his desk like a bunch of Frenchmen threatening a strike. When I stepped forward and demanded that the woodwork be redone in my boat, at no charge, the International Brotherhood of Bear Hunters declared loudly and forcefully that crappy work would not be accepted or paid for anymore (and especially not twice as in the case of John's fuel injector work). Satisfaction was the only option. To this, Philippe replied, "What is this that is so wrong with your woodwork?" and he tried to look like he didn't know.

"It's completely warped, split and coming apart," I said. "You guys did the whole job using green wood."

"This is not right," he said and laid his hands on his desk. "This must be replaced." He knitted his brow and gazed deeply into my eyes.

"Yes. It must be replaced," I said, after a second.

"All the wood," added John.

"Of course," he said and opened his desk calendar. "When will you want this work to be done?" He clicked his pen and prepared to circle the start date.

"Oh, uh, not now," I said. "My wife's here. She wants to go boating."

He stared at me for a second, then sighed and said, "She wants to go boating?"

"Uh, yeah."

He put his pen down. "When is good for you?" he said, rolling his eyes toward the ceiling.

"Tell you what. We're going home next month and you'll have all winter to do it. How's that?"

"Ah, this is fine," he smiled and picked up his pen. "We will do this job in the winter."

"With kiln-dried wood," I said.

"Of course," he said and extended his paw.

That problem satisfactorily kicked down the road, Linda and I decided to tear ourselves away from the rounds of cookouts,

Game Nights and bowling tournaments on Pontoon B and head out for a cruise. The next day, with Sarah sound asleep at my feet, we putt-putted through the harbor to the waving hankies and bon voyages of the River Rats. We had decided to do a little exploring on the Canal de Bourgogne. We had five weeks to get as far up the canal as possible and then return to St. Jean to leave *Phaedra* covered and shut down for the winter.

The Canal de Bourgogne starts, or ends, at the Saone and covers 242 kilometers and 190 locks all the way to the Yonne River at the northern end of Burgundy. It would be our most direct route to Paris so we were looking at this excursion as a sort of trial run. From St. Jean de Losne, we faced 30 kilometers and 20 locks to Dijon, all in a dead straight line. It passed monotonously through some unremarkable towns and equally unremarkable countryside spotted with grain elevators, factories and junky backyards, as it climbed a total of about 60 feet to Dijon. We pushed through and got there in two days.

A modern and well-positioned little harbor, situated in the middle of a grassy park, awaited us at Dijon. The town itself is a beautiful and historic city. It was the capitol of the Duchy of Burgundy, established in 1404 by Duke Philip the Bold, who received it from King John the Good. Philip the Bold promptly created the prestigious Order of the Golden Fleece and then passed it on to John the Fearless who fluffed it up and passed on to Philip the Good. The Order of the Golden Fleece still carries on and has never had any members named Bill the Timid or Dave the Chicken. It's that kind of stirring history that makes you want to grab your wife, your dog, and your Michelin Guide and head for the farmer's market.

I don't know who was more excited when we rounded the corner off Rue Musette and found the covered market square packed with vendors hawking fruits, vegetables, breads, cheeses, meat, and fish: Linda or Sarah. They both perked up their ears and dove in. An hour later, with bags of lettuces, leeks, baguettes, and sausages, we were sitting at an outdoor café having some wine and sampling our assortment of olives, nuts, and cheeses, when we noticed a man dressed up in an 1880's costume, cranking an elaborately-painted hurdy-gurdy on wheels. On his shoulder sat a stuffed monkey sporting a tin cup into which people were dumping coins at a pretty brisk rate. After a number or two, he picked up his cup, straightened his monkey and headed in our direction.

He parked himself right in front of our café and commenced to cranking and hooting out a new tune. He was making a fine noise. We thought this was terribly quaint and cute, and were about to drop something in the monkey's cup, when I looked down the street and saw another costumed man cranking on his own music box and setting up a competing wail. Wanting to make sure that I contributed to the best hurdy-gurdy man I could, I walked down to the corner to check out this new contender. The nearer I got, the more confused and off key his honking seemed to be. Then I looked around the corner and discovered why. Up and down the street for blocks in either direction were hurdy-gurdies. They were elaborately decorated, restored to perfection and operated by men and women dressed up in costumes that spanned at least a hundred years' time. They were all going at once, setting up a cacophony so loud and discordant it would make a bat run into a barn.

Dijon was overrun with hurdy-gurdies. It was a great gathering of them, a mad swarming of hurdy-gurdies, all come together in an annual contest for the best, most elaborate and opulent hurdy-gurdy of all Europe. There were colorful entries from Vienna, madly cranking out punch card symphonies by Mozart. There were lacquered and gilded models from Milan and

Florence setting a dower street corner mood with crank organ renditions of the arias from "Rigoletto" and "La Traviata." French, Dutch, and Polish hurdy-gurdies, with teams of costumed crankers and pushers, were supported by trained clowns and pickpockets from the animal world. There were lots of stuffed monkeys and even some live ones that would jump, twirl and beg. There were people dressed up in bear costumes who danced for the kids and even a trained crow that would jump on little boys' heads and peck at their ears. Sarah was so taken by an elaborate entry from Provence that she sat down in front of it and started to sing along. It was marvelous!

We followed the organ trail for several blocks until we found ourselves in a square in front of the town hall where the acoustics were perfect and the really big boys had set up camp. Here were hurdy-gurdies the size of semi-trucks with whole brass bands of mechanical robots blasting out perennial favorites like the themes from "Bonanza" and "Chariots of Fire." Before that day, I didn't think that there was such a thing as a maximum human capacity for hurdy-gurdy music. That's all changed for me now.

The next morning, figuring we'd experienced the best of Dijon, we cast off and headed up the canal into new territory. The Canal de Bourgogne tagging along side the River Ouche climbs through the Ouche Valley toward a high watershed and the legendary two-mile long tunnel at Pouilly-en-Auxois. Just before the tunnel is the basin at Vandenesse-en-Auxois which sits beneath the storybook castle of Chateauneuf, crowning the hilltop some five miles away.

At the pace we were going, we didn't expect to see Chateauneuf on this trip, but we consoled ourselves by consuming great amounts of Burgundian food and wine, which is regarded by the Burgundians as the best in France. The region is known for its specialties, from the mustards of Dijon, blended with wine or tarragon or champignons, to the *jambon parsille* (cold ham pressed in a white wine jelly and parsley), to the cepes, chanterelles, and St. Georges mushrooms, as well as the cheeses like the smelly Epoisse, or the creamy delights from the Abbey de Citeaux. Preceded by the local escargot or *oefs au murette*, the *boeuf Bourguignon* always went well, all chased by short shots of the local fiery digestife, Marc. We had our hands full keeping up.

Any residual stress or anxiety evaporated as we floated in a state of utter satiety through what is some of the most beautiful countryside in France. I'd pull out my painting gear in the afternoons and try to capture the passing beauty but I was never quite happy with the results. I began to realize that cruising and painting weren't compatible activities, at least not on the same day. However, Linda and Sarah and I took long walks in the mornings and afternoons and I always took a camera and took hundreds of photographs that I intended to paint from over the winter.

For days we loafed along at about three miles an hour, about as fast as a walk through a park. The locks were closely spaced as we steadily gained elevation. Most were manually operated by lock keepers who lived with their families in little lock houses surrounded by flower and vegetable gardens, decorated by Dopey, Grumpy and Sneezy, by far the most popular of the Seven Dwarfs. We would sit on the deck, holding the lines and petting Sarah as *Phaedra* rose in the locks and we'd look back over the Ouche Valley and marvel at how we had actually climbed a mountain on a boat.

When the locks closed at noon, we'd pull over, drive a stake or two into the ground and settle in for lunch. People walking or riding their bikes along the tow-path would wish us *"bon appetit"* as they went by and we'd toast them with a little chilled Mersault. Evenings, we'd often tie up along some stretch of the canal and take Sarah to explore a nearby village or farm. We usually found horses or cows or goats who liked carrots and a good scratching on the forehead. There were always villages or small towns along the way where we could stop and try out a local restaurant, visit a market, replenish the wine supply or tour a historic chateau, abbey or castle. No matter where we spent the night, a village, with a boulangerie, was within easy bicycle range.

We were two weeks out when we passed through the little village of St Victor-sur-Ouche, a tumbled collection of beautifully maintained stone cottages with a small bakery and cafe. We were tempted to stop for the night but decided to press on through one more lock to the next village, La Bussiere-sur-Ouche, where we heard there was a 13th century Cistercian abbey that gave tours. At the lock just before St. Victor, I used my best French to ask the *eclusier* where I would find the next spot in the canal that would be wide enough to turn *Phaedra* around so we could start our return trip to St. Jean de Losne. He seemed to appreciate my attempt to communicate in his language, and at some length he told me to continue on, and just before the next lock, at La Bussiere, I would find the a spot in the canal that should do nicely. We could turn around there and moor up for the night along the bank. The next day we would walk over to the abbey, take a quick tour and then start our return trip back down the valley.

The canal at this point winds above the valley of the Ouche against a backdrop of rolling mountain ridges and through a tunnel of dense flaming red maples, bright yellow walnut trees, and tall shimmering poplars, all planted in neat rows shading the tow-paths. We followed this winding cavern of trees until we finally came around a bend and found the La Bussiere lock, dead ahead. I shifted into neutral and drifted for a while, gauging the width of the canal and looking for the wide spot where we would make our turn. The lock doors were closed, but water was spilling over their tops and through the cracks, causing an easy current that helped to slow us down.

The wide spot wasn't obvious, but it looked like it might be just ahead, right in front of a lounging fisherman sitting on the bank angling his pole into the stream. He studiously ignored us as I slowly edged the boat up even with him and started my turn. I didn't have room to do any kind of a big, arching turn here. I was going to have to use the bow thruster to push the front of the boat around, while using the main propeller and rudder, hard over, to swing the stern. I was hoping the old girl would perform a sweet, stylish pirouette, spin in her own length, then do a little sideways two-step and we'd nestle up to the bank and tie off in time for cocktails. I was also hoping that the fisherman would bring his pole in during the maneuver, so I could avoid being poked in the eye.

I spun the wheel all the way over, pumped the throttle, and the stern started swinging to the right. Then I hit the bow thruster and the front of the boat began pushing to the left. *Phaedra*, with the grace of a giant, floating refrigerator, started her pivot to slowly present herself crosswise to the canal. As she came more fully around, I began to wonder if this was the right spot. My bow and stern were coming uncomfortably close to the edges of the canal where the water grew shallow and big rocks, logs, and chunks of concrete lurk, to rip holes in boats and grind off spinning propellers. As a precaution, I stopped the bow thruster and put the propeller in neutral, letting her momentum continue to carry her around.

Phaedra's bow ground sickeningly to a halt just inches from the feet of the fisherman. She sat there looming over him like some giant sperm whale that had tried to crawl into his lap. The back of the boat, just as slowly and just as firmly, became wedged against the steel revetments lining the right bank of the canal. And there she rested, aground, with the gentle current holding her perfectly across the canal.

With the rudder and propeller wedged in the mud and rocks below, I didn't dare put the engine in gear, so I grabbed our long wooden boat-pole and ran up to the bow to see if I could push us off from the front. Skidding to a halt on *Phaedra's* bow I found myself looking six feet down straight into the glaring eyes of the Frenchman who was holding his fishing pole over his shoulder and looking very annoyed. *"Pardon, monsieur,"* I said, then jammed my pole into the muddy bank next to his transistor radio and started pushing.

The pole sank into the mud and started to bend. I pushed some more. I gritted my teeth and spat profanities until Linda came and added her back to the project. I thought we were starting to move, but it was just the pole sinking deeper into the mud.

It wasn't working. The only thing to do was to jump off the boat and push from the bank. I leapt ashore, over the unhappy sportsman, then turned around and threw my shoulder against the hull. It finally started to move. Step by step, down the bank and into the shallows, trying not to step in his bait bucket, I pushed the bow back up into the stream. When she was floating free, I climbed up the anchor and back onto the deck and turned to say *"au revoir"* to the unhelpful Frenchman. As I did, I glanced down in time to see the current push *Phaedra* right back into the mud at his feet.

Feeling like Humphrey Bogart desperately dragging his *African Queen* through the swamp, I leapt back into the stream and pushed my own old iron boat off the mud again. Linda tried to hold her in place with the pole while I climbed aboard, but the current was just a little too strong. At this point I realized that this tactic was not going to work without some help from the shore. The fisherman scowled at us, shifted his fishing pole, and lit a cigarette.

No help there, so I headed to the rear of the boat to see if there was anything that could be done from there. Trotting along the deck, I imagined the rumors reaching St. Jean de Losne of a mysterious Dutch barge becoming wedged across the Canal de Bourgogne and being rammed by a 150-foot grain barge, causing a wreck that would close the canal to all traffic for months. The next barge coming around the bend or through the lock would cement *Phaedra's* name in River Rat barge history.

The back of the boat was jammed against the steel pilings edging the canal and the rudder, which had been turned all the way to the left, was folded in tight between the revetments and the hull. I pushed and cursed until I thought I'd split, but she wouldn't budge. The current that was holding me fast was the result of a lock opening downstream, which meant a boat was coming. Any second I could expect a hotel barge or some commercial monster to appear from around the bend and roll right through me. It was time for desperate measures. The steering on the boat is hydraulic. There are two-inch stainless steel rams on each side of the rudder, and when I turn the wheel, these rams push and pull the rudder from side to side. Turning the wheel now would cause one of these rams to push the rudder away from the boat and against the wall. It would either break off the rudder or it would slide us across the bottom to freedom. It was a lousy choice, but I didn't want to become famous as the stopper in the bottle of the Canal de Bourgogne, so, taking a deep breath, I gently nudged the wheel. She moved. I did it again. Slowly, *Phaedra* scraped along the rocks on the bottom, then did a dip and floated free. I jammed the pole into the bank and shoved us away until it seemed safe to put it in gear, then we backed into the middle of the canal.

Giving up on any idea of turning around, we both decided it was best to just pull to the side and moor up for the night under the trees. By the time I had our stakes in the ground and the engine shut down, Linda had fixed us a couple glasses of the Irish whiskey that we keep for special moments and we set about the process of calming down. Sarah came over and put her nose in my lap, rolled her brown eyes up at me and gave me that look that says, "I don't care what anybody says, I think you are the best boat captain in the world. Let's go for a walk."

Why do dogs always seem to have such good ideas? We decided to walk up the canal to scope out the village and although we had missed the tour for the day, we wanted to peek through the gate at the Cistercian abbey up the road. We also wanted to check out the lock house. It was the classic cute little stone house with the signature round window in the peak of the roof and regulation garden gnomes stationed around the perimeter. Standing in front of the gnomes and looking past the full lock and up the canal beyond, we discovered a great big, spacious and inviting turn-around basin. At least a hundred feet wide and clear on both banks, it was the perfect place to turn a boat around. The water was perfectly calm and smooth as a swimming pool, and there were no fishermen. This inspired Linda to pull out her French/English dictionary and research the lock keeper's phrase, "The best place to turn your boat around is before/after the next lock."

Chapter Eighteen

Dave Bowman: *Open the pod bay doors, HAL.*
HAL: *I'm sorry, Dave. I'm afraid I can't do that.*
- 2001: A Space Odyssey

We were turned around and down-locking now, which is a breeze compared to up-locking. You just drive into the lock and drop your lines over the bollards then sit and relax as you gently descend. We were lucky enough to find our old mooring at Gissey-sur-Ouche just by the stone bridge that leads to the boulangerie. The waitress at the little bistro remembered us and gave us her best table outside and even brought a blanket for Sarah to lay on. Fall was bringing crisp mornings with a foggy mist that blanketed the canals and clung to the still water. The chilly morning walks to the boulangerie were rewarded with hot, crusty baguettes that you could lay against your cheek for warmth. The poplars, maples, and live oaks were wading deep into their fall colors, their leaves raining down in glistening waves when the wind blew, blanketing the paths in warm reds and oranges. The smell of wood smoke and the sounds of rifle fire permeated the air. It was hunting season.

We went at a slow but steady pace and eventually found ourselves passing under the bridge into the little harbor at Dijon. That was essentially the end of the beauty part of our cruise, so we decided to stop for an extra day before doing the final push down to St. Jean. The hurdy-gurdies were gone, but the restaurants and cafés were enticing that evening so we eased our return from the idyllic Ouche Valley with a thick and hearty Boeuf Bourguignon and a bottle of Volnay.

Two days later, we were chugging through the last of the two-day stretch of featureless flat land on the trip back to St. Jean de Losne when, half a day from home, the boat started to shudder and vibrate in a most ominous way. I pulled to the side of the canal and climbed into the engine room, but look as I might, I couldn't find anything obvious that would be causing such a violent vibration. There were two options: Either stop and phone for an emergency house call from H2O, or try to nurse *Phaedra* along and hope that we could limp back to St. Jean without shaking the engine off its mounts and pulling out the prop shaft. Somehow, the idea of calling for the emergency attentions of Bouba seemed much worse than hoping, limping and nursing, so we pressed on. We made it back late that day, but barely, and with a close call or two inside the harbor when my bow thruster stopped working. With less than a week before we returned to the U.S., I went looking for Philippe to try to sweet talk him into fixing whatever the hell was wrong this time.

Philippe was in surprisingly good spirits when I found him lounging on his favorite forklift. He greeted me warmly and asked about my dog, my wife and my trip, then stuck a Xeroxed memo in my hand announcing his upcoming marriage to his girlfriend

Emma. From what I could tell from my own objective observation and the collective work stoppage that occurred throughout the boatyard whenever she arrived with Philippe's lunch, Emma was a real catch. She was also quite accomplished at swinging flaming torches around on short ropes toward the end of parties and late-night cookouts down by the harbor.

A quick look at the announcement in my hand revealed that the happy occasion wasn't scheduled to occur until the following April, well after my interior woodwork should be finished, so I was overjoyed by the news. So overjoyed that I suggested that he might want to send someone from his team of mechanics down to my boat ASAP, to figure out what was causing it to vibrate like a bed in a cheap motel. Giddy as a schoolboy, he promised to have Bouba clomping across my deck with his toolbox by nine a.m. the next morning.

And so it was. We barely had our teeth brushed when I heard a tapping on my hull and looked out to find Bouba with a freshly rolled cigarette, wearing his grease stained version of an Elvis impersonator jumpsuit, sporting a collection of gold chains and holding, almost symbolically, an adjustable crescent wrench in his free hand.

Bouba was the acknowledged bon vivant and 'sexy guy' of the H2O atelier crew. It was his responsibility to keep up the reputation for lechery that the H2O team had worked so hard to achieve. No matter how cold it got in the winter, no matter how many layers of fleece, wool and down the day called for, most of Bouba's chest hair would be on prominent display to warm women's hearts and drive them wild. He knew that his gift of sexiness was not his alone to covet or conceal. It must be shared, and with pretty much any breathing female in or around St. Jean de Losne. As a mechanic, he could do simple jobs, dirty jobs, or jobs where there were clear instructions with pictures. He was the star of the H2O team.

After a little explaining on my part and leering at Linda on his part, he climbed down into the engine compartment and went to work while Linda and I went off to do a mountain of laundry at the local coin-a-lav. When we returned, we found a very self-satisfied Bouba, lounging on the deck, smoking a cigarette and tanning his chest. Sitting next to him was an obviously broken orange thing that looked like it was important. Through fractured French, Tarzan English, and hand signals, I figured out that the broken part was the flexible coupling that joined the engine to the hydraulic pump.

The engine powered everything. Bolted to the back of the engine was the transmission and to that, the propeller shaft. Bolted to the front of the engine was the pump that created the hydraulic pressure that ran the steering and the bow thruster. Where each of these components met the next, there would be a minimally flexible part called a "coupling" that absorbed any shocks created by going from forward to reverse or left to right. The coupling between the engine and the hydraulic pump had started to tear apart between Dijon and St. Jean and came completely apart just as we pulled into our slip.

So, we needed a new flexible coupling. It was, of course, a Dutch part, and wouldn't be delivered from Holland until two weeks after we were back home in Sausalito. There was nothing to do but pack up our stuff, put the winter covering on the boat and promise to keep in touch with Philippe via email on the progress of our woodwork, our flexible coupling, and his own coupling with the luscious Emma.

Chapter Nineteen

"Ploink...Ploink...Ploink...Ploink"
- Trouble – Winter 2007

Once again I was caught in the throes of re-entry. The morning hankering for a fresh croissant would get so bad that I considered getting hooked on heroin as a distraction. After living happily, and media-free within the confines of a compact barge, the opulence of three bathrooms, a den and two TV's seemed to verge on the obscene. All this, and I found a leak in my roof.

That did it. It was time to downsize. We'd sell the burdensome house and move back into our little Victorian art studio. We'd live like we had when we were poor but happy newlyweds, twenty-five years ago.

Linda started jumping up and down and clapping her hands like an overjoyed circus seal when I broached the idea. In a twinkling, she had all the necessary forms filled out and I was signing a listing agreement with my wife to sell our house. She immediately started redecorating so as not to offend any prospective buyers. All my cool stuff, like my ship models and my collection of autographed boxing photographs, were hidden away.

To make the closets look bigger, half my clothes were removed and lodged in the basement of the art studio. Anything that verged on the politically incorrect, like carved bits of ivory and my stuffed parakeet, were banned, replaced by flower arrangements that made the living room look like a Mafia funeral parlor. The house was scrubbed top to bottom and all the plants in the front yard were ripped out and replaced with pots of flowering petunias from the supermarket. In short, we were "staged."

Our first open house was set to commence at eleven a.m. the very next Saturday morning. Linda got up early and ran around the neighborhood dropping "Open House" signs at every corner, then she came home and threw a frozen apple pie in the oven to make it smell like Martha Stewart lived there. Every trace of human use of any of the bathrooms or the laundry room was scooped up and jammed into my sock drawer on the theory that the hoard of eager buyers would comb through the closets and flush all the toilets, but they'd draw the line at groping my underwear. Sarah was allowed to stay, because she looked good sleeping in front of the fireplace, but I was kicked out because I didn't.

I found myself on the street with a whole Saturday in front of me. If I were in France, Sarah and I would take our sack of day-old bread down to the canal and feed the ducks. Then we could go to a café and, over coffee or wine, I'd sketch the people and she'd scour the ground under the tables for tidbits. But I was in the U.S. so that meant I had lists of things to do. Go to hardware store, sell car, wash dog, get new glasses, fix plumbing in art studio. I could be scurrying around all afternoon. Instead, I decided to go visit my father at the palatial Villa San Miguel. I arrived at noon, just in time for lunch. Visitors are encouraged to pull up a chair and help.

I never got used to feeding my father. He'd open his mouth like a baby bird until I guided a spoonful of some steamed or boiled food in. Then I'd scrape the overflow off with the spoon and wipe his chin with the bib. Between bites, I'd ask him meaningless questions like, What you been up to? How's it going? What's new around here? He'd just look at me and open his mouth for the next bite. That day he did surprise me by saying. "I got a job. I'm going to be a salesman downtown, but I need to grow a mustache first. Customers like mustaches." Then he picked up a piece of beef stroganoff from his tray and stuck it to his upper lip. "See?"

"That's great," I said. "And instead of trimming it, you can chew it off."

An attendant came by and said, "Now, Johnny, your son's here to visit you and he doesn't want to hear about your mustache."

"His name is Chauncey. Not Johnny," I said.

"Chauncey? That's nice." Then she ran off to stop a woman who was pouring her milk into her neighbor's lap.

As I wiped his face I said, "Hey dad, remember how you used to want to buy a big fishing boat and live on it, cruise around?" He looked at me and opened his mouth. I gave him a spoonful of spinach, wiped his chin, and went on. "Linda and I bought a barge in France. We're going to take it to Paris. Maybe live on it there. Want to come with us?"

He said, "I got a job."

I thought, Oh dad, I hope you're far, far away from here.

My life was now governed by the dictates of the housing market. I had to be ready to get lost at a moment's notice so some realtor could lead a pack of pre-approved tire-kickers through the house, measuring closets, knocking on walls and gobbling down endless batches of fresh baked cookies. (Linda had decided that although pies smelled just as good, they were too much mess, so she was experimenting with oatmeal and chocolate chip cookies to see which flavor would close the deal.)

I decided to focus my attention on what we were going to do when the house finally sold and we had to move. The financial plan was pretty much set. We'd bank the equity (if there was any), pay off our credit cards, move into the little art studio and then hack away at our overhead so that we could survive if Linda sold the occasional house and I was able to sell my paintings. If it all worked out, we'd be able to spend time on the boat in the spring and fall, and spend mid-summer and winter at home. If it didn't work, we were in trouble. The red-hot real estate market was looking very shaky and we both were afraid that it would collapse any time. If it did before we could sell the house, our savings and Linda's job would crash with it. I would go on trying to sell paintings, but that's not so easy when the economy's taking a dive.

We were at a critical juncture. The house had to sell. We had to get rid of all our debt, downsize our lives and start living strictly on a pay-as-you-go basis. And there was another thing jangling at the back of my mind; once we'd taken this step, we could never go back.

When we sold the house, we'd be moving from a chock-full 2,800 square foot house to one that was only 900 square feet. Things had to go. This is not so easy to do. Try looking around your house with the intention of getting rid of two thirds of your possessions (by bulk). Okay, you get rid of one old dresser, that's a big thing. Congratulations. But what about all the stuff inside it? Keep it? Where? In cardboard boxes? Then you have the special things that mean so much, like Linda's wedding dress and my collection of hats. Do we get rid of her extra shoes or my priceless library of Wooden Boat magazines?

The little house we were moving to had only two closets.

We put some hope on our two daughters. They were grown and had homes of their own so we assumed that they would want some of our prized pieces of furniture.

Not so.

How about a leather-bound set of the greatest books ever written about shipwrecks? No thanks. Please take Grandma's hutch? No room. Would either of you like this vintage hi-fi? Vintage what? Collection of records from the 60s? No, thanks, got'em on CD. Downsizing is not for sissies.

One day, I was walking out to my car with a box of old videos in my arms when a young fellow in a new Porsche convertible screeched to a halt, rolled down his window and barked, "Hey, is this house for sale?"

"Sure is," I said. "My wife…"

"Can I just take a quick look at it?" he said over the window. "My wife said I should see it, but I can't do it this weekend."

I wasn't supposed to, but I said, "OK. I can give you a quick look around, I guess."

"Cool," he said and parallel parked at sixty miles per hour.

I took him for a tour of the place and finished it up by offering him a drink on the deck overlooking the Bay. That pretty much did it. He was a rosy-cheeked young sailor and commodities broker, and he liked the idea of being able to watch the sailboat races from his own deck. We had another half shot of Power's Irish whiskey and parted company, with him begging me not to sell it to anyone else before he had a chance to write up his offer. When Linda came home with a fresh batch of frozen cookie dough, I told her to throw it away. Whiskey had done the trick and we had a buyer.

There is a mind boggling amount of rigmarole that one has to go through in order to sell a house. Most of it I never saw, but one step, the contractor's inspection, I was prepared to attend. The Porsche driver couldn't make it that day, but his wife and their ditzy realtor showed up and we all followed the contractor around the house as he tapped on things and poked and sniffed around the crawl spaces. As we were walking through the back yard, the wife noticed, mostly overgrown with ivy, an old squirrel-gnawed set of moose horns, hanging from the retaining wall. They seemed to catch her fancy, so, seeing an opportunity to eliminate one more downsizing headache, I said, "You buy the place, I'll throw in the moose horns." She made an "Oooo!" sound and then went and caught up with her realtor. I have an instinct for selling, I thought to myself. I think I got it from my father.

Of course their contractor came up with a list of critically needed repairs that included a new roof, new siding, all new windows, new plumbing and a new garbage disposal. I had to give them the garbage disposal because when they turned it on it exploded, but the rest was all fluff. We were all reasonable people though, and we wanted the same things essentially, so over the dining room table and some more Powers whiskey, we came to a final agreement and shook hands on it. The deal was done.

It took weeks for the banks and title companies to dance around and justify their fees, so we had time to plan out our next steps. The little house we were moving into had been a rental for quite a while and was getting a bit run down, which was alright for a rental, but gad, not for us! It needed a complete paint job, floors refinished, walls repaired, doors replaced and most of the plumbing updated so that the shower didn't stop when someone flushed the toilet. Both the faucets leaked and the washer and dryer just couldn't stay in the bedroom closet. More plumbing.

The house was one block from the Bay in the heart of Sausalito. It was a small yellow Victorian, built in 1876. Tourists walking by would stop and say, "What a quaint old house." For a while, Linda had one of those rubber stamps you use on envelopes for your return address that said our name and "Quaint old house" as the address. There was a market, a hardware store, a three-screen movie theater two blocks away and a hairdresser, deli, and bookstore on the next block. Just around the corner there were two places that had jazz every night. People parked across our driveway at least twice a month and drunks peed in our hedge. It was the place where we had spent some of our most fun and whacky years, and we looked forward to getting back there.

But it needed work. A lot of it. I could go into a long litany of misery here on my battles with painters, plumbers, plasterers and the impenetrable morass of the Home Depot subcontractor system, but none of that would be new unless I were to marvel about how smoothly it all went.

Our daughters, Nicole and Krista, were going to arrive a few days before our final move-out deadline to get a jump on their inheritances, or at least grab the stuff they could sell on eBay. They did a good job of it, better than we had expected. It turned out that Krista had left her husband (the story of which is a book in itself), and was in the process of furnishing her own apartment.

Her timing couldn't have been better. She took the spare bed, a couple of chairs, a couch, a dresser and the TV. She didn't want any books or clocks, but the moose horns on the retaining wall, those she wanted. She reminded us that they were a hand-me-down from an old friend of mine, known to the girls as their "Uncle Dickey," who was famous for decorating flourishes like dented coronets, rocking chairs carved in the shape of dragons, and mangy moose horns. He was their oldest hippie and bore a striking resemblance to Jerry Garcia. The girls loved him. So Uncle Dickey's moose horns came down from the retaining wall and were lovingly crammed into the back of the truck. "Say goodbye to the moose horns," Linda said, as Krista closed the doors. And I did. But they didn't say goodbye to me.

Chapter Twenty

"Life is just one damn thing after another."
\- W.C. Fields

Two days later, the moving truck arrived for the last of our goods and Linda, Sarah, and I said goodbye to our dream house and hello to the Marin Gardens Motel for a week or two until the Quaint Old House emerged from her cocoon of drop cloths and regained running water. Psychiatrists and drug manufacturers the world over love it when people decide to sell their homes and move. Few things can intensify the longing for a good psychotic episode or a fresh prescription of Valium like putting your house on the market, packing your whole life into boxes, and ending up in a motel/cathouse listening to a veritable marathon of rodeo sex thumping through the walls, ceiling, and floor.

After our first sleepless night at the Marin Gardens, I checked my voicemail to find the following message from Linda's counterpart, the realtor representing the Porsche driving buyer: "Hello, Mr. Hammond. This is Darleen. I've been told to tell you, by my client, that he is considering taking legal action against you because, when he took possession of the house, he was shocked to find the moose horns were not there. He wants his moose horns. Please call me. Thank you."

He wants his moose horns? Isn't his wife telling him that she needs all new kitchen cabinets and that the colors are all wrong? Didn't she say something about ripping out all the carpets and putting in hardwood floors? How in blazes does he find the time to sue me over a set of crappy old moose horns? He needs to get a grip. I didn't call her back.

Meanwhile, through the wonders of email, I was able to keep in touch with the crackerjack team of specialists at H2O, who were supposed to be redoing the botched interior work and replacing the hydraulic pump coupling on dear *Phaedra*. There was no Internet connection at the Marin Gardens so I'd go to the local Kinko's to check up on the progress. It seemed all was well with the woodworking project. The team of cabinetmakers and interior specialists were thrilled to be given the opportunity to apply their talents to a project that was actually meant to last and were going at it with a will. Bouba, on the other hand, hadn't had a moment free to start on the coupling project. One might presume he was otherwise occupied with coupling projects of his own. But it struck me that this was a blessing in disguise. The coupling piece had broken for a reason. If we didn't find out, then the new part would soon fail as well. I sent Philippe an email suggesting strongly that he should take care to check the alignment of all the components in the drive train, especially between the engine and the hydraulic pump, to make sure that everything was in perfect harmony with its neighbor.

That afternoon, back at the paper wall motel, Linda came hurrying into our temporary home from a quick stop at her office, breathless with news. "We're being sued," she squeaked.

"If those two upstairs don't stop, for five minutes, I'm going up there," I said, as the rhythmic thumping overhead threatened to drown out Jerry Springer.

"The moose horns! We have to give him the moose horns."

"I'm not giving him the moose horns. Uncle Dickey gave them to Krista. They're hers," I said, turning up the volume on the television.

"She says you gave them to them. They said it was part of the deal."

"Didn't get it in writing. Too bad."

"Their agent says she was there. She heard you. She's a witness," Linda said, her realtor hat planted firmly on her head.

"Oh no," I said, as the couple next door woke up from their rest period and resumed slamming the headboard against the wall behind the TV set.

The next day I went back to Kinko's and checked my email. There was one from Philippe at H2O telling me that Bouba had been down to my boat to check the alignment on everything and had reported back that the hydraulic pump was mounted on a fixed mount that was not adjustable. Philippe was very unhappy about this but he had an idea. He suggested that they should take the whole pump off, then fabricate a new, adjustable mount out of stainless steel, and put it all together again, perfectly adjusted.

This sounded like a perfect example of "project creep." A basic two-hour job had just morphed into an engineering and stainless steel fabrication project with untold riches flowing into the coffers of H2O. I emailed back that he should send Bouba down one more time to confirm that there were no adjustments possible with the mount as it was. It didn't seem likely, I told him, that any self-respecting Dutchman would install a hydraulic pump in that way. I hit send.

The next email was from Mr. Porsche. He was outraged that I hadn't left the moose horns on the retaining wall for his wife. She was from Wisconsin or some such place, and moose horns reminded her of home. These moose horns in particular had touched her heart and she wanted them in her new home. Deliver them or face legal action.

I wrote him a scathing response, then deleted it. Instead, I simply replied that the moose horns weren't mine to give away. They belonged to my daughter, a beloved memento from her dearly departed Uncle Dickey, a Vietnam war hero, and I couldn't, in all conscience, take them away from her. Then I got on eBay and started checking out the going rate for moose horns. The highest bid, for a set that had reportedly resided above the pool table in Graceland, was $150.00. Being unemployed at the time, I figured I could afford to spend a lot of time defending myself.

Days were spent thus. Emails in the morning and fussing and fighting to get our house finished the rest of the day. I'd make an occasional visit to the Power's bottle in the evening, hoping to sleep through the Olympic shagging taking place in the adjoining rooms.

Two days later, the young, mostly inebriated son of our house painter, who had taken on the job of refinishing the hardwood floors in our little house, allowed his industrial sized floor-sanding machine to get away from him and it drove itself through the living room wall, condemning us to another week at the No-tell Motel. I was in the basement, sorting books when I heard the crash so I ran upstairs to see what had happened. I turned the corner from the kitchen and my foot rolled over the sanding machine's power cord. I did one of those feet-above-the-head, fly-through-the-air, whahooo-o-o body slams that you see in the cartoons. I lay there on my back, staring up at the ceiling, thinking, "I've seen this before on TV. Old guy retires to live his dream, buys himself a barge to float around France, eating cheese and drinking wine, moves into his romantic little artist studio, trips on power cord, gets incurable whip-lash, gets hooked on pain pills, his wife leaves him, and he ends up living in the gutter, crippled, wearing a neck brace, drinking six-packs of canned wine and peeing on himself." I wiggled my toes as a test.

The pain was beginning to spread from my butt to my neck and my mood was turning dark when I checked my email that afternoon. There was another harassing missive from the demented, moose horn crazed, Porsche driver, which I ignored. Then I opened a message from Philippe with the news that Bouba was convinced that the hydraulic pump was *not* adjustable but he was quite excited about trying his hand at making me a brand new mounting block that would, no doubt, move all over the place. He also liked the idea of redoing all the stainless steel tubing for the system. He thought it would be creative and fun. What's this gonna cost me? I thought.

Chapter Twenty-One

"You're making Hulk mad."

\- Hulk Hogan

It was the first week in November and we were finally in our little house. Pictures were still leaning against the walls, un-hung, and we were shuffling around, knee deep in crumpled newspapers and bubble wrap, starting each conversation with, "Have you seen the...?" The faucets didn't leak, the walls were freshly painted, the floors had a new coat of Verathane, and you could flush the toilet and run the shower at the same time. No randy executives were spending romantic afternoons with their administrative assistants just through the wall and if Sarah had a call of nature, she just had to go out the front door and into the flower patch.

But it was not all skittles and chips. My neck and back had fused to the point where my head had the turning radius of a frog. And we were still under threat of legal action from the unhappy moose horn guy. We had decided not to make any decision about the coupling project on *Phaedra* until things had settled down at home, but it was still adding to the twinges in my neck. Stacks of euros would dance in my head like sugarplums, and images of Bouba, with his prominent chest hair, trying to figure out how to weld stainless steel or how a ruler works, would trigger my fight-or-flight response.

So, it was with mixed feelings that I opened a fresh email from Philippe. My feelings clarified quickly when I read that Philippe had taken my lack of a definitive "NO" as a "YES" to his plan to replace just about everything and he had dispatched his top man to the task. Bouba had gotten as far as trying to loosen the first bolt in the job when he found that the area in which he had to work was so cramped that he couldn't wield his favorite big wrench to full effect. His inspired solution to this problem was to cut a hole in the teak floorboards in the main salon and chop a chunk out of the main settee so that he could get his wrench in place and loosen bolt number one. Philippe was emailing me to get my approval for this butchery. Upon my consent, he'd set Bouba loose with his saw and his wrench and, if all went well, proceed to bolt number two.

With my head seized at a thirty-degree angle, I sent an immediate reply, "DO NOT TOUCH A THING. I'M COMING OVER THERE!"

That was a rash thing to say. One doesn't just jump on a plane these days unless the ticket is being paid for by your boss. The fare I could afford was two weeks off. As much as Linda loved being on *Phaedra*, a trip to St. Jean de Losne in the dead of winter to fight with Philippe and Bouba wasn't appealing enough to override her nesting instincts. She and Sarah weren't going to budge for a while. It wasn't a trip I was looking forward to either but *Phaedra* was our baby and I had to go over there and keep the wrecking crew from tearing her apart.

But the prospect of sitting on an airplane with my knees crammed under my chin for eleven hours had all the allure of a long day of waterboarding, so I called my HMO doctor and requested emergency prescriptions for pain drugs and sleeping pills, big ones. He refused to do it unless I came in for an appointment, in about six to eight weeks. Then he asked me if I'd like to speak to someone from the suicide help line.

Tired of watching me move around the place like Frankenstein, Linda shoved a phone number in my face and said, "Call Dr. Darleen. Now." A large, muscular woman, adept at twisting necks and popping backs, Darleen was Linda's chiropractor and she was happy to see people just about any time. I went in to see her that very afternoon. She took one look at me and started licking her little chiropractor chops. She put a protractor under my chin and told me to try to turn my head so that she could measure my range of movement. I had none. She immediately had me lay down on her table to be aligned. This is done by having Dr. Darleen hoist herself onto your back, balance there on her hands and knees, and bounce up and down until she hears a pop. It's surprising how loud it can be.

After that, it was time to pop my neck. I really didn't want to do this one, but I was in the hands of a professional, and very insistent, chiropractor who had just bounced on my back, so I somehow had lost my will to resist. In a twinkling I was sitting in a straight-backed chair, with the lady chiropractor standing behind me. She spoke calmly and in an almost motherly way, reassured me that I had nothing to worry about, all the while sneaking one beefy arm around my neck and under my chin. The other arm snaked up and pressed against the back of my head. I thought I recognized the hold as "The Sleeper," made famous by Hulk Hogan.

She was talking softly and soothingly about her dog, I think, gently rocking my head from side to side, when she suddenly let out a yell and ripped my head around like Linda Blair. My eyes popped out, fireworks exploded in my ears and my right leg shot straight out in front of me. The bones in my neck made noises like someone crunching a water bottle and explosions of light blasted through my cranium and bounced around behind my eyes. With my head still firmly clamped in her thick arms I opened my eyes expecting to see my headless body slump slowly to the floor.

As I rolled my eyes and tried to touch my face, through the ringing in my ears I heard her whisper, "OK, just relax. Now we'll do the other side."

I didn't last the full ten rounds. I had to lie down until my eyes uncrossed and I regained feeling in my feet. Lying there in her darkened recovery room, with an icepack on my head, I thought about my decision a year ago to take charge of my life, simplify it, and go for the joy. So far, my body was wracked with pain, I was being sued over moose horns, my father was playing with meat mustaches, the dream house was gone, and I had spent my savings on an old boat in France that currently had a sex-crazed mechanic hovering over it brandishing tools of mass destruction while his boss conjured up new ways to pick my pocket. I'd also learned an important lesson, one that should have been obvious to me from the start, but that I had somehow overlooked. The world isn't going to suddenly decide to stop messing with you just because you've decided to downsize and go simple. There are still going to be bad clams in the pasta, seaweed in the plumbing, and raccoons in the trashcan.

But we had made some progress. We were out from under the big house, I was painting again, and I was beginning to get some feeling back in my toes. But there was no getting around it. It was becoming painfully clear that building a simple, joy-filled life can be goddamn complicated and stressful as hell sometimes.

Chapter Twenty-Two

*"What I need is a list of specific unknown problems
we will encounter."*

- The Management

Late November is a cold and dark time to land in St. Jean
de Losne. A quick, nasty rain was falling, driven by winds that
clawed through my jacket and slithered up my pants legs. It was
nine o'clock in the morning and I was walking back to *Phaedra*,
carrying my breakfast croissant and holding a warm loaf of bread
against my cheek. I was exhausted from the flight but I was
looking forward to having a sit down with Philippe.

Savoring my first sip of coffee, I felt the boat take a dip as
heavy boots landed on the deck, signaling the arrival of the boys
from H2O. I offered Philippe and Bouba black coffee and we
stumbled through the small talk. The flight was fine, the train was
fine, the weather in California was fine, fine, fine. "So," I said,
"let's take a look at this pump thing."

"Yes, this is a problem," Philippe said, "Let us look at it."

"You're sitting on it," I said. "It's under the seat." I pointed
at the settee.

"Oh yes. Of course." Philippe jumped up.

I started dismantling the settee, handing cushions and wood panels off to the two of them, who stacked them outside in the cockpit. In a couple of minutes, we could see the hydraulic pump, mounted under the floorboards in the darkness by the inner hull. I shined my flashlight down into the hole. Philippe followed its beam until it landed on the bolts connecting the pump to its mount.

"Hmm," I said. "What's that look like to you?" I met Philippe's eye as he looked up at me.

"A bolt?" he made a guess.

"Actually, I was looking at the hole the bolt goes through." I wiggled the light. "Right there."

"Oh." Philippe pulled on his chin.

"You see the hole? It's slotted." Then I moved the light toward the back of the pump and found another bolt. "Oh look," I said. "That hole's slotted too. See there?" Philippe craned his big head around so he could see way in the back.

"Doesn't that mean that the pump is sitting on an adjustable mount?"

"Mon dieu!" Philippe exclaimed. "I think you are right!" Then he called to Bouba and they palavered a while in French.

"So, if it's an adjustable mount after all, can't Bouba just adjust everything and bolt it all back together without having to reconstruct anything at all?" I asked Philippe. Which prompted another debate in French with Bouba.

When they were done, Philippe turned back to me and said, "Oh, but there is still this problem that the piping is not flexible.

And you see this grand pipe?" He pointed at a two-inch curved piece of stainless steel tubing. "It must be loosened for the adjustment." He sat back on his heels and shrugged. Bouba leaned in, blew smoke all over everything, and nodded his agreement.

"And that's the one that needs the big wrench, huh?"

"Yes, yes," Philippe said. "And you see, the big wrench will not fit. There is no room to move here." He pointed out a large solid looking cylinder next to the pipe.

"This thing is in the way?" I asked, shining the light on it.

"Yes. The wrench will not go around. That is blocking it, you see there."

"That thing is the oil filter," I said. "It screws off."

"It does?"

"Yes. So, to sum this all up," I said, turning off the flashlight, "the pump *is* on an adjustable mount. Which makes it *adjustable*. And, if you simply take the filter off there, you *don't* need to cut any holes in my floors. Correct?"

"Eh, *oui*."

"Aren't you glad I flew all the way over from California to point these things out to you?"

"Hmm," he said.

"So, when can he start?" I asked, nodding toward Bouba.

Philippe and Bouba had another conference. "This morning he can make a start."

"Good. Does he mind if I watch?"

The job was done by four o'clock that afternoon and my back and neck pain was gone by five. I figured I'd avoided being fleeced for about 5,000 euros.

After disposing of one big H2O problem I had six days to tackle the other one before my flight back. After Philippe's glowing email reports about the progress on the interior work, I was surprised to see that the only thing that had actually been accomplished was that two doors had been removed from their twisted frames. When I asked him about the doors, Philippe said that his eight-fingered woodworker, Pascale, was working on them over at the atelier. That afternoon I dropped by to take a look. When I got there I saw my old, twisted doors clamped flat to a big table in the workshop. When Pascale wandered in a few minutes later, he proudly explained that they had been clamped like that for a month in the hope that they would eventually warp back straight again.

In the best French I could muster, I said, "You're crazy." And together we freed the captive doors. As soon as we took the clamps off, they sprung back into their warped and twisted selves. In the face of this, he had to admit defeat, and he promised to start making new ones the very next day.

That night, while staring at the wall inside the boat and sipping on my six p.m. glass of wine, I came to the realization that the entire crew at H2O wasn't worth a fart in a bucket.

The next day, I walked over to the little tourist office by the harbor and checked my email messages. There was one from my brother that was two days old. It said that my father had pneumonia and was in the hospital. It looked like he wouldn't make it. There were no emails or phone messages from Linda but I learned later that she had no idea this was going on. It was three in the morning in California, so instead of calling home, I called Villa San Miguel and got the night nurse. "Yes, Mr. Hammond," she said. "Johnny is very sick. He's not expected to last the night."

It took almost three days to close the boat, find a flight and get in the air. The first two days were lost in a slow motion, dream-like haze. I felt like I was underwater, trying to run through a wall of emotions that careened between frustration, impatience, and anger. The world just didn't seem to realize that I had to get back there to say goodbye before it was too late. Then, on the second night, he died, and it was too late. Reality slowly filled back in.

At the ticket counter at Charles de Gaul, the agent looked at her computer screen and said, "I'm so sorry for your loss, Mr. Hammond." She was being kind, but her words meant nothing to me. I got on the plane. We took off. I put the seat back, closed my eyes and asked myself, What's the matter with you? Your father died. You loved him. Isn't this when normal people start coming apart? Why can't you cry? I was alone, six thousand miles from anyone who knew me, or my father. It's alright to cry. But then suddenly I could see that on the inside, I really wasn't sad.

The truth was that I had said goodbye to my father months before when I realized that his mind was no longer there. That sad crumpled bundle hunched in its wheelchair at Villa San Miguel was not my father. That wasn't the man who had bought me boxing gloves as big as my head when I was four and then stood me up on the top bunk bed to box with him. He wasn't the one who spun around in a circle when I hit him, then fell on the floor howling, the victim of my terrible right hand. The person who opened his mouth for spoonfuls of chipped beef had no stories to tell about roaming the dives of the world on a merchant ship, or repossessing cars from gangs of "narcotics smugglers" in Houston. My father was the best man at my wedding and he had danced with my wife. The man I went to visit all those times didn't remember that I had a wife.

The memories that made him, the humor that sparkled in his eyes, the love for his family that filled his heart, all these things went away when his mind crashed. I said my goodbyes a little bit each time I went to Villa San Miguel and searched those vacant eyes for a sign that he was in there. But then I came to realize that in my heart I was dreading that I would see some image of him appear though the fog. I was afraid that I'd see him suffering, begging to get out. Well, now there was nothing more to fear. He was finally released, and it was over. I would miss him but my grief had been spent long ago.

Chapter Twenty-Three

One time I saw my daddy dancin'
Watched him movin' like a man in a trance
He brought it back from the war in France.

- James Taylor

Chauncey's mortal remains were soon residing in a bronze box on a shelf in the Crematorium Columbarium in Oakland. There was a service and a reception at my brother's home, and then we had our own celebration of my father's life afterward back at home. Linda and the girls and I went through boxes of old pictures and souvenirs, drank wine and cooked his favorite dinner, corned beef and cabbage. We laughed and told stories, but we didn't cry. There was sadness, yes, but not crying. The sadness was not because he was gone, but because he had had so many ideas, inventions, imagined possibilities, and schemes that he never completed. I remembered back to when I was just fourteen and he lost the used car lot. He had to move our family of seven into a dreary little two-bedroom house. He and my mother took one bedroom and my sisters the other. My brothers and I slept in beds set up in the garage under the house.

That winter I spent every afternoon swinging a sledge hammer, breaking up the concrete floor in the storeroom off the garage so that he could lay plumbing for a second bathroom down there for us. By spring, the last thing to do was to install the door, which he did one Saturday morning, and we all cheered. Except the door didn't have a doorknob on it. The hole for it was there, but no doorknob. Twelve years later, I bought the house from him and there was still no doorknob. He had a problem finishing things. He'd get bored before the end and move on to something else, which meant that the big things he wanted to do, the grand schemes he hatched in his imagination, never fully materialized. One day, after watching another plan fall away, he gave up dreaming. He sat down in his little apartment and became a spectator.

To him, the doorknob was nothing. He never even thought about it. But I sat and stared at that damn hole in the bathroom door all though high school and I took a lesson from it. I'd always finish what I started. This has become to my daughters, who have heard it countless times, "That Stupid Doorknob Story."

The dark days and long nights of that December hung around us like a drunken uncle. We discovered that Sarah, at fourteen years old, had cancer. Soon, she could barely stand and I had to carry her out and help her to go "walkies." We did all we could but it rapidly progressed and when she let us know that the pain wasn't going away and she wanted rest, we had to let her go.

That's when I finally broke down and cried, and darkness seemed to tuck in around me.

In an effort to lighten the mood, Linda decided to fill the house with Holiday Cheer. What she did was fill it with a Christmas tree that I could've built a fort in. Our little place had high ceilings and this thing went all the way to the top, then spread out at the bottom so that we could barely get in the same room with it. She then proceeded to hang everything she could think of on it and cover every other surface in the place with boughs of holly and tinsel.

I was up a ladder in the kitchen one afternoon, putting a decorative string of lights around the pie tins and boxes of macaroni that Linda stored on top of the refrigerator, when the phone rang. Linda, who was directing from across the room, recognized Nicole's number on the caller ID, grabbed the phone and wandered onto the front porch. In a minute she was back, hopping from foot to foot going, "Oooo!! Eeeee! Nicole and Clint want to have dinner with us this weekend. They have something to tell us."

"Uh-oh." I foresaw doom.

"Oh My Gawd. I bet she's pregnant." Nicole and Clint had been married for three years and Linda had been waiting for this phone call since the last dance at the wedding reception. "I know it. She's pregnant! She's pregnant."

"If they are pregnant, you realize that will make you," I prepared to duck, "a grandmother."

"I know. Isn't that great? And you'll be a grandpa."

"Linda, you'll be a grandmother. A little kid will be walking around calling you grandma."

"No, he won't. He'll call me Gigi. Isn't that cute?"

"Who's Gigi?"

"No one. It's French. I'm going to teach it to speak French." Then she went out for a whole new round of Christmas shopping.

There was indeed to be a blessed event. Nicole, Clint, and Krista all came up to the house for dinner and to make the announcement that there was to be a new child and heir in the family and we were all invited to attend the birth sometime in May. Nicole has always been pretty, with her olive skin, pale blue eyes, auburn hair, and her mother's radiant smile. That night it seemed to me that she had gone beyond pretty, past beautiful, and on to lovely. Maybe I was looking for something to open up and let the light back into our lives, or maybe it was the radiance of a pregnant woman, but that night I saw in her what I imagine Leonardo Da Vinci saw in Mona Lisa: a warm, mysterious power that comes from discovering another dimension of life existing entirely within her.

I looked around our little kitchen as Linda and her daughters tasted the sauce, then stirred more fresh herbs into the pot. Clint rooted around in the fridge for a beer. The little house had been a refuge for us in the past, a place we retreated to when it seemed the sky was falling around us. I was a single man when I brought an old schooner up from Los Angeles to Sausalito and started living on it there. Just one block up from the harbor I found this little house, rented a room in it, and turned it into my art studio. When Linda and I got married, I sold the boat but kept the studio. Within a year we had scraped together enough for a down payment on a house near a school. Six months later, we lost the house in a flood and took shelter back in the studio with what few possessions we had saved. It was tiny, but cozy and dry. We were wiped out, but we sat down in this kitchen and began the job of rebuilding our lives. Thirty years gone, and we were back, not refugees this time, but starting again nonetheless.

The room was draped in Christmas decorations that Linda had been collecting for over fifty years. My paintings from France were leaning on the floor next to empty dog bed, where Linda had placed a photograph of Sarah smiling in a restaurant in France. On the bookcase, through the pine boughs, angels, and red-nosed reindeer, peeked photos of kids, cars, vacations, graduations, and smiling, healthy friends and grandparents.

We had come a long way together and if you judged by the pictures on display, we'd had a blast. But of course missing were any photos of car accidents, hospital stays, briefcases, bounced checks, scheming lawyers, or chiseling bosses. In the ebb and flow of life, it's usually during the flow that the cameras come out. Our latest shots, stuck to the refrigerator under a Santa magnet, were of *Phaedra*, moored by a vineyard along a canal in France. Soon, there would be pictures of a new baby, learning to walk, petting a horse, riding a bike, and maybe one day, helping grandpa steer the boat in France.

"We have another announcement." Nicole broke my reverie and was handing me a glass of champagne.

"Well, nothing could top the last one," I said. "But I'm all ears."

She pulled Clint forward. "We've decided that if it's a boy, we're going to name it Chauncey, after you and your dad."

"Really? He'll be Chauncey Wilbert ..."

"No. Not the Wilbert, just the Chauncey," Nicole said. "And only his middle name."

"Probably best." I took a sip. It looked like the ebb was turning and the good times were about to flow again.

Over the next six months, Nicole blossomed, or bloated, depending on her mood of the moment. Linda's business had slowed considerably so she had lots of time to plan showers, shop for showers, cook for showers, and attend them. I kept painting, and in March we turned the studio into a gallery and I had my first one-man show, which was an unqualified success. Over two weekends we poured gallons of wine, shoveled tons of cheese onto baguettes and sold every painting but one. And that one was claimed by Linda and hung in the bedroom. With that encouragement I set to work painting more.

In April, I caught Linda surfing dog rescue sites and a week later we had Billy, a Schipperke (pronounced skipper-key), better known as a Belgian barge dog. Billy was seven years old, all black with the stature of a chesty Pekinese and the heart of a Doberman. Linda said he was perfect because he fit under an airline seat and wouldn't have to ride to France in stowage.

Boatyard Billy Bones

On May the fifth, our grandson was born and was duly burdened with the name of Daven Chauncey. The arrival of the Little Prince was not noted on the front pages of the *New York Times* or the *Wall Street Journal*; however, I'm certain I saw a mysterious star cross the heavens and shine in his hospital room window. There were also rumors of three wise men being stopped by security downstairs, carrying strange packages. But none of this is confirmed. What I can say is that he was a beautiful, blue-eyed little boy whose earliest memories of his grandma Gigi will be of her telling him stories of something called *Phaedra* in a language loosely related to French.

I got to hold him sometimes, under tight restrictions and close supervision. About a week into it, Nicole sat me on the couch, propped pillows around me and said, "Put out your arms like this," and she demonstrated the 'baby-holding pose.' I did as I was told; right hand against my belly, palm up (to hold the butt), and left arm bent at the elbow, straight out, palm up (to support the head). Once she was happy with my stance, The royal Daven was ceremoniously placed in my arms. "There you go, dad. What do you think?"

"He's cute. Oh look. He's smiling, or something." His face went into a strange, spastic kind of grimace, he screwed up his eyes, spit bubbles, and then looked shocked.

"That's the future you're holding," Nicole said proudly.

"Well, I think the future just pooped all the way up my sleeve." Then I did what grandparents do best: I handed him back.

That night, Linda and I decided that it was once again time for us to go back to France. Our winter of sadness, disappointment, and frustration was behind us, and our optimism and faith had reappeared in the spring like the leaves on the trees. Our spirits had been revived when we learned about Daven coming, and took wing as we settled into our little home and new life. It felt good to be a painter again. Linda loved watching her daughters' lives fill in, and Billy had so much love in him that he eased the pain of missing Sarah. Now it was time to take the barge and go exploring again.

We decided that I would go the third week in May alone, de-winterize the boat, give it a mechanical run-through, fix any winter rust, and put a few coats of varnish on the hatches. Linda would tear herself away from her grandma duties a couple weeks later and she and Billy would fly over. We three intrepid explorers would then start our journey north, toward Paris.

Chapter Twenty-Four

"Time to blow this fascist popsicle stand."

\- Homer Simpson

It was cocktail time when the taxi from the train dropped me at the foot of Pontoon B and no sooner had I unlocked the boat and dumped my bags than Bob came running over with a cold beer and some exciting news. There was a car for sale and it was a *really, really good* car too. It belonged to friends of his who, for the last two years, had been living on a big barge moored down river at an old abandoned lock. They were giving up the barge life and moving back to Arizona. Everything was for sale, including a 1990 Renault Espace with only 186,000 miles on it. They were ready to make a deal.

La Belle Espace

Until that moment, I hadn't realized that I was in the market for an Espace, but given my heritage, I have a hard time passing up any car with a For Sale sign in the window. I had no idea what a Renault Espace was, but when Captain Bob says something is "really, really" anything, it's worth checking out. So, the next morning I went with him down the river to take a look at it. It turns out that an Espace is a sort of six-passenger van that's made out of fiberglass. This particular one had been living under trees beside canals or rivers for so long that it had acquired a striking similarity to Huck Finn's raft. It appeared to have once been painted a maroon rust color, with a shiny clear coat finish, which was peeling off in big ragged sheets, making it look like it was suffering from a horrible skin disease. It had hubcaps, but the owner, a bearded haystack of a guy named Jack, kept them in a plastic bag in the back so they wouldn't get stolen.

There had once been three rows of seats in the van, but Jack had taken the last row out so that he could carry his scooter in the back. It had electric windows that worked if you weren't in a hurry, and a hole in the dash where a radio had once been. It had five doors in all, and each of them had its own unique trick to open, close or lock. A five-speed manual transmission, two new tires, middling brakes and a tired battery comprised its high points. It was about the dirtiest car I'd ever seen. Jack called it Pierre, and wanted a thousand euros for it.

We took it for a little spin around the town with Captain Bob bouncing around in the back. Most of the roads in France were made for cars much smaller than Pierre, which might prompt some novice Espace drivers to slow down and make their way carefully between parked cars and outdoor café tables. But using the brakes is a sign of weakness in France, and slow drivers are roundly booed and run into ditches, so putting my faith in Jack's assurances that "it'll fit, keep going," I shut my eyes and hoped the Force was with me.

It was really fun. This was the perfect car. It was so ugly that I'd never have to lock it, and another scratch or a dent now and then wouldn't be noticed. The engine purred, it steered and stopped and had all its windows. I offered him $900 for it. He thought about it for a couple of minutes then said, "I'll take it on one condition."

"What's that?" I asked.

"I've got a load of stuff to take to the dump this weekend," he said. "I'll need to borrow it for the trip. It's just a one day run."

"No problem," I said, and gave a tire one last kick. "I've got no place to go until my wife gets here. I'll pick her up at the train in it."

"She'll be thrilled," he said, and stuck out his hand. I had myself a car. The next couple days were spent discovering the bureaucratic ins and outs of buying, registering and insuring a car in France. But the fun part was getting the insurance, because it involved Martine.

Martine worked in the little insurance office in St. Jean de Losne. She was about twenty-eight years old, big boned, and came to work looking like she'd just survived last call at a disco. Her English was the kind you heard in those old movies where the American G.I. saves a poor little Parisian cocktail waitress by giving her nylon stockings and Hershey Bars. On the day I arrived in her office, Martine was sitting all alone wearing stiletto knee boots, a mini skirt that was mostly a slit, some sort of flimsy sequined blouse and makeup designed to be seen in strobe lighting. Her hair was moussed and gelled into spikes and curls that stuck out in all directions. She had two cigarettes going and her fingernails were multicolored works of art two inches long. She greeted me in English and we got right down to business. Martine was a whiz at insurance and it took only three visits in two days to collect all the data, fill in a pile of forms, inspect the car, fill in more forms, and pay the bill. I was insured.

When Jack showed up early Saturday morning for his dump run, all was a go. The car had only been mine for two days, but I felt a little sad handing him the keys. Watching it bounce off down the road, I was reminded of the old '52 Ford panel truck I'd had in college. I made a mental note to call Linda and ask her to bring a Grateful Dead window sticker with her when she came over.

That evening, I was lost in a book and enjoying a young but astute Aligote that had been chilling in the bilge all winter when Jack's clomping across the deck brought me around.

"How'd it go?" I asked when he poked his head in the door. He didn't have to answer. "What's wrong?"

"It wasn't my fault," he said and started pulling papers out of his pocket.

"What happened to my car?"

"There was this old guy, in this roundabout." He started shuffling his papers.

"Uh-huh."

"He hit Pierre! He sideswiped me."

"You got in an accident?"

"It was his fault," Jack said, and he waved the papers around. "I filled out the accident forms. Here."

"But? You got in an accident?"

"Yeah, sorry."

"How bad is it?"

"It kind of tore off the back corner, on the right side," he said. "But the tail light still works. I stuck it back with duct tape."

"Now what do I do?" I still couldn't believe it.

"You got insurance, right?"

"Yeah, yesterday." I thought of Martine.

"I'll go in with you on Monday," he offered. "I'll help sort it out."

"I just got it yesterday. Two days later I go in with a claim?"

"Well, it wasn't your fault. Hell, you weren't even driving."

"I wasn't even there!" I said. "What am I gonna tell Martine?"

Monday morning, when Jack and I walked into her office, Martine was wearing sheer vinyl pants that made her look like she had been dipped in chocolate sauce. She wore fur-topped spike-heel boots with spurs, a lime green mesh blouse highlighting her flowered pushup bra, and her Cleopatra makeup. *"Bonjour Monsieur Cris,"* she said and stood up to show me the vinyl. "You have come to see me?"

"Bonjour, Martine," I mumbled. "Yes, we have a little problem we need to talk with you about."

"I am all for you," she said and bounced around getting a chair for Jack. When we were all seated and Martine's hair had been fluffed and tossed, we got down to business.

"Martine, the Espace, he has been in an accident."

She stuck out her lips and knitted her eyebrows, "But, it is so soon."

"I know. I'm sorry. It wasn't his fault." I nodded to Jack, who gave her a warm smile and held up his papers.

"Is your fault zen, Cris? Zis is not so good." She pouted and frowned.

"No, no. I wasn't driving the car. He was," and I pointed to Jack.

"Pourquoi he is driving?"

"I leant the car to him. Just for one day." I looked over at Jack, who was being too quiet. "I bought the car from him but he gave me a good price because I promised to lend him the car, just to drive some things to, uh, the dump. See, he's moving to Arizona—"

"What is Arizona?" Martine interrupted my story.

"It's in America," Jack answered. "Lots of desert. Do you know Taos?"

"I don't understand," Martine said, and pointed her lips in my direction again. "You have an accident, but you don't drive zee car? Eee does?"

"Right," I said. "He was driving."

"But is not eez fault, the accident?"

"No."

"Who is fault?"

"The other guy."

"Oh. It is no problem then," she said and sat up straight. "Zat man must pay."

"Really?" Jack and I said together.

"Yes. Have you zee report of zee accident?" Jack nodded and handed her the papers. She looked them over for a few minutes, puffed her cheeks, went "poot-poot" with her lips, spun her chair around and did something on the computer, then announced, "Voila!" Then she got up and, spurs jingling, strutted over to the copy machine. Jack watched her intently as she reloaded the paper. Soon she was back. "Alors! You must go to the

Renault, eh, the shop, and ask him how much to fix. Then you bring the paper back to me, and we will pay to fixing this Espace."

"That's it?" I said, amazed. I had expected the usual insurance company run-around. If Martine's English weren't so good, I'd have been sure that something was wrong. "That's it? That's so simple," I said. "Martine, you are great."

"Zis time, *oui*," she said. "It is not you fault, eh?" Then she wagged a long fiberglass fingernail painted in the colors of the Dijon soccer team, and said, "If it eez you fault, you pay beaucoup euros." And she rubbed her two fingers together under my nose.

All went smoothly and a week later I rode my bike over to pick up the Espace. When I arrived, my new car was sitting out front, forlorn and alone with paint peeling off in chunks, and spider-webs catching flies in the wind. It looked like the "before" picture in a body and fender shop ad. But when I walked around to the back, I saw that they had actually done a great job. The right rear corner sparkled with a brand new bumper and taillight, all beautifully painted and polished up. Poor Pierre looked like a wino wearing one patent leather shoe.

Linda and Billy would be arriving in a few days, eager to be heading up the Canal de Bourgogne, and I was working through my list of chores. *Phaedra* was looking like a debutant, ready for the dance. I'd put coats of varnish on her hatches and touched up the paint around the decks and cabin sides. Then, I spent a day checking out all the various systems that could break, fail or explode. The engine started fine. The bow thruster was working like a champ and my auxiliary generator consistently started on the first pull of the rope. I detected a small oil leak at the back of the engine that wasn't severe, but made a mess, so I decided to see if something simple could be done about it.

A friend of mine, an American from California who owned and operated a B&B barge, had the name of an honest and reliable mechanic who worked out of an old Mercedes station wagon. His name was Herby. He was a young Brit who had spent his whole life in France, living on, driving, and repairing barges. His father had a boatyard on the Yonne River where Herby had been raised and learned his art. The Mercedes was his new shop and his first crack at setting up his own business. Figuring that a brain dead drunken goat would be better than Bouba, I called him up. We made an appointment for him to come down to the boat at two o'clock for a look-see.

Two o'clock came and went and no Herby. At three, I called his cell and reached him somewhere on the road near St. Symphorien. "Herby. This is Hammond," I yelled, above the clattering Mercedes.

"Hey," Herby said.

"Where are you? I thought you were coming by an hour ago. What happened?"

"I was there, mate," he said. "But big Philippe wouldn't let me on the dock."

"What?" I sat up.

"Philippe wouldn't let me come down the dock. He said I couldn't do any work on his docks."

"Did you tell him you were coming to see me?"

"Yeah. He didn't care. His docks, his customers. That's what he says."

"No shit. OK. Thanks, Herby," I rung off.

That settled that. It was goodbye to St. Jean de Losne and any association with H2O. I took on the oil leak myself and fixed it by the next day. The following morning, I drove the car up to Dijon, parked it at the barge basin, then took the train back. Early the next morning, clutching a stack of phone numbers and email addresses from the River Rats, I cast off my dock lines and left the H2O docks for good. I made it to Dijon in two days of easy cruising, just in time to meet Linda and Billy at the train from Paris. I was so glad to see her that I put a flower and a mint on her pillow. Billy got cookies. Two days later, after Linda had rested and done her traditional reorganization of the kitchen drawers, and Billy had laid claim to every bush and hydrant in the port, we left Dijon and headed north, back into the Valle de Ouche.

It felt wonderful to be on the canal again. The engine was purring along, the weather was perfect and the countryside was every bit as beautiful as it had been in the fall. But this time it was summer and the days were getting progressively hotter, the trees more lush and green, and the long evenings languid and warm. We stayed at familiar moorings in Plombieres-les-Dijon and, one of our favorites, at Saint Marie-sur Ouche, a beautifully restored village set around an ancient stone bridge.

Giselle, the waitress in St. Victor-sur-Ouche was saddened that Sarah wasn't with us, but she welcomed Billy with a kiss and his own bowl of treats. Billy proved himself to be a perfect barge dog. He loved to scamper all over the boat, following at Linda's heels, standing guard against ducks and swans and striking a bulldog pose at the bow like the hood ornament on a Mack Truck.

We'd cruise at a laid back five knots. I'd stand back at the wheel, captain of the ship, and in the afternoons, Linda would carry a chair out onto the bow and sit there, holding an umbrella, reading a book and watching the canal open up before her. On those occasions she was supremely and entirely happy. And that was the most important thing in the world to me right then.

As we got farther from Dijon, we saw fewer and fewer holiday rental boats until we eventually had the canal to ourselves for days at a time. There are seventy-five locks from St. Jean de Losne to the summit of the canal at La Lochere, some fifty miles away. Most of them manually operated by lock keepers, many of whom handle two or three locks in a row. That many locks gave us the opportunity to experience the full range of lock keeper, from the "Happy-to-See-Ya" college student with the dream summer job, to the "Oh hell. What're you doing here? Can't you see I'm busy?" third generation lock Nazi who's been living in that tiny lock house with his six kids and four dogs, working on his truck and polishing his garden gnomes since puberty.

In the beginning, we covered six to ten miles a day. We'd stop for lunch but then continue on until about five o'clock, when we'd start to look for a place to tie up for the night. Once we'd secured everything, shut down the engine and set the wine to chill, we'd get the bikes off the deck and ride down the towpath beside the canal all the way back to where we'd started. It would usually take about forty-five minutes, a good workout after being confined to the boat all day. Then, we'd find the car, load up the bikes and drive back to the boat just as the wine reached the perfect temperature.

As time went on, we grew a bit less energetic and would go right to the chilled wine at the end of the day, leaving the car where it was. It made for a longer bike ride the next evening, but the towpaths were flat and well groomed, and we weren't in anything like a hurry, so we let it slide. By the time we got to Vandenesse-en-Auxois, near the summit, we had let it slide so much that we had forgotten exactly where we'd left the poor Espace and had to take a train to the stop that sounded familiar and hunt for it.

Phaedra was performing beautifully but a boat is a boat and eventually disturbing noises did start grinding up from the engine compartment and we had to pull to the side and call Herby. He jumped in his car and in two hours his old Mercedes was rattling down the towpath to the rescue. He had his girlfriend with him, a pretty young English lady who glided over to the canal and sat there like a nymph, tossing flower petals into the water. She managed to do what I had heretofore thought impossible: she made me think dreadlocks were sexy.

Meanwhile, Herby, with barely a pause for introduction, dove head first into the engine compartment and in less than a minute declared, "Sumpin's been burning down 'eer." Herby was about twenty-six, average height with a shaved head and a bushy red beard. He had some sort of spike in one ear, and what looked like a jib-sheet fairlead in the other. He had his share of tattoos, most of which were your garden variety crosses and death's heads, and he was one of the best mechanics I've ever seen. Within a half hour, working almost entirely while hanging upside down with a mirror in his teeth, he had removed and dismantled the alternator and found that its innards were melted to death. He then called his father, a renowned expert on such things, and got the names of a couple of alternator shops in Dijon.

After a few more calls, he and his Rasta Nymph were off to find a replacement, promising to return the next day. And he did. They were actually back the next day. As it turned out, this was a very complicated job, in that my original alternator was made in Egypt, and not compatible with anything in France. Back in Dijon, Herby was able to find two different sized English alternators that he could take apart and reassemble into one that had the same dimensions as my original. He brought it back to the boat that afternoon and worked until midnight installing and testing it until he was satisfied. He didn't go on strike, took no holidays and didn't disappear for days at a time. I was flabbergasted. For the first time since I had owned the boat, I didn't feel one breakdown away from total ruin.

Herby didn't take credit cards and I didn't have cash, but I did have wine. So over a couple of glasses, we decided that I would drop the payment by his father's boatyard on the Yonne

River, just past the end of the canal. We'd be there in two to three weeks and like the perfect mechanic, he was in no hurry to be paid.

At Vandenesse-en-Auxois, just before the summit of the canal, Grandma Gigi made an appearance. Linda had held off calling to check on Daven for almost three weeks, but she'd hit her limit. The news was that he was sleeping most of the time, eating well, and no, he had not been asking for Grandma Gigi. "I'm sure, once he learns how to talk," Nicole said, "he'll be crying for you constantly."

"Well, you just tell him that Gigi is thinking of him, and she'll see him soon."

"Do you want to tell him yourself?" Nicole asked. "He's right here."

There followed fifteen minutes of Linda making goo-goo sounds and listening to corresponding gurgles in reply.

We had been climbing in elevation since leaving the Saone and just past Vandenesse, at the little hamlet of La Lochere, we reached the highest point on the canal. At La Lochere lurks the entrance to the 2.6 mile tunnel through the mountain to the port of Pouilly-en-Auxois. We had, of course, been anticipating this tunnel since leaving Dijon. I hadn't met anyone who had actually been through it, but everyone talked about it in terms of its dimensions, as in, will your boat fit through?

The tunnel is a straight hole in the mountain, arched at the top, ten feet high in the center and six and a half feet high at the sides. There is no walkway inside the tunnel. The walls drop straight into the water. It's about fifteen feet wide and there are no lights. As my dad would say, "It's as black as a pawn broker's heart."

It's obviously a one-way-at-a-time tunnel. The rules are: you check in with the La Lochere lock keeper who asks if you have life jackets for everyone aboard and some kind of a light. You say yes. Our light was provided by an old car headlight propped on my cabin top, and Linda hanging off the side with a flashlight. This seemed to satisfy his minimum requirements so he called the people at the other end, got the "all clear," and then waved us off.

We pulled away from the dock at La Lochere, cruised across the pond and into a dark and dismal ravine covered in clinging brambles and gray emaciated trees. As we crept round a tight bend, the hole in the mountain came into view. Lichen-covered stones arched over a cave so black and forbidding that I found myself pulling the throttle back and coasting forward, as if I really didn't want to go in there. The milky green water turned dark and oily inside its mouth, then murmured and slapped at us as we entered the tunnel.

Pitch black and straight as an arrow.

I switched on my headlight and was able to see almost as far as the front of the boat. The rest was utter and complete blackness. It's hard to imagine how black. Close your eyes. It was blacker than that. There was just one tiny pinpoint of light, floating straight ahead, like a tiny star you can really only see if you don't look at it. I thought it might be a single bulb from an air vent or emergency alarm, but it wasn't. Through my binoculars I could see that I was looking at the exit, over two-and-a-half miles dead ahead.

In the blackness it was impossible to keep my orientation. I was steering like a bat, by sound. *Phaedra* has a radio antenna on the cabin top that we'd folded down, but its tip was still a foot above the roof. If I let the boat get too far to the right, the antenna dragged on the sloping stones above and made a noise like hubcaps grinding against a curb. When that started, I'd try to move her to the left where Linda, with her flashlight, would yell, "Go right! Go right!" just as the hull started banging and grinding along the stone wall at her elbow. I'd maneuver it off the stones and back to the right again, which would start the antenna screeching and knocking small stones loose to rain down around us. This would send me edging back to the left again and so on. If we were dead center in the tunnel, I had headroom and almost two feet on either side, but unfortunately I only passed through the center on my way from crashing into one side or the other. I left a lot of paint on the sides of that tunnel.

It seemed about twelve hours later when, feeling like a couple of Tennessee coal miners, we emerged from the blackness into another deep, tree-shrouded ditch, which we gratefully followed until it opened onto the basin at Pouilly. We were suddenly back in fresh air, gazing at a radiating pink and orange sunset over the Morvan, the legendary "tunnel on the Bourgogne" behind us. We found a place in front of a small park and tucked in for the night.

Chapter Twenty-Five

"We'll always have Paris."

- Humphrey Bogart

We had made it to the high point on the Canal de Bourgogne, and it was, as they say, all downhill from here. Sounds good, right? Swooping down a water slide, laughing and screaming with joy until we drift to a gentle stop in front of a vineyard where we're handed chilled glasses of Chablis and bits of creamy cheese on freshly baked baguettes. We might get to that, but first, directly in front of us were 56 locks to do in the next 19 miles.

Our first lock of the day was only 100 feet from our mooring so when the lock keeper arrived for work at nine, we put our breakfast down and shoved off. That first one was a breeze. It was full and waiting for us with open doors, so we drove right in. The water drained easily and lowered us gently to the next level. The doors opened and we slowly moved out and then stopped because the next lock was directly in front of us, doors shut tight and the chamber empty. We sat there idling while the startled lock keeper finished his cigarette then went about the process of closing the downstream doors, opening the upstream valves and filling the chamber. Twenty minutes later he opened the doors for us and we motored in, ready to be lowered.

Down-locking on the Bourgogne

Another twenty minutes and we were released to find ourselves immediately in sight of the next one. It too was closed, so we drifted and waited. This is not everyone's favorite part of the Canal de Bourgogne. The views are pretty spectacular because you're up on a hill and can see out over the valley, but there's not a lot of progress made. At the next lock, we asked the lock keeper if he would telephone ahead to tell them we were coming so they'd have the lock prepared for us, but we were told that they didn't have phones. I didn't believe him, but there wasn't much choice, so Linda went ashore with her bike and she pedaled ahead to sound the alert. When I emerged from the next lock and moved *Phaedra* slowly around the bend, I could see Linda pulling and straining against one of the long iron bars that open the door. I put it into neutral and drifted slowly toward the lock, while Linda went to work earning herself an official lock keeper's hat.

This turned into a little system. Linda worked the bank on her bike and I guided *Phaedra* through the flights of locks. By lunchtime, we had done eight locks and covered something like two-and-a-half miles. We had provisions. We could do this for days. And we did.

Toward the end of that first day as we were nearing our mooring spot at Gissey, we saw off to our left a lovely old fortified *chateau ferme* (large farm house and compound) standing across the fields just off the A6 motorway, it's stone walls glowing a pale ochre in the afternoon sun. As we looked we could see that the walls were standing, but large chunks had fallen in and the rest seemed, despite their massive appearance, rather fragile. At the same time, the grounds were planted and ordered gardens were blooming. As we looked more closely we noticed that the southern wing looked as if it were being restored. This intriguing sight turned out to be the 18th century castle of Equilly. This exquisite old pile of rocks had been in a state of restoration by two private individuals since 1983. The were doing it on their own, without the help of the government, which is undoubtedly why it was going so quickly.

The next day our first lock keeper was a young student named Luc, who told us that he would be our personal *eclusier*, accompanying us for the rest of the flight of locks as far as the town of Venarey-les-Laumes. We were facing two flights in close succession. The first would be thirteen locks in 3 miles and the second flight was twenty-five locks in about 5.5 miles. With our own dedicated lock keeper, we hoped to cover these 8.5 miles in two days, dropping almost three hundred feet toward the Alesian plane where Gaul finally fell to Caesar in 52 B.C. And where we would no doubt feel as beat up as the Gauls.

Luc was a college art major, spending the summer learning the finer points of opening and closing lock doors and zooming

around on the company moped. He had been issued a green VNF (Voies Navigables de la France) polo shirt, the official moped (which he adored because he could take it home with him at night and ride it around  his village) and a helmet that he wore at a jaunty angle, cocked at the back of his head so it wouldn't interfere with his cigarette. He was at our service. This was the only sane way to navigate this section of the Canal de Bourgogne. Luc would ride the moped ahead to prepare to the next lock while *Phaedra* was being lowered through the previous one. Then he'd zoom back in time to open the doors for us to let us out, then haul the moped back to the next lock, which would be full by then, and open the doors so that we could drive straight in. As soon as we were in, secure and descending, he'd take off for the next one and do the same thing all over again. It was a great system and we made good time all that morning.

Luc was young, enthusiastic and new at the job. We were his first charges. The first few locks we encountered had been updated with the new hydraulically powered doors and gates that were operated simply by pushing red and green buttons on a control panel. The grueling old system of swinging the gigantic wood and steel doors by pushing on heavy iron levers had been thankfully replaced by neat electric boxes with buttons to push. Luc had been thoroughly trained on the new system and he was moving us through locks in record time and without a hitch.

As we were preparing to leave our third lock of the day, Luc gave us a wave and hopped onto his moped and scooted off to prepare the next one. We were getting used to his cool efficiency so when we rounded the bend and came in sight of the lock in front of us we were surprised to find that the doors were still closed and it hadn't been filled. At first I thought Luc might have fallen off his moped. He was still learning that skill too. But then I caught sight of him and I realized that we had a whole new problem.

See, Luc had gone through a complete orientation for his new job, so he knew about the old system and how it worked, but he had never actually operated one. He knew about the big hand crank that opened the gates and which of the nine-foot iron bars to push around to get the doors open. He had the theory to do it, but he didn't have the muscle. As we drifted closer I saw that he was at the far end of the lock, pulling and pushing and straining with all his might to move that ancient iron bar. His feet were sliding and kicking up the gravel as he shoved and shoved again but the bar wasn't budging.

He clearly needed help. I put the boat against the shore and Linda jumped off with her bike and pedaled to the rescue. Through the binoculars I could see that he was glad to see her, but a little abashed. Linda talked to him nicely and patted him on the shoulder, then they both put their backs into it and the iron bar started to move and the door slowly swung closed. Working as a team, they prepared the lock the old fashioned way, with bars and levers and hand cranks, and eventually *Phaedra* made her way in. When the doors were shut behind me and the water was draining out, Linda and Luc went by bike and moped to the next lock, got it started on its sequence, they came back in time to open the doors for me. As I moved out, I turned around and waved to Luc who was pushing his moped down the slope from the lock to get it started.

Luc and Linda made a terrific team of *eclusiers* and for three days they worked together like a couple of stevedores. He left us at the end of the third day with samples of his art, his website address and promises to keep in touch. That section of the Canal de Bourgogne is as breathtaking as any in France but it can be trying at times. I'm convinced that Luc and the rest of the kids working that section are one of the main reasons that we were able to enjoy the trip so much without obsessing about locks every half a kilometer.

With 19 miles and 56 locks behind us, we still had 54 more locks and about 79 miles to go before we reached the end of the Canal de Bourgogne. After the endless flights of locks of the last few days, the forests, fields and chateaux of this next leg were a cruiser's dream. We stayed a couple days at a cozy little mooring spot next to an old stone bridge that connects the towns of Cucy and Ancy-le-Franc. The best mooring spots were on the Ancy-le-Franc side so we pulled over and settled in, just behind a boat that we soon found out was carrying the self-proclaimed Grapefruit King of France. Monsieur Alain claimed to have made his fortune importing grapefruits from warmer climes, and was traveling with his party on a rental boat overflowing with sacks of grapefruit. He was so charmed by Linda that he gave her a dozen.

Ancy-le-Franc is known for its beautiful Renaissance chateau designed by the Italian architect, Serlios. Tearing ourselves away from the Grapefruit King and his friends, we got out our bikes for the short ride up the tree-lined lane to the old town and the gates of the chateau. By the time we arrived the grounds had been closed for the day, but peering through the bars we could see the immense house of grey stone with tall roofs, massive towers and an ornately decorated central front entry. A magnificent park laid out with hedges, lawns and flower beds surrounding the elegant building. We resolved to return the next day for the tour.

The next morning we got there just in time to join a whole busload of Germans on a specially arranged guided tour of the chateau that was conducted entirely in English. It became apparent very quickly that only two of the Germans spoke English. The rest tramped through the chateau grumbling and saying, "vas?"

At Tonnerre, a quiet town with an 11th century church and lots of fountains and statues, we drove in our stakes and rested for a while on the edge of a grassy park. We were getting near the end of the canal and in five days we would be at the town of Migennes, on the Yonne River. This was a crossroads of sorts for us. At the Yonne, we could either turn right, and travel down the river onto the Seine and into Paris, or hang a left toward a town we'd heard about named Auxerre, situated at the beginning of the Canal du Nivernais. The Nivernais is regarded as the closest rival to the Bourgogne for the title of the most beautiful canal in France, and Auxerre, a beautiful city with a history dating back to the time of the Romans, was its crown jewel. In addition, we were told it had a welcoming, charming, and fully equipped harbor. We'd be flying back to the U.S. in three weeks and we needed to find a secure and comfortable place to leave *Phaedra* until we returned. A decision was looming. Should we turn left at the Yonne and make our way to this ancient and intriguing city, or go downstream and push on to the Seine and into Paris.

Paris would be only about six or seven days of cruising beyond Migennes, but there were complications with this option.

There were no guarantees that we would be able to leave *Phaedra* at Paris' Arsenal yacht basin for an extended period of time. They had a waiting list that was legendary for its inscrutability. Some said the key was a wad of cash placed in the right person's hand at the right time. Others said that the list had become one of the more ironclad examples of scrupulous behavior in all of French bureaucracy. Brits who had been there said that only the French were offered spots and it was whispered by the French that the French had no hope. There were different rates for all the seasons: prices for the day, the week, the month, the season and the year, but nobody could get them for the year and the only season available was the dead of winter. All the rates were expensive. We had put an application in with the harbormaster's office on a trip through Paris months before, but it only put us on the list. It was a notoriously slow moving list.

It would take us five days to reach Auxerre if we went by boat, but only a half hour by car, so we decided to jump in the Espace and take a short road trip to check it out. Tonnerre, Chablis and Auxerre are in the Auxerrois area of Burgundy and are famous for their delicate and utterly lovely Chablis and the flinty Auxerrois red wines, which could be considered by some as the poorer cousins of the elegant Burgundies of the Cote de Beaune. The auto route from Tonnerre took us straight through the little town of Chablis, surrounded by the rolling, vine-covered hills of the Auxerrois. We couldn't resist stopping for a stroll and lunch, accompanied by some serious wine tasting in the cool cellars that are set to lure you in every fifty feet throughout the village.

Arriving well fed and mellow at Auxerre, we easily found our way to the port, situated across the river with a storybook view of the medieval town. Two major cathedrals and one white wedding cake of an abbey dominated the skyline of the old town that sits above the anchorage. The Paul Bert Bridge, built in 1857, takes traffic into the old town just upstream from a sleek, modern footbridge that crosses at the center of the harbor. We parked the Espace under a tree and went looking for the harbormaster to inquire about the possibility of getting a long-term berth in what was looking to us like a mini paradise. The harbor office was closed, but we spied a small barge that was being used as a souvenir shop at the waterfront, so we went in.

We were greeted in perfect Brigitte Bardot English by a warm and bubbly young woman named Dominique. With batting eyes and a brilliant smile, she informed us that she and her husband Paul, a tall, thin Dutchman with coke bottle glasses and Albert Einstein hair, were the owners, masters and hosts of the harbor. Dominique made it abundantly clear that their world would not be complete without *Phaedra* living happily in a place of honor along their waterfront for as long as she floated. She gave us a card with her cell phone number on it and told us to "joost call to me when you come near, and I weel av Paool greet you at zee spot, she eez perfect for you."

"Do you people work on boats here?" I asked. The lessons of H2O still burned in my mind.

"Uh, yes, yes," she cooed. "You av problem?" She looked suddenly sad.

"No. Not right now," I said. "But, you know, with boats, eh?"

"Yes, yes, we av many peoples to work zis boats, you know?"

"It's just that, where we were before, they were not good mechanics."

"Where were you before?" she asked with a frown.

"Down on the Saone." I said. "H2O."

Her brows came together and she made a little pout. "Oh! Yes, we know zees people. We don't say about zem, eh? But we are not like zem, no, no," and she wagged her finger in the air.

That was good enough for me. "OK. We'll call you when we're near."

"Oh, zis eez perfect," she cooed.

On the drive back to the boat, we conferred. "So, what do you think? Auxerre or Paris?" I asked Linda.

"Oh, Paris definitely," she said, "only Auxerre first."

"Really? You'd pass on Paris?"

"No way! We're going to Paris, but when we get there, I want to have plenty of time to hang out and get into it," she said. "Plus, we can leave the boat in Auxerre while we go home and visit Daven. Then, when we come back, we'll get her all spruced up and take her on down to Paris."

"Up," I said.

"What?"

"It's *up* to Paris. It's north."

"It's *down* river."

"Good point," I said. "So we're going up, or down, no, over…"

"We're going to Auxerre."

To take *Phaedra* to Paris and live on her there was still our dream. But it seemed that a fundamental change had crept upon us during this voyage. The drive to get that boat to Paris had mellowed. To paraphrase Jimmy Buffett:

> *"The warm summer breezes,*
> *The French wines and cheeses,*
> *Had put their ambitions at bay."*

Our ambitions now, if there were any, were simply to see what lay around the next bend. We had learned that we could indeed take *Phaedra* anywhere the rivers or canals went. She was a good boat, comfortable, easily handled and, within the limitations of any boat, reliable and dependable. We had also realized that what my friend Phil had said was true. To hurry was to miss the point of it all.

We had become accustomed to staying in a village for an extra day, waiting for a restaurant to open if it looked interesting.

A lunch stop might present a painting opportunity that couldn't be missed. If we came through a village and it was market day, we'd stop. The idea of simply cruising through France, with no fixed destination and no deadlines, had taken hold.

Back in Tonnerre, we loaded up with supplies of food and Chablis wine and set off. Four days later, late in the afternoon, we entered the last lock of the Canal de Bourgogne. Past those doors flowed the Yonne River. To the right was Paris, to the left, Auxerre. I swung the wheel to the left.

Chapter Twenty-Six

*"There is one way to find out if a man is honest.
Ask him. If he says 'Yes,' you know he's a crook."*

\- Groucho Marx

The first thing we saw once we were on the river was Herby's father's boatyard. He'd said we couldn't miss it and he was right. It looked like a combination of boat and scrap yard. There were all sizes and types of floating derelicts tied in gang rafts five and six hulks deep, as if they were poised at the starting line of some race to a barge graveyard. Old stone buildings that resembled WWII rubble, topped with odd sheets of rusting corrugated iron and surrounded by a sculpture garden of broken engines and ancient cranes, lined the quayside. I was reminded of the many happy Saturdays I used to spend with my father poking around wrecking yards looking for useable parts for some car he'd be fixing up in our backyard at home. I felt strangely drawn to the place.

It was late in the day, the boat was running a little rough and we owed his son some money, so we decided to pull in and meet the maestro of it all, Joe Parfit. With Linda stationed on the bow gripping her rope, coiled and at the ready, I angled us in toward the only spot on the quay that didn't have some big ugly boat already there. Joe had seen us coming and was waiting to take our lines. A Brit who'd been working the French waterways for over thirty years, Joe had a scraggly salt and pepper beard, thick glasses and wore what appeared to be a suit fashioned from old oil rags, worn through at the knees and elbows. He spoke French all right, but with a strong British accent that signaled that he wasn't ready to go completely native just yet.

"Running kinda rough," was his greeting.

"You think so?" I said. "It was sounding funny to me, but I wasn't sure."

"I'll get someone on it tomorrow," he said. "Or maybe the next day."

That was a nice thought, but we weren't there to get into a mechanical nightmare this close to our destination. "Well, two things," I said. "First, I have some money for you."

"For me?" His eyebrows went up. "That's nice."

"Well, it's not exactly for you," I said and watched a puzzled look begin to form through his beard. "It's for your son, Herby."

"Oy, bugger!" He said. "Ow much?"

"Hundred forty euros," I told him. "He fixed our alternator."

"Right. You'd be the bunch he called me about then. Happy to take it off your hands." And he put out a palm. "Probably owes me at least that much anyway. What's the other?"

"Well, we were just wondering if we could tie up here for the night," I said and handed him the envelope full of cash. I looked around the boatyard and said, "We'll be off tomorrow, first thing."

"Right then." He scratched his beard and the money disappeared into a pocket, "I'll just have a look at it now then." And he planted a size 18, grease encrusted boot on my deck. "Engine's down there I imagine," he said and pointed under my feet.

For the next hour *Phaedra* had his undivided attention. He slithered around the engine like he'd been de-boned, sniffing and tapping on things and sticking his finger into the bilge, judging the scent and texture, no doubt. He told me to fire it up again and then he went and got some tools. By the time he was back, Linda and I were ready for a beer, so he sent us off to the train station, where the nearest bar was to be found, and then ducked his head back into the engine compartment.

We returned later to find the deck resembling the oil bay at a Jiffy Lube. Obviously something mechanical had been done but there was no sign of Joe. I followed some grease stains that led off toward the paint shed but found it locked. A quick tramp around the place turned up nary a soul, so we just settled in for the night.

Linda and I were about to sit down for dinner when a smoking and backfiring little boat bumped up against us and tied on. Seconds later, a desperate looking young man, dressed in what appeared to be a pile of laundry, jumped onto *Phaedra* and bounded across to the quay. He tore around the paint shed and disappeared, abandoning behind a confused elderly lady and a hairy white dog.

These sorts of things need to be investigated so I put down my wine and hoisted myself onto the deck. While Billy performed a background check on the dog, I engaged the wide-eyed woman in a conversation of sorts. The gist of the situation seemed to be that the absent young man was her new boyfriend and he had some important business with some guys who he was, for the time being, running away from. This I reported to Linda, who was not pleased. I volunteered to stand guard all night to see that nothing bad happened.

I might have nodded off once or twice but as far as I could tell, the reclusive young businessman remained at large through the night, much to my relief and the further confusion of his anxious girlfriend. By the time a light appeared in Parfit's office the next morning, Linda had started the engine, warmed it up and was ready to hightail it out of there. But nothing's free in this world, so she agreed to wait long enough for me to run over and settle up with Joe.

I found him buried at his desk behind piles of odd papers, old and new engine parts, two loaves of bread and a large fan big enough to blow it all away if he ever turned it on. "Mr. Hammond," he said after my greeting. "Did you pass a pleasant night?"

"Not entirely, no," I said, and related the night's events.

"Ah, Migennes," he sighed, like a disappointed father. "We do have some colorful sods dropping in from time to time. They don't often steal anything though."

"That's good. So, I wanted to find out if I owe you anything for yesterday." I sat down on a well-used kitchen chair. "Did you find anything to fix on the engine?"

"Ah, yes." He cleared a space in front of him and laid his elbows down. "Throttle linkage had gone dicky and she wouldn't idle. Also, bit of an air leak in your uplift pump." He scowled. "Put it right. Ticks over nicely now."

"What do I owe you?" I braced myself.

"I dunno," he said. "How's thirty euros?"

"That's it?"

"Could make it more I guess, but then I'd have to put it in my books, wouldn't I."

"Thirty is fine. No problem. But, um, I just gave you all my cash yesterday," I said. "How about I bring it down to you after we get to Auxerre and I find a cash machine?"

"That's fine." He said, and went back to pawing through his stack of papers.

"Right then, we're off." I stood up. "See you in a few days."

"Cheers," he said, as he pushed his chair back and disappeared under his desk.

Nine locks and seven easy hours later we were being greeted by Dominique at our new berth beneath one of the lovely cathedrals at Auxerre. The trip up the Yonne River took us through green forests and small picturesque river villages. Joe's attentions to *Phaedra's* engine had made her purr. We had covered over 150 miles and negotiated more than 200 locks in our cruise through Burgundy, and we were ready to settle for a while in a new home base.

Auxerre looked perfect. After we'd shut everything down and set ourselves up with shore power and water, we set off to explore the town. We crossed the river on the footbridge just behind the boat, and chose a narrow, winding street that led up a steep hill toward the old town center. Along the way we passed ancient stone houses built into the walls, and leaning, half-timbered buildings decorated around the doorways and windows with elaborate wooden carvings of saints and sinners. We found a café at the top of the hill where we had coffee and watched the locals streaming by the shops, which were chic and selling the latest Paris lingerie. There were bookstores, patisseries and restaurants scattered throughout the old town and at least three places that sold Italian gelato.

The boat was within easy walking distance of a major supermarket in one direction and cafes, restaurants and even a cheese shop in the other. We found a theater where live music and plays were performed and a riverside park with swimming and tennis. Another park, just next to the harbor, was setting up stages for live concerts that would be happening the next week.

That evening, Linda was hit with one of her cooking inspirations that I love so much. She dashed off to the supermarket and came back with her arms full of the makings of a world class rabbit Bourgogne. While she set to work with her pots and pans, I put a couple bottles of red into the bilges to cool. Soon, the cabin was filling with the aroma of sautéing onions, garlic and lardon, which had Billy so excited that he got himself evicted from the kitchen. I took him outside to the cockpit and settled down with a book.

St. Etiene Cathedral from Phaedra's deck

A few minutes later I looked up and noticed Billy staring intently across the river. I followed his gaze and my eyes fell on the single gothic tower of the giant Cathedral of Saint Etienne, rising above the crest of the town. The stones of the tower glowed golden in the light of the setting sun, creating sharp, crisp shadows that traced the intricate lacework of the carved stone decorations covering the building. I looked to the right, along the jumbled tile rooftops of the town, to the Abbey de Saint Germain. Its white stones and flying buttresses glowed like sugar frosting supporting one, slender tower that shot into the air like a highly decorated needle.

Abbey St. Germain from Phaedra's deck

As I watched, the light on the clouds changed from pink to orange, then light yellow, and the brilliance of the tower of Saint

275

Etienne faded to a frosty silver against the pale blue sky. The shadows lengthened and the air was growing chill. Suddenly, from the west, a flock of small black starlings appeared. The leaders flew over the town and led their followers toward the harbor. Then, another flock appeared behind them, and another, and another. The sky was suddenly filled with the birds, calling, spinning and diving in wild crazy waves in the sky over the river. Rolling clouds of black birds instantly changing course became undulating rivers in the sky, diving and scolding and dancing in fluid, amoeba-like formations.

One gliding ribbon of birds rose and spun in the air and then, as if on cue, dove headlong into a stand of trees lining the river. They disappeared from sight, but their chirping and calling still floated across the water. One by one, other flocks followed with sprints and dives and swoops until the trees were alive with the sounds of millions of birds, settling in until the morning when they'd sally forth for another day of foraging in the fields surrounding Auxerre.

The sun sets late in June in that part of France and it was almost ten o'clock when the lights on the Abbey and the Cathedral came on. The Abbey became a glowing white monument, reflected in the river. The Cathedral was floodlit from the outside, but lights glowed from inside as well, illuminating the intricate stained glass windows lining the Choir and the Apse. Linda and I raised our glasses and toasted each other.

We had two weeks to settle in before we were scheduled to return to California, so we got comfortable. Each morning we set out to find the best patisserie for our breakfast croissant. It quickly boiled down to three, with the tiniest and farthest away, holding the lead. Some mornings, the walk up to the Paul Bert Bridge, across the river and up the hill to the hole-in-the-wall shop across from the Cathedral St. Estephe, would seem daunting, but the warm smile from the patissier we came to call "Skinny Arms" was too much to resist. She knew exactly what we wanted every morning and always offered tastes of some new treat that her husband was experimenting with. Skinny Arms started our days and made Auxerre begin to feel like a second hometown.

We quickly discovered that Friday was market day in Auxerre. With Billy pulling on his leash, we'd set out for the covered market at the top of the Rue de Temple in the old town. Inside the place was bustling with hungry Auxerois, haggling with butchers and fish mongers, examining the fruit and squeezing the small wheels of Brie de Meaux to judge its degree of runny-ness. Chablis, only a fifteen-minute drive away, had a food market on Saturday and a wine market on Sunday. We found that it is possible to be over-marketed on occasion. We had to learn to pace ourselves.

We also made friends in the harbor. The local ducks and swans became very attached to us and brought their extended families around for daily morning and evening stale bread feast.

Antique Brocante in Auxerre

By the end of the first week we were beginning to feel quite at home in Auxerre. We'd found a couple of pretty nice restaurants, shopped the weekly market, toured all three churches, and, a magnificent find for boat dwellers, we discovered a really wonderful Laundromat. The public pool was big and beautiful and set in a park by the river. Unfortunately, they required that men wear those tiny Speedo swimsuits, so I stayed away, although Linda seemed to enjoy it.

One afternoon, the quiet of the town was shattered by someone blasting an air horn, directly across the river from us. We quickly identified the noise as coming from a large tractor-trailer rig, painted all over with clowns and hippopotamus'. Over the last few days, we had begun to notice colorful posters appearing on telephone poles and walls around town, announcing the imminent arrival of "Le Cirque de Guignol," France's most famous puppet. The model for Punch of Punch and Judy fame, Guignol was a fiesty little fellow with a devoted following amongst the children of Auxerre. Apparently, the little fellow and his entourage had finally arrived. We pulled our chairs out onto the deck to watch the excitement.

Guignol's semi was idling in the parking lot that ran along the water where most of the inhabitants of the lower town parked their cars. It was also the site where the occasional small circus, carnival, or traveling merry-go-round would set up shop. This however, required some coordination between the city fathers, the car owners and the carnival guys. You can imagine the problem when a fleet of trucks show up, ready to assemble the Thrilling Tilt-a-Whirl or the Mickey Mouse Space Ride, only to find their intended site filled with parked cars. In the case of Guignol's traveling puppet show, about forty cars had to move immediately or a certain dwarf, who had been cooped up in the back of the Magic Puppet House all day, traveling down the A6 from Paris, was going to have someone's guts for garters.

The driver of the truck was attempting to solve the problem by leaning on his air horn, thereby alerting all of Auxerre that they had better drop their aperitifs, grab their cigarettes, and hoof it down to the riverfront to move their damn cars or the dwarf would do it for them. Of course honking one's horn in the street, no matter where in the world one honks, can be construed as the opening challenge to any idle "back-honkers" within earshot. Auxerre, as we were beginning to learn, was a hotbed of drivers just itching to honk-back at the slightest provocation. In no time at all there arose a magnificent cacophony of air horn, "HOOOONNKK!," followed by an irate Citroen's "hinnk-hink!", which required another "HOONNNK-HOOONNK!," which brought back the Citroen, two Opals, and a Renault's "Honk-toot-hinnk-hink." The puppet truck was honking at empty parked cars. Cars were honking at the truck hogging the parking lot. Traffic was slowing down to see what all the noise was about and the ones in back were honking at the rubber-neckers who were naturally honking back. Scooters were beeping just for the heck of it. Billy started barking.

A crowd was beginning to gather in the parking lot when, after about fifteen minutes, one harried woman dragging a shopping basket arrived and moved her car. They had to restrain the dwarf.

"You know, with stuff like this, who needs Paris?" I said, as Linda and I dragged our chairs off the deck.

"I think I'll go to the pool for a while." she said.

"Dear? Paris? You still want to go, right?"

"Of course. When we come back in the fall, or maybe next spring." she said. "Where's my book?"

"I was thinking. The boat looks pretty shabby. Rust is popping out all over and she needs to be hauled out and have the bottom tarred."

"Yeeaaahhh?"

"I just thought, when we come back in the fall, we'll head for Paris but," Linda shot me a look. "Just hear me out. On the way, we make a quick stop at Parfit's boatyard, get the bottom done, touch up the paint then dash into Paris with the boat looking brand spanking new."

"What's that gonna cost?" She said. "How long will it take?"

"I'll call Parfit and see if he'll come up and give us an estimate."

The next morning, Joe Parfit stood on the quay pulling his beard. "So, what'd'ya think?" I asked.

"Not too bad," he said. "Three weeks, four, tops."

"Have you done this kind of job before?" Linda asked.

"All the time. We've got a boat just about this size in the yard now for a paint job. Come on down and have a look if you like. Give you an idea what we're talking about."

The next day, while Linda started the packing for our return to the U.S., I drove down to Migennes to have a look at the sample paint job and get a feel for what we were facing. Joe met me in his office then took me down to the quay to admire the boat in question. It was about the same size and shape as *Phaedra* and although there was no work going on at the time, from the tools lying all over the deck it was apparent that this boat was indeed somewhere in the process of being painted. Joe proudly pointed out the areas around the deck and cabin that had been chipped and ground down to bare metal and were currently covered with a bright orange primer. As I looked the boat over, I could see that the job was in its beginning stages and there would be lots more orange before the poor old thing settled down to its final colors. However, satisfied by the evidence before my own eyes that there were others before me, I followed Joe back into his office for the palaver.

After some talk, some beer and some more talk, we arrived at a price for the whole job. I agreed to bring the boat down in the second week of August. Joe would lift it out of the water with his crane and then his crackerjack crew of professionals would jump right on it. With everybody turned to, Joe estimated the work would take about three weeks. Linda and I could live on board during, which would be miserable, or find some place to camp for the duration. We shook on it. Done.

When I got back to the boat I couldn't wait to tell Linda. "Guess what?" I said. She looked up. She'd been crying. "What?" I asked.

"It's Phil, Sue called."

"What's wrong?"

"He has a tumor. In his brain."

By the time Linda and I got back to the U.S. the doctors had removed as much of the tumor as they could find. Phil was in a fog, weak and the victim of a very bad haircut. Although we all hoped, and many even prayed, that the tumor would stay gone, its tiny cells had their own agenda and they fought on. The doctors began to make predictions: a month, a year, can't tell.

He still had two comic strips to put out every day, but the papers had agreed to publish re-runs until he got back on his feet. As his strength began to return, sometimes I'd go over to his house and we would write gags and draw cartoons. Even though he'd occasionally fall asleep in the middle of it, at least he'd nod off with a sketchpad in his hand. One day we were in his studio trying to find the punch line in a bunch of press clippings from the day before when he looked up and said, "Did you ever get that boat to Paris?"

"Not yet," I said. "Maybe in the spring."

"Don't wait too long. You never know." Then he smiled and lay down on his sofa, and went to sleep.

Chapter Twenty-Seven

"We have met the enemy, and he is us."

\- Pogo

Eight months later, in early May, I arrived in Auxerre to take *Phaedra* to Joe Parfit's boatyard for the work we had talked about doing the previous summer. On the phone, he and I had compared calendars and fixed the date for her haul-out in just two days. Three weeks of his tender loving care would have her spruced up and shining like a new car, and then Linda and Billy would come over and we would finally set off for Paris, the dream realized.

It was an easy one-day run to Migennes, which I planned to do on my own. There were only nine locks to get through, but the mooring situation at the boatyard was an unknown, so I decided to take a little reconnaissance run to boatyard in the car to check it out. I rolled across the dirt parking area and left the car by the dumpsters then walked around to the quay. A raft of barges six deep stretched out into the river in various stages of repair. It looked like my best approach would be to tie *Phaedra* to the last barge and then bring her against the quay the next day to be lifted out.

As I started to make my way out to the furthest barge for a closer examination, I realized that I had stepped onto a familiar boat. It was quite like mine. It also needed a paint job. It was the same boat that Joe had shown me almost ten months before! And it was exactly as it had been those ten months back. The spots of orange primer were now black with dirt and mold, and tools were still lying on the deck exactly where they had been last July. Leaves had piled up behind them, but that was the only progress I could see.

As this was sinking in, I noticed some movement to my right. I turned and saw an old couple painfully climbing out of a chipped and faded barge and making their way along the quay toward me. They wore a dazed expression but they were coming at me with a purposeful, shuffling intent.

"Oy, what're ya doing here?" the old gentleman wheezed in cockney English.

"I'm bringing my boat down tomorrow for some work and I'm just checking out the mooring situation," I replied.

"What're ya havin' done then?" they demanded in unison.

"Re-tarring the bottom and then touch up the paint job."

"Oh. Nothin' mechanical then?" the woman asked, gripping my arm.

"No, haven't planned on it."

"That's fine then, fine." She released me.

"Why?" I asked, like a fool.

"Oh nothin', nothin'. We're just hoping Joe'll be getting to us next week. But he won't be foolin' with you, except for the crane and liftin' you out is all. No, Sally'll be workin' on you. Sally, ya, that'll be fine."

Questions were beginning to form in my mind. "Who's Sally?"

"Oh, Sally does all the paintin' around here. I saw her 'round yesterday. Paintin' that blue boat, back o' the yard," said the old lady.

"Joe does the mechanical," added her husband. "He said he'd be gettin' to us next week is all. Thought you might be jumpin' the queue."

"Sally? She runs the crew?"

"Oh, no crew. Just Sally," said the old woman. I thought I smelled gin.

"You been waiting long?" I asked.

"We came in last August. Broken rudder. Joe said he might get to us next week. But if you're just getting a paint job, well, that's no problem for us then."

"You've been here since August? Last August? Waiting for Joe...?"

"Can't go far with a broken rudder, can we. Joe says next week." The man's voice trailed off as he gazed into the distance.

I looked down again at the tools lying on the deck where they had been dropped all those months ago. Then I looked around the rest of the yard. I noticed boats leaning on crumbling stands that seemed to be growing out of the tall weeds. Fading hulks littered the yard like gravestones, their tattered canvas, fluttering ghostlike in the wind. Rust, like dried blood, streaked their flaking sides. Disgorged innards lay in heaps and pieces on the ground. Had I found the fabled place where boats go to die?

A little voice inside me was screaming, "Run!" But instead, I went looking for Joe.

I walked around the boatyard, poking my head into dark cavernous shops, pulling corrugated iron doors open against protesting hinges and banging on the hulls of boats that had ladders propped against them as if someone had once intended to climb aboard with tools or parts for repairs. I woke up a dog, but never a sign of Joe or Sally or anyone who looked like they might be a boatyard worker. In the dirt parking lot I found a couple sitting in folding lawn chairs in front of a small RV, drinking beer and reading. They looked up as I walked over.

"Bonjour," I said. "Have you seen Monsieur Parfit, s'il vous plait?" A large greyhound got up from the shade of their awning and came over and goosed me.

"Stop that, Daisy!" the round, sunburnt woman hollered. "Sorry 'bout that," she said. "She's bored." More Brits, I realized.

"No problem. Got any idea where I can find Joe Parfit? I'm bringing my boat in tomorrow and I just wanted -"

"What're you bringing it in for?" the man asked, putting down his beer.

"Bottom and paint."

"Oh, that's OK then," he said.

"It's nothing mechanical," I said reassuringly.

"That's fine. No Joe so far today," he said. "He was here yesterday, wasn't he?" he asked his wife. She nodded absently, having gone back to her reading and beer drinking.

"You, uh, you got a mechanical problem going on?" I asked.

"Oh, yeah. Joe's redesigning our 'hole prop and rudder. Boat won't steer. Bad design. 'Ad to rip it all out. Start over. That's 'er over there. Names *Moya*. 'Ole back end's off, isn't it?" he said.

"Sounds big. Been here a while?"

"'Bout six months."

"Seven, months and more, Roger." his wife corrected him.

"Well, we went home for a while in the winter, didn't we," Roger said. She nodded. "Joe says maybe he'll get back at it next week. Finish it up. Go cruising." He picked up his beer. "Haven't seen him today, though."

I thanked them and wandered back toward the river. As I was taking one last look at the poor abandoned boat with it's orange primer, I was surprised to hear someone calling my name. I turned and saw a familiar figure climbing across the raft of barges and waving at me. As he got closer I recognized Jack, the fellow who had sold me the Espace a year ago. At the time, he and his wife were selling their barge, and going back to the States so I was surprised to see him in Migenne.

"Jack! I thought you moved to Arizona."

"Aw, that didn't work out. We sold out and bought another boat. She's over there. Name's *Deja Vu*." And he pointed back at a beautiful Luxemotor barge with a fresh load of laundry drying from her rails. "What'er you doing here?" he continued. "Still got the car?"

"She's right over there. Uglier than ever but it runs great. I'm bringing *Phaedra* in tomorrow for a haul-out." Jack just kept his smile and nodded his head.

"OK, Jack, tell me the truth. If I bring my boat in here and have it hauled out, will I ever get it back in the water?"

"What're you having done?"

"Bottom job, tar and stuff, and fix up the paint job."

"Nothing mechanical?"

"Don't think so."

"Well, if it's just paint and tar, that'd be Sally. She's not too bad," he said. "How long's it supposed to take?

"About three weeks."

"That what Joe said?"

"I'm thinking four."

"Oh, at least," he said and scratched at his grey beard. Then he looked me in the eyes and said, "Nothing mechanical?"

"Not that I know of. I'm getting the feeling I should avoid that."

Jack nodded. "The thing is, all the mechanical work is done by Joe, see. And, well, Joe works when he feels like it. Can't push him."

"So, if I can avoid Joe, I should be all right," I said.

"Keep your fingers crossed."

"So, what are you doing in Migennes?" I asked.

"We bought the boat in Holland and brought it down to have a new engine put in."

"That's *boucoups* mechanical," I said.

"Uh-huh." Jack looked at his feet.

"You came from Holland?" I asked. "To Migennes?"

"Uh-huh, last November," he said.

"Seven months ago…?"

"Yup. That's the engine, right over there." He pointed at the hulking iron shed behind us. "They delivered it last winter." Through the doors, in the gloom, sinking into the dirt and grease floor, I could just make out a bright yellow diesel engine and gearbox, strapped to a wooden palette.

"Oh yeah. I see it. It looks good," I said, working up a little enthusiasm. "Shouldn't take too long to get it from just over there into your boat."

"Well," Jack said, "first they have to start taking out the old one.

Joe said, maybe next week."

Chapter Twenty-Eight

"As long as it's not mechanical."
- Roger the Rudder

With teeth clenched, a fixed set to my jaw, and a persistent voice in my head screaming, "Don't do this!" I set off in *Phaedra* for the boatyard. If all went to plan, I'd make it to Migennes by nightfall and spend the night on the boat. The next day, Joe would haul her out and Sally would jump into action while I got settled into a tiny trailer at a nearby campground called The Confluences. Perched on two wheels and a cider block and offering running water and a Western style toilet just a short walk away, the trailer would be mine for three weeks, with an option for a fourth if things took a bit longer than planned.

Bachelor Unit #23

The trip was progressing along nicely until, around lunchtime, I began to notice a growling vibration whenever I used the bow thruster. By the time I reached Migennes five hours later, a grinding howl had joined the other noises and the bow thruster had completely packed it in.

Whatever noises I made, crunching *Phaedra* into the abandoned river tug on my approach to Joe's quayside didn't attract an audience or disturb anyone's afternoon nap, so my arrival went unremarked. Once I was securely tied off I poured myself a measure of brandy for warmth and set about assessing the damage. Another scrape, a small dent, no big deal. I'm here to fix the paint. Bow thruster kaput; bad, very bad. This was mechanical.

I had another brandy, this one for strength, then went looking for Joe. Out behind the tool shed I found old Margaret, wandering around with a teapot in her hand. "Hello Margaret," I said. "Say, have you seen Joe?"

"What'ya want him for?"

"Oh, I just wanted to let him know I'm here."

"Why?"

"Well, he's hauling my boat out tomorrow and I…"

"Tomorrow? What's he doing to it?"

"Uh, just some paint," I said.

"Oh, right. That'd be Sally," she said. "Last I saw Joe, he was heading toward *Rosey*." She pointed her teapot toward the back fence.

Rosey was perched on piles of railroad ties and propped up by metal boat stands. There was a ladder leaning against her side. From inside the boat, I heard a muffled pounding, so I climbed aboard. I found Joe deep in the gloom at the back of the boat, crouched on the floor between two beds. He was peering at the ground through a great gaping hole in her stern. He seemed almost pleased to see me.

"Oy, you made it then," he said and whacked on a fresh weld with a wrench.

"Just tied up," I said. "She'll be ready to come out of the water first thing in the morning. What time do you think?"

"Might not be tomorrow. Could be, but probably the day after. Got a few things to get on to tomorrow." He scowled down the hole. "Probably the day after."

"OK. That's fine. I'll start taking things off tomorrow, clearing the decks and stuff. It's probably easier to do that while she's in the water anyway," I said. "Oh, by the way, I think my bow thruster's packed in. Maybe you can take a look at it soon as she's out. Best time to take care of it, while she's out."

"Probably got water in the fluid. I'll have a look at it tomorrow." Then he went back to peering at the ground through the hole.

"Right. Good. See you tomorrow then." As I was climbing down the ladder, I saw Jack sitting slumped in the wheelhouse of his boat, and the little voice once again said, "Run!"

The next morning I moved officially into my temporary aluminum bachelor pad at the Confluences and then went looking for Joe.

I wanted to see if, by chance, he'd haul *Phaedra* on schedule. After all, he had said, "might not be tomorrow." In my book, that meant that it still might be tomorrow, right?

I caught sight of him climbing up the ladder into *Rosey*. I trotted over.

"Morning, Joe," I said, bounding up with a smile that said "I'm a good guy." He stopped on the ladder and looked me over.

"Morning to you, *Mr.* Hammond," he said.

"So, you think we'll be hauling her out today?"

"Not today, no, don't think so. Got this lot here to deal with today. Probably tomorrow," he said.

"Tomorrow. Right. OK, I'll just go ahead and get things cleared off and ready to go. Tomorrow then." I smiled at his back as he disappeared into *Rosey*. "Great."

The next day I was ready, but Joe wasn't. "Not today. Looks like it'll have to be tomorrow," were his words.

"Right!" I said.

I was even more ready the following day, but not Joe. "Tomorrow," said he.

"Right," I said. But the voice inside said, "You don't really need a bow thruster to get to Paris. Run away!"

The day after that, he wasn't to be found. I trotted off on a round of the boatyard, asking the rest of the inhabitants, "Seen

Joe?" Then it dawned on me that I was the only one who did that. Everybody else just sat there from one day to the next, on their boats or in their lawn chairs, never knowing, beyond hoping, afraid of caring. Where is Joe? Will he work on my boat today? No? Well, maybe tomorrow, maybe next week...I looked around and told myself, I'm not like these people. I won't end up like this. Joe likes me.

So I went looking for Sally. I'd seen her a couple of times, putting the finishing touches to a paint job on a small boat in the back of the yard. *Phaedra* was supposed to be her next project and I'd spoken to her a couple of times about it. She was about forty years old, tall and strong, with an unruly mop of curly brown hair that she tied up in a bandana.

She was never without a hand rolled cigarette in her teeth, which served as a sort of jagged sieve for odd shreds of tobacco. By lunchtime, the dust and residue from her grinders and sanders would stick to the sun block she rubbed on her face and streak it black. She worked all day alongside her portable radio, which played sappy French disco songs at volumes sufficient to be heard above the noise of her power tools. She and Joe, and Joe's mechanic, Jeff, were, I came to learn, the entire crew of Mr. Parfit's boatyard.

I found Sally in her paint locker, pounding the lid back onto a can of blue paint. She was full of information. "Oh, Joe's gone north to pick up a boat. Won't be back 'til sometime next week," she said and spit a shred of tobacco at a bucket on the floor.

That night I was on the phone with Linda, "Is *Phaedra* out of the water yet?" she asked.

"No, not yet," I said. "Maybe next week."

There was a pause. "Cris, you're becoming one of them."

On the tenth day, I was driving from the campground to the boatyard when I thought I saw the massive arm of Joe's crane, moving slowly above the trees. My pulse quickened. When I pulled into the yard, I found I had driven right into the middle of a major event. The dispossessed, the hopeless, *les miserables* of Joe's private purgatory had come out of their boats, RV's and cardboard shelters, and were gathering in awestruck silence around the great yellow crane. Its giant diesel engine belched black smoke as Joe, seated on his lofty throne, pulled levers, pushed throttles, and tread on pedals. The sixty-foot cantilevered arm swung in a majestic arch until it pointed toward the back of the yard then slowly, oh so slowly, it moved on clanking steel treads toward a line of small boats leaning amidst the weeds. These were good signs, hopeful signs. The crane worked! (There had been rumors that it didn't.) And Joe was going to move boats!

Through the rest of the morning, I watched as Joe and Jeff, with the help of a shuffling gang of volunteers, positioned the pair of lifting slings beneath the newly painted boat and then, at Jeff's signal, Joe reved the engine and the crane gently lifted her off her stands. Then, after some ominous gnashing of gears, Joe put the crane into gear and crept toward the quayside to set her in the water. Jeff was just getting ready to release her from the slings so her happy owner could finally take her away, when the lunch whistle blew at the slaughterhouse next door, signaling that all French workers within earshot must immediately drop whatever they are doing and go to lunch. The siren froze all progress in place as Jeff bolted for his car and Sally dropped her paintbrush and shoved her hands in her pockets. Joe silenced the belching diesel engine, descended proudly from his crane, and sauntered toward his office. As the crowd wandered off, I caught up with Sally. "So, Sally, ya think he'll get to my boat this afternoon? Since he's already got the crane going and all?"

"Yup. You come out today. Right after lunch," she said.

I was stunned. Today! Today we start on the project. It was ten days later than I had planned and I only had my trailer reserved for another ten days, but TODAY we'd start! Woo-hoo! See? I told myself. You're not like those other people, pathetically sitting around waiting months and months for Joe's attention. No. Joe likes you!

But the little voice whispered, "They aren't waiting to be hauled out of the water, stupid. They're waiting to be put back in."

"Shut up," I said to the little voice.

After lunch, as Joe was climbing up into his crane, he called me over and told me go on out to *Phaedra* and start warming up the engine. He'd wave me in as soon as the blue boat was away from the quay. I watched for a few more minutes just to be sure that the crane engine would start, then I made my way out to my boat.

From my deck, six boats out at the end of the raft of barges, I could see the process on the quay as the boat's owners and friends scurried around, freeing her from the slings and untying her lines. It was almost a half hour before I saw the puff of smoke from her engine as she began to creep away. I untied and shoved off.

In five minutes I was at the quay, tied against the bank, and Joe was pacing off the length of the boat, trying to estimate the balance points for the slings. "She's a bit bigger than I thought," he said. "You don't think it's over 20 tons, do you?"

"Don't know."

"Oh well, let's give it a go." Joe climbed up into the crane and took the controls.

The engine revved and my heart swelled with joy as I watched the slings, dangling high over the deck, begin their wonderful descent. I was on the cabin top with Jeff, eagerly waiting to catch them and walk them forward to the bow so they could be dragged under the boat and positioned at the lift points. They were just about three feet beyond my reach when, out of the corner of my eye, I caught sight of Margaret shuffling up the quay toward the crane.

She carefully made her way to the side of the crane and in her little old lady voice, started screaming up at Joe. The engine dropped to an idle. The slings stopped in place. Joe said, "What is it, Margaret?"

"Joe?" She yelled. "Would'ja like a cuppa tea, Joe? I've just put the kettle on."

"Cuppa tea?" Joe yelled down at her.

"I've just put the kettle on."

"Sounds lovely, Margaret. I'll be right there."

"Right, then." Margaret waved, and shuffled back toward her boat.

Joe, on his throne, pulled a few levers, pushed a button, and the great diesel engine fell silent.

The slings stopped dead. They hung there in mid-air, silently swaying, just out of reach, tormenting me. I jumped and clawed at them. "Jeff! Jeff, lift me up," I called. But when I turned he was gone. I just caught a glimpse of his ponytail, as he followed Joe into the shed for their tea party. They left me standing there like a beagle tied to a parking meter.

They were about forty-five minutes into their tea break when I couldn't stand it anymore. I walked over to the shed where Margaret had set up her dainty porcelain tea set. I found them all sitting around with saucers balanced on their greasy knees, sipping tea and nibbling biscuits.

"So, how's the tea coming along?" I asked.

"Lovely," Joe said.

"Bout ready to, uh, you know, start up that crane?"

"Oh, I'll just clean up here," Margaret said. "You boys go on." She started to fuss with the crockery.

"Uh-oh. What's this then?" Joe said, looking over my shoulder.

I turned and saw a red faced gentleman hurrying our way with "uh-oh" written all over his face. I recognized him as the owner of the boat that had gone into the water just before I had pulled up to the quay. "'Ello, Dave," Joe said. "You don't look happy."

"Aye, got a bit of a problem, Joe," Dave sounded like he was choking.

"What's that then?"

"I've got a leak."

"That doesn't sound good," Joe said and reached for another biscuit.

"How big of a leak?" I jumped in. "Don't you have a pump?"

"It's coming in pretty good," Dave said. "The wife, she's out there pumpin' now but it's not helpin' much."

"But you're keeping up with it?" I put it to him.

"Sort of," Dave said.

"Fine. No problem," I said and turned to Joe. "So, Joe, ya ready to fire up that crane and haul me out?"

Dave butted in again. "Kinda worried about that leak, Joe. I think I'm sinkin.'"

"Can't have that, Dave," Joe said. "Better bring her round, we'll pick her up and see what's what."

"I'll tell the missus." Dave turned and trotted off.

"But, but…" I said.

"Better move your boat outa the way," Joe said as he got to his feet.

"But, but…"

"We'll get your *Phaedra* out, maybe next week."

Chapter Twenty-Nine

"Life is a moveable shed."

- Joe Parfit

It took only two more days for Joe to finally get around to pulling *Phaedra* out. I really tried to be filled with joy at the occasion, but instead I felt a cloying sense of dread. It was painfully obvious that I had now put myself high and dry on Planet Parfit. A place where you can get on your knees and pray to God for deliverance, but only Joe Parfit can put your boat back in the water.

I would tell myself, "Hey, we're only two weeks behind schedule. With three weeks for the paint repair and maybe another week to fix the bow thruster, we'll still have plenty of time to get to Paris and settle in." And in fact, now that *Phaedra* was out of the water and sitting proudly on her railroad ties and boat stands, work had started almost immediately. Sally had rigged up her pressure washer and had begun blasting scads of dirt and grunge off of the bottom of the boat and, unfortunately, great clouds of loose paint off of the rest of it. After she had finished with her power washer, so much paint had been blown off the boat that the simple paint repair job was shaping up to be more like a full blown paint job. Hard to do in three weeks.

The next day Joe once again fired up his crane and carried his brand new moveable boat-shed across the yard and proudly lowered it over *Phaedra*. Not a small part of Joe's original estimate of three weeks for my paint job rested upon his assurance that he'd have this spanking new shed by the time I brought her in, and with *Phaedra* sheltered beneath it, his crew of painters would be able to work on the boat rain or shine. As Joe slowly lowered his latest piece of technological boatyard gadgetry over *Phaedra*, a fundamental shortcoming became painfully apparent. It was a twenty-five foot shed, protecting a sixty-foot boat. "No matter," he assured me. "We'll just work on the parts that are under the shed, then move it along as we progress."

Joe was so proud of his new shed.

Two weeks had passed since I had brought *Phaedra* down for what was supposed to be a three week job and aside from the power washing and the shed, virtually nothing had been done. It had also become painfully obvious that I had to be in the boatyard every day to prod things along or *Phaedra* would end up overgrown with weeds and future generations of Migenne-ites would walk by on Sundays and say, "See son, that old boat is still here."

Just standing around fussing at Sally was making us both crazy, so I decided to keep myself busy by refinishing all of *Phaedra's* decorative, carved wood pieces. They had to be removed anyway for the paint job, so I set to work. The mast, a pair of deeply carved oak swans, two mahogany skylights, a pair of carved oak 'eyes' from the bow, the giant oak tiller with its bas-relief floral motif cap, and the combing around the cockpit would be stripped, sanded and then brought back in six coats of oil. I found a couple of unused railroad ties lying around the yard and dragged them over and laid them in the dirt under *Phaedra*, then dropped a piece of plywood over them and, voila! I had a desk. I found an old seat cushion from an abandoned couch for comfort and went to work sanding wood and making my presence felt in the silly hope of keeping the boat work humming. I had a lot to learn. A typical day would unfold as follows:

Sally would arrive at the boat around 9:30 a.m. and start organizing her tools for the day's labors. Extension cords laid, air hoses coupled, radio tuned to the proper station, vacuum cleaner at the ready, tobacco and papers fully stocked, one final trip to the loo and by 10:00 a.m., an electric tool would usually be switched on.

At 10:30, Margaret would come tottering over from her barge and ask if Sally would like some tea. Then, all work would stop for tea and biscuits until 11:00, then cigarettes. Back to work at 11:15 until 11:45, when Sally would stop work to begin preparing lunch for Joe and Jeff. Lunch: Noon to 2:00. Clean up from lunch and back at it until 2:30 when Margaret, bored and thirsty, pops up with her damn tea-kettle again and all work would stop for more tea and cookies. The whistle at the slaughterhouse would blow at five. Days turned into weeks.

One day, about the third week into it, I was surprised to arrive and find that Sally had a helper. His name was Gil and I discovered him sitting on the scaffolding around the hull, wielding a grinder. "Now we'll see some action," I told myself. Soon he was joined by Sally, who was carrying a strange tool that I soon learned was her "needle gun." A needle gun is a long metal tube, about as big around as a half dollar, with about a dozen thin metal rods protruding from its end. When you hook up compressed air to the other end and hit the switch, the metal rods shoot in and out and knock the bejezzus out of anything it touches. With that and the grinder going I was ecstatic. The din they made was "The Lovely Sound of Progress."

The Lovely Sound of Progress only lasted for about ten minutes before Gil's grinder fell silent. I looked over and saw him making his way along the scaffolding to the short ladder at the end of the boat. He climbed to the ground and sauntered past me, across the yard to the main shed and ducked inside. He was back in ten minutes, looking rested and puffing on a fresh cigarette as he climbed back onto the scaffold. He made his way back to his grinder, fiddled with it for a few minutes, then switched it on and got back to the business of grinding paint.

For the whole day, he would repeat his mysterious trek every ten or fifteen minutes, effectively reducing the French seven-hour work day to something more like two and a half. After two days of this, I couldn't take it any longer, I had to find out what kept calling him back into that shed. I followed him.

Parfit's main warehouse was a dark, cavernous space, filled with piles of unidentifiable engine parts, coils of wire, and giant, pre-war machine tools, all covered in black grease and seemingly sinking into the spongy dirt floor. The only light filtered through a filthy window over a jumbled workbench at the back of the room. Gil was intently bent over a small box he had pulled off a shelf above the bench. As my eyes adjusted to the gloom, I realized that he was holding a box of thin sandpaper disks for his grinder. He took one out, turned it over in his hand and examined both sides, then slipped it into his pocket and replaced the box. Then he lit a fresh cigarette and sat on a stack of boxes and smoked.

Gil had been grinding through one of these paper disks about every ten minutes. His solution? Stop what he was doing, walk all the way back to the shed, get a new one from the box, grab a smoke, then carry that one single piece of sandpaper back to the boat and attach it to his grinder for another ten-minute session of labor.

After Gil had returned to his grinder, I went back to the shed, picked up the whole box of sanding disks and brought it out to him. I set it on the scaffold next to him, gave him a thumbs up and went back to my desk in the dirt. The next day, Gil walked off the job and never returned, but he had set the pace.

Sally's needle gun had been knocking great chunks of rust and old Bondo out of the decks, leaving behind areas that had to be cleaned and smoothed over with new body filler. These cancerous holes were appearing all over the boat and she had begun filling them with epoxy filler that had to be mixed with hardener then spread around before it hardened. She would go into her paint shop in the main shed, and then, on a paper plate, mix up a batch about the size of a golf ball. She'd then walk back to the boat, climb aboard, and with a small blue square piece of plastic, meticulously spread it on the metal. She'd watch it harden for a while, then climb back down and go to her shed for a cigarette and another paper plate's worth of stuff. I was pulling my hair out.

Finally, I couldn't stand it any longer. I approached her as she was carefully spreading epoxy on the deck. "Sally, how about, the next time you mix up a batch of that stuff, you mix up two batches. Then I'll take one and we can both be spreading it around. It'll go twice as fast."

She looked up from her latest spread, frowned, and said, "I don't think that will work."

"Why not?"

"Because I only have one of these." And she held up her little blue plastic spreader.

Chapter Thirty

"Pins and needles, needles and pins,
It's a happy man that grins."

- Ralph Cramden

Linda and Billy arrived toward the end of my fifth week in Parfit's gulag. It was well into June and it was raining when I took them to see poor *Phaedra* sitting on her props in the muddy boatyard by the river, her paint a disaster of primer, bare metal, and blotches of exposed rust. I had kept Linda up to date on the state of the project, so she wasn't too shocked by what she saw, but the reality was disheartening. Even though it was obvious that we were not going to be taking the boat to Paris any time soon, I had begged them to come over anyway to share my incarceration.

I went to the proprietor of the campground and asked for an upgrade to a mobile home with a little more pizzazz, and he found me a nice one with fake styrene shutters screwed to the siding around the windows. It also had a tiny kitchen, indoor plumbing and a small deck in front so we could sit outside on the rare evenings that it wasn't raining. I bought a bunch of flowers, which pretty much filled the place, and some mints for her pillow. Billy got a boiled chicken breast. Linda brought a suitcase the size of a

Buick, filled with things too numerous and weird to mention. But the two of them also brought a fresh dose of enthusiasm and buckets of love, which seemed to brighten even the weather in Migennes.

The news on Phil wasn't good, but it wasn't expected to be. He had come to a state where he was in no pain, and holding on. Linda had been doing what she could to help Sue deal with it but it only made her more conscious than ever of how precious little time any of us have together. We both felt it, so even though she faced flying six thousand miles to spend her summer in a trailer camp next to a dead-end boatyard, she did it so we wouldn't be apart.

Linda hadn't been in the yard an hour before she started meeting the other inmates of the asylum. Lawrence and Elizabeth were two Brits who had been living in Joe's parking lot in a caravan parked near Roger the Rudder and his wife in their cab-over camper. Lawrence's boat had been in the yard for nine months awaiting Joe's attentions. When they couldn't take it any longer in Migennes, they would flee to Panama, where they were building a small hut on an island near Boca Chica where they actually could have the experience of seeing things get done. Roger and his wife, Sally and their dog Daisy, had been in Joe's dusty hell for at least eight months hoping Joe would fix the steering problem on their boat. He had acquired the name Roger the Rudder, because that was all he could talk about any more.

Ken and Sheila were from Northern Ireland. They and their boat *Aquabelle*, had been mired in Joe's swamp for over six months with rudder problems of their own. Ken was tall and lanky with a soft face nestled between a set of ears that would have looked normal on a Bassett Hound. Sheila's red hair and rolling laugh belied the fact that she had been blown up once while standing in front of a chip shop on the High Street in Belfast. She miraculously survived with only a few cuts from flying glass. Joe Parfit didn't phase her a bit. Ken and Sheila were my neighbors in the campground where they were proud of their plush location, near the public showers and toilets.

Linda had arrived on a special day. It was the opening day of the Tattoo and Body Piercing Convention at the Auxerre Expo Center. I had seen the posters all week, but had forgotten about it with Linda's imminent arrival, but the refugees from Migennes were going en masse, so we all piled into a couple cars and took off (driving on the wrong side of the road at first, since they were all Brits.)

We arrived at the Expo Center and immediately realized that we stood out like a bunch of Jamaicans at a Klan picnic. We were wearing plaid. We wore not an ounce of leather. We hadn't shaved our heads, and we had no tattoos or facial piercing. We displayed no rings, studs, spikes, bones, or chrome skulls stapled, pinned or otherwise implanted into our flesh. Our bodies were free from permanent detailed renderings of Johnny Halliday, Jesus, Charles Manson, busty female lizards, or barfing Death's heads. We had no Chinese sayings, Maori talismans, glowing crosses, serpents, flames, or spider webs on our elbows. In short, we were uniquely weird.

Once inside, we moved around in a tight little group, the women clutching their bags under their arms and the men squinting due to the fact that we'd taken off our glasses because we didn't want to look like wimps. The Auxerre Expo Center is a fairly sizeable auditorium with a stage at one end and a wine kiosk at the other. It was only eleven in the morning, but we all agreed that the wine booth would be our first stop. Once fortified with plastic cups of the local *Vin d'Parking Lot*, we set off in small groups to learn the latest in body art.

Almost immediately Linda found a booth giving away temporary tattoo kits so she grabbed a bunch and the three ladies adjourned to the loo to apply them. We men fanned out to watch tattooing demonstrations and shop for body jewelry. The most interesting booth I found was one that didn't offer tattooing, but did a thriving business selling little dolls based on the possessed child in the movie The Exorcist. It had influenza green skin, tiny, needle-sharp fangs, and yellow reptilian eyes. She had artfully applied blood dripping from the edges of her mouth and from randomly placed gashes in her forehead and cheeks. Young, black-clad couples, covered in tattoos and metal attachments, pushing young toddlers in strollers, would stop to marvel at the way the eyes closed when she laid down for her nappy.

The doll and the photo album of "Body Jewelry For Private Places" were the big hits of the show as far as our innocent group was concerned. We left after an hour and retired to the Paul Bert café for more wine, where the ladies displayed their tattoos and the men dared each other to get real ones. The next morning, Sally screamed and spilled a gallon of paint on the floor when she turned on the light in her paint shed to find a little Linda Blair, bleeding from the head, sitting on her work bench.

Chapter Thirty-One

"Start every day with a smile and get it over with."
- W. C. Fields

Joe Parfit's mechanical team is Jeff. He was raised on a farm somewhere east of Tonnerre and is said to have been weaned on a hydraulic pump. He looked to be about twenty-five years old, although that's just a guess because he was usually covered pretty thoroughly in grease and dirt from his forehead to the soles of his cracked leather boots. He had long black hair, which he wore in a ponytail, and a shaggy mustache and beard. Jeff lived at the boatyard in a teardrop trailer balanced on two flat tires and an engine block. It sat boxed in a hole made up of a decaying old boat that will never move, two remaining sides of some forgotten cement shed, a wall of weeds, and the rusting gutted chassis of a 1953 Citroen. There was no running water or toilet, so he did his sprucing up in the back of Sally's paint shed. His work clothes were suitable for shimmying into the bilge under an engine in a coal barge or cutting quarter-inch steel plates with a torch. His dress-up clothes were the same. Joe figured out what was wrong with your boat and what will fix it, then he'd send in Jeff.

We lost souls on Planet Parfit would eagerly track the comings and goings of Jeff. Sightings would be noted, confirmed, and discussed. If he is heading toward your boat, your pulse quickens. Like a lost swimmer at sea, your strength about gone, you see on the horizon, a light! Rescue! Jeff is coming. A tiny light in the darkness of Migennes.

At first I thought it was my mind playing cruel tricks so I looked away and then quickly back again, but he was still there. Joe Parfit, freshly scrubbed and looking sober, and proclaiming this to be the day that he'd take a look at my pesky bow thruster problem. I was climbing up the ladder to the boat to change into my grubby, paint stripping outfit for the day and I admit that I just said, "Uh-huh," and kept on climbing. I was a bit shocked to find that he was climbing the ladder behind me.

"Let's fire it up and see what happens," he said.

"Sure," I said, still not really believing that this was real. But I found the keys, gave it a turn and the engine quickly roared to life, sending its signature black cloud of smoke out the exhaust pipe and directly into Sally's hair as she walked by dragging her favorite industrial vacuum cleaner. Joe paid no mind to her yells and put his attention on manipulating the hydraulic controls that ran the steering and bow thruster units. He discovered, as I had told him almost two months before, that the steering worked fine but when he tried the bow thruster itself, a horrendous grinding and shuddering hit the boat, so he shut it off instantly.

"Well, it doesn't seem to be the fluid," he said, stroking his chin. "Sounds like the bow thruster motor itself might be knackered."

"That's not good," I said, not particularly surprised.

"I'll get off the boat and go up front. When I tell you, hit the lever left and right," he said as he headed for the ladder. I stood at the controls and waited for his signal. "Okay. Hit it!" he yelled. That old grinding and shuddering erupted through the hull and I could only stand it for a few seconds before I had to stop. It gave me goose bumps.

"Hold it," he called out. "I'm gonna try something." And he walked off and disappeared around the edge of the building. I figured I'd never see him again, but to my surprise, he was back in a few minutes carrying a branch of a small tree in his hand. "Okay, let's try it again. Push the lever when I tell you," he yelled, and ducked back under the boat. I stood at the ready. "Okay, hit it!"

That awful noise came rumbling through the boat until suddenly, there was a massive CLUNK and BANG and a sound I hadn't heard since the time in high school when, on a dare, I threw my dad's car into "Park" on the Bayshore freeway.

"Okay, shut it down," Parfit yelled from under the boat. He walked around and stood at the base of the ladder. "Looks like the motor's ruined."

"So, what's next?"

"Well, we'll take a look at the valves and the pump, to make sure they're okay, then I imagine we ought to take that motor off and see if we can fix it, or if we need a new one."

"Fine!" I said. "Let's get started."

"Not today," he said. "Maybe next week." And he walked off.

I was still standing there ten minutes later when Linda arrived with Billy. "What's the matter with you?" she asked.

"Joe was here," I said.

"Really?" she said. "What'd he want?"

"He came to look at the bow thruster."

"Get out!"

"No, really."

"What'd he do?"

"Well, I got it going, then he jammed a log into it."

"A log?"

"Then he said he thinks the motor's broken."

"So, what happens next?"

"Said he'll be back next week," I said and sat down.

"No shit."

The following Tuesday morning started like all the others: waving good morning to the slaughterhouse workers huddled over their cigarettes, bouncing through the dusty parking lot of the boatyard and rolling to a stop in the shade of *Phaedra* and her shed. I noticed the yard was eerily quiet. The great boat crane was still and birds were nesting in its rigging. There was no sound of machinery from the machine shop and Sally's grinders and needle gun were silent. The barges tied to the quay were deserted and Jeff's radio was unplugged. It was a sunny morning and there were ducks foraging along the riverbank, but even they were not speaking.

I took a deep breath and climbed resignedly out of the car to begin another day. I skirted the muddy lake of spilled diesel fuel, climbed over the abandoned tractor tires to the ladder propped against *Phaedra's* hull and dragged myself aboard. As soon as I entered the main salon I realized there was something very wrong. Just inside the door, on the right, the cushions from the built-in settee were pulled off and the boards under them were removed and stacked against the wall, revealing the major components of the hydraulic system. Obviously, someone had been working down there. Someone must have shown up to do some work! Yes, there were greasy handprints all over the place! Jeff had arrived. My long dark night would soon be over!

But then, in the silence, I heard something that I couldn't understand. It sounded like running water. I should not have heard that. There wasn't a faucet or a toilet or a water pump at this end of the boat. Within seconds I traced the gurgling sound to the dark space under the settee. I was bending down to look into the hole when I heard heavy footsteps hurrying up the ladder and across the deck. Before my eyes could adjust to the darkness, Jeff burst into the cabin. He had several wrenches in one hand and a shiny yellow quiche pan in the other. He dove straight for the opening, reached down into the space and came up with the end of a hydraulic hose that was gushing oily fluid into the bilge. Being the expert in hydraulics, he put his thumb over the end of the hose.

Since Joe's entire mechanical team is Jeff, he works alone. Sometimes this can lead to really stupid problems, like when he takes a hydraulic line apart and can't put it back together again without some special tool that he forgot to bring along, and he can't go get it because he's taken the line apart and if he removes his thumb gallons of fluid will come gushing out and fill the bilge of the boat. But after a half hour of vainly calling for help, he has to just let it go and let the hydraulic fluid pour out into the bilge while he runs to the shop and finds the goddamn tool and then runs back again to put the damn thing back together again and also grabs a quiche pan on the way to bail out the oil before the owner comes back and shits a goddamn brick.

I looked into the bilge area and saw my reflection in the oily lake that was sloshing in the bottom of the boat. It wasn't deep enough for the automatic bilge pump to come on, but it would be soon if Jeff didn't get to work with his "proper" tool and stop the leak. I didn't quite know what to say. "What the hell?" came to mind, but I didn't know if that would be helpful. "Can I give you a hand?" wouldn't really be much use either, seeing as he'd already passed the point where another set of hands would have made a difference. Various colorful expletives ran through my head, but I took a breath and simply said, "Jeff, is that hydraulic fluid in my bilge?"

"Oui," he grunted as he reached around and started reattaching hoses.

"Um-hm." I said. "That what the quiche pan's for?" I asked.

"Oui," he grunted again.

"Ah, good." I said. "Well, I'm just gonna get into my work clothes. If you need anything …"

"Oui."

I put on my raggedy clothes then left Jeff to bail with his quiche pan. Then I climbed onto the deck and let out a string of profanities that would have won me an ovation in a Teamster's convention. I heard a gasp and looked over at Sally peeking at me over the cabin top, looking like she'd just seen Jack the "effing" Ripper. I turned toward her and she stepped back, and fell right off the scaffolding into the mud. "Oh great," I thought. "I've broken Sally. Now we'll never get outta here."

It was subtle at first, but things started to change after Sally fell off the scaffold. Jeff would take off his shoes when he came onto the boat, so as not to track grease around. He showed up three days in a row and had the bow thruster motor off, and in pieces in two more. Sally started using a bigger spatula to spread her filler, and I saw two occasions when she told Margaret that she didn't have time for tea. Joe even came by once and chatted. He never chatted.

Linda noticed it too. "I think they're afraid of you," she said one evening outside the mobile home.

"Because I got mad?"

"Yeah. And plus, you're an American. They know what we're capable of."

"Well, if calling in air strikes will get us out of here, I'll put in a call to the Pentagon. Oh, did I tell you? Sally brought color swatches by today."

It was mid-July when Sally started applying primer to the boat. The next steps would include actual paint. The bow thruster motor was pronounced dead and a new one was on order, scheduled to arrive on some imaginary date in the future. I was still maintaining the 'cranky' act and would curse for effect once in a while over my wood refinishing projects. This would encourage Jeff to drop by with the news that the motor had not been delivered yet, but maybe next week.

Linda and I were working side by side at our desk in the dirt next to *Phaedra*. She was painting final coats of oil on the refinished wood bits and when that work began to peter out, she took it upon herself to stay busy by applying white paint to the framework for the cockpit awning. In the afternoons she would check her email using the wi-fi she discovered floating around the parking lot. This was how we got the news that Phil had finally died. Sue was hoping we would come to the memorial. Two days later, we were on the plane.

Memorials are rarely remembered as being fun, but this one got close. We were a small group of friends and family and we all knew how to eat, drink, and laugh at Phil stories. A few days later, the city of San Francisco put on a parade in his honor through North Beach. The place was taken over by people dressed up as his cartoon characters, dancing and cavorting until sundown. We went with our girls and the little prince, Daven, who loved the dancing bears and beavers. It was quite a send-off.

When things calmed down, I called Parfit for an update. He gave me the happy news that the bow thruster motor had arrived and Jeff was in the process of installing it, and Sally was busy as a beaver applying paint. None of this did I believe, of course. The motor might be somewhere in the shop, but the idea that it had even been unpacked from its box was absurd. I confirmed this by my next phone call to Ken and Sheila, who said they hadn't seen Sally in a week and Jeff had been buried in the bowels of Jack's boat, installing the new engine.

Going back for another endless stay in Migennes was not an option for Linda or me, so I called Joe back and used a little leverage. "Joe, it's all set. We'll be back to pick up the boat and head for Paris in two weeks," I said into the phone.

"Right. No problem. Should I call the Confluences?" he said, being the full service boatyard owner.

"No way. We'll just pick up the boat and go. Can't wait to see the new paint. How's the bow thruster coming along?'

"Um, oh, Jeff…I'll ask Jeff when he gets back."

"Oh, did I mention that we're bringing our daughter Krista back with us? She's a writer for the *New York Times*. She's going to do a series of articles on the cruise into Paris, and she's really anxious to do a big piece on you and the boatyard," I said. "Get a haircut. She wants pictures."

The next day I got an email from Ken announcing that Sally was back and working like mad, and Jack was fuming because Jeff had ditched him to work on *Phaedra*.

Chapter Thirty-Two

"Rick, there are many exit visas sold in this café, but we know that
you've never sold one. That is the reason we
permit you to remain open."
- Captain Renault, *Casablanca*
-

The train dropped us at Migennes just after noon on a hot
and muggy afternoon in September. Krista had indeed come back
with us for the trip into Paris, and, despite being a mere thirty-six
years old, and a physical trainer, was stumbling and babbling from
jetlag. With Billy still groggy from his drug-induced sleep under
Linda's seat on the plane, the lot of us made a pretty pathetic group
of refugees as we shuffled through the dust into that all too
familiar parking lot.

It looked, on first glance, unchanged. The same sagging
crop of bedraggled and neglected boats, impaled on thin iron props
loomed above piles of refuse, seemingly dumped at random from
some psychotic's immense junkyard. I started recognizing the old
landmark boats: *Moya*, with its eternally broken rudder, *Titan*, with
its weed patch grown all the way up to its waterline, and *Sheridan*,
a partially burned wooden yacht with smashed windows, gutted
interior, and holes in the hull that kids would kick soccer balls

through. If Satan ever made a brochure for his boatyard, Sheridan would be on the cover.

As we dragged our bags toward the quay, familiar faces emerged from the campers, lean-to's, barges, and workshops. Sally peeked out of her paint shed, saw us and jumped back inside. Jack waved from the deck of his boat, but didn't come down, and Roger the Rudder brought his greyhound over to say hello to Billy.

We spotted *Phaedra* as soon as we came around the main shed to the river side. She was floating daintily at the quay, radiant in her bright new paint. She'd been freshly washed and small puddles of water sparkled on her deck and cabin tops. Krista had only seen pictures of her before and her first response was, "Oh, she's beautiful. Let's get her out of here."

"She's all ready to go." It was monsieur Parfit himself. He'd come out of his office when he'd spotted us limping across the yard.

"The paint looks good," I said. I couldn't help noticing that he had shaved, and possibly even brushed his hair. "Oh, Joe, I'd like to introduce our daughter, Krista."

"It is a pleasure indeed," he said, and held out a hand that had been recently washed.

"Ah, so you are the famous Mr. Parfit." Krista had been briefed. "Interesting name. How do you spell that?" She took his hand and as he opened his mouth, she continued, "Oh, we'll get all that later. Right now, let's get all this stuff aboard and get settled in."

"Right," he said. "I'll get Jeff to help you with…"

"No need," I said. "We can manage."

As soon as we'd unpacked and Linda and Krista had gone off on a market run, I started up the engine and tested the new bow thruster. I held my breath and touched the control that used to push the bow to the right, and by God, it did it. I held it there for a few moments and let *Phaedra* strain against the dock line, then I reversed it and watched the water churn up under the bow as she leaned with all her might against the stone quay. It was working like new, and that meant there was nothing between us and Paris but water.

The engine was still running when the girls got back I gave them the news that all was good to go. "I'll just pop up and see Joe," I said. "Then we're outa here."

Joe ran his fingers through his hair and looked past me expectantly when I walked in.

"I tested the bow thruster and she seems to work just fine," I said.

"Yes, she works now. We had a spot of trouble with the starboard indicator light. Bloody bulb seems to have gone. That's a problem. It's Belgian, you see. Have one on order," he said. "Be here next week."

"Forget it," I said. "Don't need it. Have you got our bill ready?"

"Ah, yes. It's here somewhere." He started pawing through piles of flotsam on his desk. A grimy, dog-eared piece of binder paper floated to the surface and he grabbed it, "Here it is. You must be proud of that daughter of yours," he added. "Reporter for the *New York Times* and all."

"Oh yes."

"I'm available any time she wants to sit down and ask me any questions about, well, whatever…"

"Oh, she's eager to. Not today though. Maybe next week."

Back at the boat, Linda and Krista were waiting with their dock lines in hand, ready to cast off. I jumped aboard, they gave the ropes a flip and after almost five months in Parfit's boat dungeon, *Phaedra*'s prop turned over and she was once again free. A touch of the lovely new bow thruster and her nose slipped away from the boatyard and onto the river. I swung the wheel over, gave her a little throttle, and she moved into the current. The water giggled and sang down her sides as we gained speed and headed down river. Billy started running around the deck, barking goodbye to Roger the Rudder's greyhound while Krista coiled down her line and Linda sang out, "We're going to Paris. We're going to Paris. Eeeeeeee!"

Chapter Thirty-Three

"Ballerina, you must have seen her dancing in the sand."
- Elton John, Tiny Dancer

Our first day of cruising was a short one. We were so anxious to get moving that we shoved off without even caring where we'd end up that evening. Luckily for us, just two locks and about eight and a half miles down river was the little town of Joigny. We found a sweet little mooring at the end of a short pier across the river from the old medieval town, with a perfect view of the ancient churches of St. Thibault and Saint Jean.

Linda and Krista had a bottle of wine open by the time I had the motor shut down. The weather was still warm, with a slight breeze off the river cooling us. Linda raised her glass, "To Krista's first locks, and her first day of barging. To Paris!"

"What do you think, Krista?" I asked.

"I get it now." She laughed. "You know, losing the job, buying a barge, selling the house, doing art again...God, Nicole and I thought you had gone crazy."

"Not that far off really," I said.

Krista pointed at the arched stone bridge that crossed the river to the old town. "How old is that?" she murmured. "It's gorgeous. And the churches…" Her voice trailed off.

I looked at the notes on the chart. "Well, the churches are medieval, so that makes them maybe eight or nine hundred years old."

"Tomorrow, can we go there?" Krista asked.

"Um, hm." Linda smiled and touched her knee. "First thing."

Joigny from Phaedra's deck on the Yonne River

Everyone's eyelids were beginning to droop so I suggested that we put down the wine and walk into town for a quick dinner.

This was Krista's first trip to France and she had a whole list of French dishes she wanted to try, so in spite of barely being able to move, the motion was carried and the crew of the good ship *Phaedra* staggered ashore for a night on the town.

We walked along the main road leading away from the river towards the shops and cafes. We passed a few brasseries that didn't look very inviting before we came upon a small restaurant with lace curtains in the windows, it was called "Le Paris Rouge." The waitress brought us menus, and water for Billy, then announced that Chef Claire was home taking care of their fourth baby, so Chef David was on his own that night. Lucky for us, she said, because Monsieur David was very creative, a master in the kitchen. Without Claire to hold him back, we were in for a treat.

We each ordered the special two-course menu of the evening then sat back to see what the chef would produce to dazzle us with. What landed on our table was indeed creative. David appeared to be into a fried spaghetti phase. Our salad plates were bedecked with long sticks of dry spaghetti, fried into needle-like harpoons, spearing small fruits and vegetables that floated above our plates. Red and yellow cherry tomatoes bobbed among bright yellow pineapple chunks and dripping wedges of ripe watermelon. Slivers of smoked duck breast were impaled on spaghetti, while giant purple grapes nodded like politicians over it all on their own spears.

Linda was about to mix her salad together when suddenly she froze. "Oh my God," she gasped and held up a plastic syringe.

"It looks like a syringe," I said.

"It's in my salad!"

I reached for it, held it up to the light and flicked it with my finger a couple of times like they do on TV.

Krista grabbed the syringe and boldly squirted some on a spoon. "Salad dressing," she said. "Mustard vinaigrette."

"It's in a syringe." Linda was having trouble with this one. She put down her fork. "What's the next course?"

"Surprise du Chef."

"Oh great."

The next morning the sun glowed across the vineyards creeping over the hills behind the church on the hill. The river flowed quietly by, shedding a feathery blanket of mist that rose in tiny swirling towers in the sunlight. The girls had gotten up early and were off wandering around the old town, so it was up to me tend to Billy and hit Joigny's covered market for supplies. I got our bread for the day, a basket of apples from a local orchard, a couple wedges of cheese, some slices of meat pie, and a dozen eggs. I found no syringes, but I did find a man selling an assortment of tapenades and olives, which I bought in case Linda was inspired to fry spaghetti spears and needed something to stick on them.

The girls were back by 10:30 proudly bearing a glistening pear tart, some sweet figs, and more bread. It was time to shove off so we bid adieu to Joigny and pointed the boat down river once more. Almost immediately we were directed off the Yonne into a diversion canal that bypassed seven kilometers of un-navigable shallows and rapids. The canal was quite narrow and wound through a tunnel of trees lined with an overgrown wall of camellias crowding the shoreline. Krista and Linda made friends with a pair of swans who escorted us through their domain, while a great grey heron majestically lifted himself into the air at our approach and glided ahead to show us his next fishing spot. He stayed with us the length of the cut until we arrived at the closed lock at the end. Waiting there, we found a small boat moored to the bank where her captain had set up a picnic table. We pulled up next to him, wished him *bon appetit*, and asked if he was intending to proceed soon, or if we should go on ahead of him.

"*Groses peniches, alors,*" he said. "*Deux.*" And he pointed in both directions. "*Ils ont prioritie.*" He was waiting for two commercial barges to pass and he simply decided to take advantage of the stop and get comfortable. Commercial barges always have priority over us pointless wanderers, so if one is on its way, we will simply have to wait. In this case, there were two. The one coming up stream would pass first, then the next one, coming from our direction, would arrive sometime after that. We would try to squeeze into the lock with the barge coming down.

This would be our first encounter with one of the truly enormous commercial barges. Frankly, I was none too excited about sharing confined spaces with one this early in the day. But there was no avoiding it, so we got ready by pulling to the side, driving our stakes into the ground, and double tying our lines.

We didn't have long to wait. In only a couple of minutes, the first barge appeared through the trees from downstream and moved heavily into the lock. She was traveling empty, and her faded black flanks rose almost seven feet above the water with a greasy stripe that once might have been yellow defining the upper limits of her deck. When this 125 foot long wall of steel came nosing out, we all took hold of our lines and braced ourselves for a thrashing. If he came through fast, the massive barge would push a huge volume of water ahead of her which could drive *Phaedra* onto the bank, then suck her into its side as he went past.

It never happened. The boat went by so slowly and carefully that she made no more wake than a duck. As the stern came alongside, the captain looked down at us from his Barca

Lounger pilot's chair and called out, *"Bonjour."* Then he smiled and gave us a wave.

With a deep rumble like a locomotive he picked up a little speed and disappeared around the bend, leaving us with just the sounds of the birds and the cicadas again. Not for long though. From around that same bend came an ominous metallic banging and crashing echoing through the trees. I turned toward it and saw the bow of the next barge appear and move slowly into view. This one was fully laden, showing less than a foot of hull above the water. The skipper was walking around on the deck adjusting the metal hatch covers over his load, wedging them into place and battening them down with a hammer and a crow bar.

The other barge had carried most of her bulk above the waterline. It drew less water in the canal and pushed less out of its way. This one, fully loaded, was just the opposite. Almost its entire bulk was under the water. Her bottom was actually dragging along the floor of the canal, carving a groove in the mud. Her captain had to stay near the center, where the water was deepest, which meant that he'd pass us with less than three feet of clearance. We took up our positions again at the ropes.

No need. This captain was as courteous and skillful as the last one. He maneuvered his ship by us like a mother whale, so slowly and precisely that we almost wanted to reach out and pet it. As he slid past, we could see that he was alone on board, steering his vessel from outside his wheelhouse with a hand held joy-stick. He too smiled as he passed, gave us a nod, and moved sedately into the lock, where he took up its entire length. He had left us just enough room to squeeze *Phaedra* in beside him on the left.

Slowly we followed him in and prepared ourselves to take on our first commercial lock on the Yonne River. The Yonne locks are unique in that their walls slope inward. As the water drains, the sloping walls force the boats closer together at the bottom. There are so many impractical points to this design that I'm convinced its designer had never tried to actually take a barge through one himself. Linda and I had done hundreds of locks by this time and we had learned to expect the unexpected, but Krista was getting nervous. As the water drained, she had to let line out so that we wouldn't get hung up on the sloping sides of the lock on our way down, but this meant that we were inching closer and closer to the freighter next to us. "Are we gonna hit?" she called back.

"Don't know. Never done this before," I said.

"We're not going to hit," Linda yelled forward, then she turned to me. "Are we?"

"Not if we hold our lines, dear. These guys know what they're doing. Please take your fingernails out of my arm. You're hurting me."

When the draining was complete, and the lock doors started to open, we had more than enough room to fit a loaf of bread between us and our lock partner. Once out of the lock, we followed him through the rest of the diversion and back onto the river where he put the hammer down and that lumbering behemoth turned into a greyhound and left us struggling to keep up.

Krista had three locks under her belt now, and she was already handling the lines like a pro. She used the bollards on the boat with a double wrap and a flip that allowed her to manage tons of pressure with simple movements of her wrists. It was a pleasure to watch her and Linda working together on the bow, giggling and playing, excited to be finally on their way to Paris. Between here and there, all the locks would be scaled to handle the massive big-rigs of the river. The one we had just gone through was big enough to handle one full-sized 125 foot barge and a small cruiser or two. From here on, they would be big enough to hold nine full sized commercial barges. If all the captains were as skilled as those last two, we'd have no problems. That is, of course, if we were as skilled as they were. If there were a slip-up, especially on the Seine, it could get ugly fast.

We had the river mostly to ourselves for the rest of the day as we pressed on to our mooring spot for the night, about nine miles away at the medieval town of Villeneuve-sur-Yonne. Massive stone arches, crenulated towers, and ominous-looking keeps still guard the gateways at either end of the little red-roofed, 12th century town. Linda and I had visited once for lunch and ended up spending an afternoon at an antique flea market by the river. We'd walked the riverfront enjoying its tree-lined park and the ancient arched stone bridge. There was a long stone quay where we hoped to spend the night, just down from a small sailing club and yacht harbor.

We had the quay to ourselves so we tied to stone bollards in the welcome shade of a leafy plane tree and made fast for the evening. Linda and Krista had whiled away their afternoon cruise by reading cookbooks, so they had some specific ideas for dinner, which called for a visit to the local shops, so while they trotted into the village, Billy and I secured the boat for the night then ran over and rolled in the grass. By the time the sun touched the top of the church bell tower, the delightful aroma of shallots and white wine was filling the air and we were officially another day closer to Paris.

The next morning broke bright and balmy, promising a lovely day of cruising. The river widened immediately after the first lock and became even more lush, with thick green forest coming right down to the banks on both sides. Sunbathing and reading between locks kept the the ladies of the crew busy while I stood at the wheel, captain of my vessel. We had eighteen miles and six locks to Pont-sur-Yonne, our next stop. We were making less than four miles an hour, so including the six locks, we were looking at around eight hours of non-stop cruising for the day. The locks along this stretch of river were, aside from their absolute dimensions, often quite unique. Some of them had river hi-tech control towers with hidden lock keepers pushing buttons in air-conditioned command centers while others had small, obscure houses. Some had doors that rolled up out of the water and others had a single door that swung away like a giant garden gate. Often we would pull to the side in front of the lock, tie off, and with *Phaedra* idling, I would ride the bike to the lock keeper's office for instructions. We saw only a few commercial barges along this stretch and shared a couple of locks with them, but for the most part, it was another day with the whole river to ourselves.

Phaedra was running beautifully the entire time. She started right up in the mornings and ran without a hitch for eight hours straight every day. She never burned or leaked a drop of oil either from the engine or the hydraulics and our fuel consumption was a fraction of what I'd anticipated. Her new bow thruster was smooth and quiet, her paint job sparkled and her freshly refinished woodwork glowed golden in the sun. In short, *Phaedra* seemed to know she was going to Paris.

We arrived a Pont-sur-Yonne well before the locks closed for the night at seven. We tied up to a small floating pontoon by a park and Billy leapt ashore like a dog on a mission. Pont-sur-Yonne is named for the remains of its old arched stone bridge that was reportedly blown up by the Nazis. They've put the one end that is still standing to good use by putting a pub on it, so we collected Billy and went off for a beer. The bartender told us that the next morning would be market day in town, so we started making lists of things we'd need like cheeses, pates and, for some reason, eggplants. Maybe it was the beer.

We spent a quiet night at Pont-sur-Yonne. Krista and Linda had been back at their cookbooks and our little kitchen was never happier. After dinner, we ate peaches and raspberries on the deck and watched the stars filling the night sky like they do only in Burgundy. Before retiring, we took a final walk around the little town. The streets were narrow and winding with rugged stone houses backing up to planted fields, surrounded by stonewalls. Amber street lights cast a warm tone that clashed with the occasional flickering lights and artificial sounds of televisions leaking through shuttered windows. A final glass of wine back at the boat and we went off to the kind of blissful sleep that I think one can only get on a river flowing toward Paris.

The next morning we set off early hoping to cover the nearly thirty miles to our next stop, on the Seine. Thirty miles doesn't sound like a terribly long way to go in a day, unless you're in a barge on a river. It was a full ten hours, only stopping for locks, (eight of them) to the small pier at the waterfront town of Saint Mammes (pronounced San Mam-ay). We could have made it a shorter day by stopping at Montreau, a fairly large city located at the intersection where the Yonne disappears into the Seine, but we were anxious to finally make it onto the mighty Seine so we pushed on.

Saint Mammes is the first good mooring spot below Montreau. It lies at the junction of the Canal du Loing and the Seine, just forty-five miles from Paris. The Canal du Loing connects the Loire River to the Seine, the Marne and the Yonne rivers, which has made Saint Mammes a major hub for commercial barge traffic since 1726. Commercial barges still stack up there four deep along its waterfront, waiting to be dispatched to take on cargo anywhere in northern France.

Lately though, the commercial traffic has been dwindling dramatically. Except for bulk shipments like grain or gravel, today most cargo travels on wheels. In response, bent on attracting more private boats and holiday travelers, Saint Mammes has spruced up its waterfront. They've planted trees and created a grassy park next to a small marina where pleasure boats can moor for the night. It's a tiny waterfront town, with some interesting old buildings and a pleasant walkway along the river to the estuary that leads up to the first lock on the Canal du Loing. I had heard that this estuary was a place where some people left their boats for the winter so I grabbed Billy and we set off to check it out.

The approach to the Loing is about a mile long and lined with hard working barges of all vintages and descriptions. Many will never move again, but some are trying to keep up at least the hope. I like wandering among these old ladies. Their battered and scarred hides, dismantled machinery, painted over names, dried up herb gardens and rusty bicycles seemed to be presided over by only a few agile cats. Standing there looking back across their jumbled decks, I hoped that the life stories winding to a close behind those darkened portholes held at least some tales of adventure and romance, and not just hard, hard work.

On the way back to the boat from our walk I noticed a poster on a tree announcing a concert that very night in the park by the water. I rushed back to tell the girls and immediately set about chilling some wine and setting up chairs on the deck so that we'd have front row seats. By seven o'clock the lawn was filling with families spreading their multicourse picnic dinners across long tables set up for the event. The band had arrived and was tuning guitars, testing drum sets and setting up a sound system for a night of heavy rock. Five or six haggard and starved, post adolescent rockers were coughing and sniffing and struggling with their inner demons as they tapped on microphones and said, "une, deux, trois, testing!"

Along about eight o'clock, the first guitar screeched to life. The rest of them jumped right in and they all lit into a French accented version of the Rolling Stone's "Sympathy for the Devil." The pain that it inflicted on the lead singer was heartbreaking, but he found the strength to press on with "Tombstone Shadow" by Credence Clearwater.

That got 'em going. The audience down front was on its feet and dancing like crazy. They were whirling and twirling, spinning, jumping, and running around with their eyes closed, screaming and laughing in ecstasy. And not one of them was more than three feet tall. No, that's not accurate. There was one little girl who was maybe three and a half feet. She was in a pink dress with fairy wings on the back, a sparkly tiara and white shoes. She was twirling a baton and prancing around like she expected the band to get up and follow her down the street. She's the one who ended up causing the trouble that brought an end to the concert. It might have been that she was carried away, but during the thirty-seventh verse of "Highway to Hell," when she tossed her baton into the air and did a spin-around move while it was up there, her tiara flew off, which broke her concentration so she missed the baton and it came down and hit a five-year-old boy in the head and made him cry. This started an imbroglio that Linda described at the time as "heated" between the mother of the injured boy and the mother of the baton twirler. This grew to the point where both extended families packed up and left, right in the middle of the band's version of "Cocaine" by Eric Clapton. That pretty much cut the attendance at the concert in half and took the wind out of the sails of the band. They weren't the same after that.

We finished our night in Saint Mammes in a pub just down from the boat that had an accordion player. The accordion player never played his instrument though, which, according to the bartender, was a good thing.

We were in bed by ten. The last thing Linda said was, "Two days to Paris. Eeeeeee!"

Chapter Thirty-Four

"Left bank café,
Strollin the quays
Watching the boats on the Seine
Come back again."

- Duke Ellington, Paris Blues

The difference between the Seine and the Yonne was apparent immediately. The Seine is wider for one thing, but the main difference is the amount of traffic. Despite the fact that commercial barge traffic is down, coming off the Yonne onto the Seine was like moving from a country road onto a freeway, merging into a regular stream of 100-150 foot barges barreling up and down the river at twice our speed. The barges by themselves were imposing, but at least half the time they'd be doubled up. Two barges, tied end to end, would make up a 300 foot long monster dead ahead or coming up fast from behind. These were often run as family businesses with the husband, wife, kids, dog and car, all living, traveling and working on board.

On the Seine, priority was strictly enforced. The guys making a living went in and out of any lock first. A lock might be empty and its doors open, but if there were a commercial barge coming from the other direction, the lock keeper would close the doors in our face to accommodate the working barge. We learned to hold back and wait for permission to enter a lock that was open. If it was set up for a big boy coming from behind us, we'd pull over and wait until he was inside before we entered. In the beginning, we went right in if the doors were open, only to look back and see a double rig of fully laden barges come gliding in behind us, and keep coming and coming....

The first few times sharing locks with these guys was utterly nerve wracking. We'd be sitting there, tied in an empty lock for twenty minutes wondering why the doors weren't closing. Then we'd see a couple of empty barges barreling down river pushing big bow waves and heading for the lock. We'd pull *Phaedra* all the way up to the doors at the front and sit there, convinced we'd never all fit and praying they'd see us and not crush us like bugs against the stone. Then, we'd see another one come around the corner and we'd know we were dead for sure.

In fact, the locks were big enough to take three barges end to end, and three abreast, nine barges in all. The captains knew their dimensions, down to the inch. We had to learn it. At one lock, just before we reached Melun, our final over-night point before Paris, we waited outside a lock with another small boat as eight commercial barges went plowing past us and on in. I figured that was it and we expected to wait for the next one, but the doors didn't close. Then the lock keeper called us on the radio. "Eh, petit bateau vert. Why you don't come inside l'ecluse? Eh?" his voice scratching through the static of my hand held radio.

"Monsieur, do you have enough room for us? Over," I said into the mouthpiece.

"Oui, oui. Bien sur. Mais vite, vite alor. We must hurry."

I looked at Linda and Krista and said, "Put Billy downstairs. We're going in."

"No, we're not," Linda said. "I like this place." She looked at the parking lot by the river. "Look, there's a dumpster. Let's stay the night."

"But they're pulling that big double rig up a little, 'specially for us." I pointed to what looked like a 14 foot-high elephant's behind that had just moved three feet forward. "You'll see. It'll be fine." I put it in gear. The water churned behind us as we moved slowly forward into what had looked like an impossibly tiny spot at the back corner of the lock. But the big fella kept inching forward and by the time we got there, they'd made a space for us that was almost a hundred feet long and fifteen feet wide.

We had lots of room, but still, when the doors closed and the water started filling the chamber, I felt uncomfortably like a wedding cake on the floor of a cattle car.

After a while we got used to the commercial guys and began to appreciate how professional and skillful they were. If we paced it just right, we could slide right through every lock on their green light, like an ambulance chaser beating the rush hour traffic.

As we got closer to Paris, we began to see even more and more elegant old estates and castles of the upscale suburbs of Paris. Beautiful pocket chateaux country homes with steep pointed roofs and tiny spires were set in their own forests and garden parks that led down to graceful pavilions and private docks on the water.

At Melun, the last stop before Paris, we took the first mooring spot we saw, on the river-side of a small island where the original city was founded. We moved two hours later when we realized that we were right behind a floating discothèque that was warming up for an epic battle of the bands that night.

The next morning we were under way by eight o'clock. We had thirty-six miles to go to reach the lock at the entrance to the Arsenal yacht harbor in Paris. That distance, plus five locks, would make it our longest day of running so far. It was by no means certain that we would make it before the gates of the Paris yacht basin closed for the night. The river environment would also be changing dramatically as we got closer to the city. For the past five days, we had been a cruising through beautiful countryside, villages, and towns but as we got closer to the city, we would be entering the industrial outskirts of Paris. The chart we were following had been depicting the areas surrounding the river as miles and miles of forest with the occasional town or village. But now, the forests were receding, replaced by highways, rail lines, storage tanks, fuel depots and grain elevators. If it looked like we weren't going make it to the Arsenal by seven, we'd be hard pressed to find a safe place to moor in this industrial no-man's land. I pressed the throttle down a little more.

At five o'clock, I was searching the chart carefully for icons indicating secure, overnight mooring facilities among the storage tanks and train yards crowding the banks of the Seine. One spot had a plethora of little blue icons, including ones for showers, a lift, and a mechanic, but reality revealed a few very distressed boats, held in place by a half submerged dock and their own tangled gardens of river kelp. We were still seven and a half miles and two locks from the Arsenal, so I got on the phone and called the Captainerie at the Paris harbor and told him we were cutting it close, and that prince of a man said that if we made it through the last river lock by seven, he'd stay late and let us in. This drew rounds of applause from the whole crew, including Billy.

But we weren't there yet. At our top speed, we would be very lucky to cover the six-plus miles we'd have to do to put the second lock behind us by seven o'clock. If we did that, we'd still be almost two miles from the Arsenal lock. I pushed the throttle to the peg, hoping to squeeze just one extra kilometer per hour out of our straining engine, then prayed for open lock doors, no break-downs, and no commercial barges coming against us.

Ahead and around a slight bend, we finally sighted the towers of Pont a l'Anglais, the 1912 suspension bridge across the Seine that marked the entrance to the last lock between us and the Arsenal. It was ten minutes to seven. Through the binoculars I could just make out the doors to the lock. They were closed. Linda and Krista grimly prepared their lines while I swept the river with the binoculars, hoping for a sign of a commercial barge that would compel the lock keeper to open his doors one last time before he shut down tight at seven on the dot.

And I saw it. Just nosing around the bend behind us I caught sight of the bow of a heavily laden commercial ship plowing full tilt toward the lock. The captain was in a tearing hurry, his bow-wave driving white water over his forward hatches and pushing a small tsunami in a rolling "V" toward the riverbanks. He wanted to make it through that lock before closing and judging from the smoke billowing from his stack, he wasn't taking no for an answer. I swung the binoculars back toward the lock gates. They were still closed, but then, as I watched, a tiny sliver of light appeared through the crack in the doors. They were opening!

Those doors were not opening for us, though, but for Mr. Commercial Job, so we dutifully pulled *Phaedra* to the side and let him barrel past, then floored it, slipstreamed his wake and surfed into the lock behind him. The girls were cheering as I hit full reverse to slow us down so they could tie us off.

We were just setting up our dock lines when I looked up and saw, advancing along the edge of the lock, two serious looking gendarmes with notebooks in their hands. I prepared my most sincere smile.

The French police are an imposing bunch who, in my experience, rarely smile, but I'd never had any real trouble with them. I'd been flagged down several times at checkpoints while I was driving the Belle Espace, but that was because they couldn't believe that something so ugly was being driven on their streets. I had learned from these experiences that when the French police get bored, they get really interested in paperwork. So, when I saw these two bastions of officialdom approaching, in their crisp blue uniforms with their pants tucked into their shiny black parachuting boots, I knew I was in for a thorough document check.

I had my annual permit from the VNF, *Voies Navigables de France*, the agency regulating the canals and rivers of France, my documents of insurance, and my boat registration number freshly painted on the outside of the boat. What I didn't have was a license to actually drive the boat. It's pretty much a rule in France, well, actually, it's a law, that to operate a boat over fifteen meters long, one must have an operator's license. *Phaedra* is anywhere from 15.5 to 16.5 meters long, depending on how you measure the rudder. So, technically, I should have gotten a license that I could show these gentlemen of the law. That was one of those details I had been meaning to get to for the longest time.

Of course, the first thing they asked me for was that operator's license. They asked it, though, in French. So I smiled broadly, nodded my head, and in English, said, "Yes, yes. Thank you. We love France." They both rolled their eyes and asked again, this time with hand gestures.

"Oh, yes," I said in English. "I have it on the boat." And I smiled and pointed at the boat. Then I stood there and smiled some more. The big one, the one with the shaved head, put out his hand. "*Donnez le moi*," he said. (Give it to me.)

I smiled and took his outstretched hand and shook it. "Hello Donny. *Moi* name is Cris. Nice to meet you."

The muscles around his jaw flickered, but the younger one, the one with hair, stepped in and said, "*Non, non monsieur. Le permis. S'il vous plait.*" Then, almost instantly, he lost interest in the whole thing when he noticed Krista at the front of the boat.

Krista, I may have mentioned, was a personal trainer. She did sit-ups for a living. She was also a wind surfer and a sponsored long-board surfer. She stood about five foot seven with thick blonde hair and a pair of Paul Newman blue eyes. She was standing on the bow in her running outfit and California tan, setting up her dock line. The young gendarme took off his sunglasses and went to investigate.

As he walked away, his partner snapped his fingers at me and said, "*Le permis, monsieur.*"

"Oh. The permis," I said with a smile. "I'll get it." I was back in a jiffy with the copy of my VNF permit to have the boat on the canals. This was something he'd be asking for eventually, so he took it and wrote down the number in his book, handed it back and said again, slowly, "*Le permis, s'il vous plait.*"

"Oh. Wait a minute. I know…" Then I jumped back onto the boat.

"What's going on?" Linda looked a little worried.

"Oh nothing, dear. Just a routine document check."

"You don't have a license, do you," she said.

"No."

"We're screwed! I told you. Ohhhhh."

"Look, don't worry about a thing. I'll handle this."

"Paris is right up there. I can see it."

"Right." I grabbed the boat registration and climbed back up to the policeman. I handed him the blue laminated placard with the stamp of Belgium on it, proving that *Phaedra* is a Belgian vessel and I am her owner.

"Belgique?" the officer said with some surprise.

"Oh yes," I said and smiled, even more warmly.

"Avez vous un permis pour le conductor le bateau?" He growled and this time he put his hands on an imaginary steering wheel and made putt-putt motor sounds.

No mistaking that. "Ah," I exclaimed and smiled. "Yes, yes." I reached into my back pocket and pulled out my California driver's license and handed it over.

He looked at it and started to inflate. His shoulders went up toward his ears and his eyes crushed to a squint just as I held up one finger and said, *"Regardez,"* and pointed toward the front of the boat.

He turned in time to see his fellow officer with his shirt-sleeve rolled up, flexing his bicep, and Krista poking at it, going, "Oh, wow. Niiiice."

"Jean-Phillipe! Allons!" he roared. He shoved my driver's license at me, threw up his arms and stomped off muttering some words in French I hadn't heard before.

The water had already begun to drain from the lock so I pocketed my driver's license, jumped on board and took Linda's line. She was smiling as she punched me in the stomach. As we rode the lock down, Krista came back and said, "He was cute."

That was our last lock except for the one that would take us off the river and usher us into the heart of Paris. Linda got on the phone right away to the port captain at the Arsenal to let him know that we were through the lock and on our way. *"Tres bien, Phaedra.* We will prepare the lock for you," he said.

I pushed the throttle down a little further. The current seemed to add to our speed as we flew past the junction of the Marne, and Paris began to unfurl herself all around us. Off to the right, we could see Sacre Coeur, atop Montmarte, catching the rays of the lowering sun. And in the distance, past the towers of Notre Dame, we could just make out the top of the Eiffel Tower. We started giggling, and laughing, and singing,

"Hold me close and hold me fast
The magic spell you cast
This is la vie en rose..."

Our voices rose up in a joyful shout that echoed back as we charged under the eight bridges marking our approach to the city. The river traffic became more congested with double grain carriers weaving among Bateau Mouches filled with tourists. *Phaedra* galloped like a filly heading home, seemingly heedless of the fact that everything else on the river was so much bigger and going so much faster.

We passed under Pont Austerlitz, the last bridge before the Arsenal entrance and I slowed the engine as we all scanned the right bank, searching for the traffic lights that mark the opening to the Arsenal and the Bastille. Red lights would mean that the lock was still being prepared and we would have to tread water and dodge traffic until it was drained and the doors opened. Green lights would mean the captain had set up the lock and we could drive right in. Krista pointed toward the bank. The lights were red.

I put it in neutral and drifted with the current down toward the lock doors. Just over the bow was the tip of the Ile Saint Louis and beyond, the Ile de la Cite. The twin towers of Notre Dame, the Palais de Justice, and the sharp spire of St. Chapelle were in sight, and the magnificent Hotel de Ville cast its reflections in the river. I put the engine into reverse to hold us against the current. After all the years that Linda and I had strolled along the Seine and watched the barges steaming by, here we were. Our voyage had taken us longer than we had planned, but we had stuck with it and, almost miraculously, we were finally here, just outside the gate.

Standing at the helm of that old boat, watching my wife and daughter on the bow, jumping and dancing and hugging each other, I thought of my father and the dreams he'd had, of casting off in an old purse seiner chasing adventure up and down the coast of California. I remembered Phil's advice; "Take your time, but get there." My eyes were hot and I felt my chest swell. I realized this was a moment that I wanted to remember for the rest of my life. I reached out and did something I'd never done before. I pushed the red button that set off the burglar alarm. *Phaedra* exploded in screeching and wailing as her air horn and deck-mounted loud-hailer blasted out a warbling, ear-spitting noise that bounced all over Paris, and almost knocked Linda and Krista into the river.

It also woke up the captain at the Arsenal, because the lights turned green, and the lock doors swung open. I slipped it into gear, swung over the helm, and we nosed into the final lock on our journey. When the doors opened at the other end, I pushed the throttle forward and *Phaedra* motored proudly into Paris.

EPILOGUE

Lists. Krista had lists, lots of them. She had to see the *Tour Eiffel*, the *Arc de Triumph*, the *Louvre*, the *Musee D'Orsay*, the *Tuileries*, the Rodin Museum, and everything on the "Left Bank." She had to stroll down the *Champs Elysees*, and climb to *Montmartre*. She had to have crepe's in Luxembourg Gardens, falafels in the Marais, and coffee in a sidewalk café, any café.

The coffee was easy, so that's where we started. With *Phaedra* safely settled into her new berth in the crowded *Port de l'Arsenal*, we gathered up our guidebooks and Paris maps and set off in search of a suitable café where we could sip cognac-laced coffee and plan our immersion in all things Parisian.

We climbed the stairs at the eastern end of the port and emerged into an entirely new reality. From the idyllic, riverside villages of Burgundy and the upper Seine, we were suddenly transported into the swirling chaos of the frenzied roundabout at the *Place de la Bastille*. The air vibrated with the cacophonous roar of hundreds of cars, scooters, motorcycles, buses, and, it's worth noting, claxon blaring police cars.

There were people moving everywhere. Couples holding hands, people jabbering into cell phones, tour groups straggling behind raised umbrellas, there were joggers, skaters, skateboarders, and dog walkers, all flowing around us at a pace that would have gotten them all speeding tickets in Auxerre or St. Mammes.

Krista summed it up when she said, most eloquently, "Wow, so this is Paris, huh?"

There's an energy to the city that is contagious. Having just come from six days of cruising the river at five miles an hour, we were particularly vulnerable to it. Krista's lists ruled our first week in Paris. We marched through the *Louvre*, the Catacombs of Paris, the *Musee D'Orsay* and the Rodin Museum with barely a break for crepes and cafes. We walked the streets for hours until our feet couldn't take it anymore, then flopped once again, into the nearest café and let Paris walk by us for a change. In the evenings, we searched for bistros where we could eat outside and revel in the cool air while we watched the lights come on and change the entire color pallet of the city.

On the fifth morning we came up from the harbor to find that it was market day on the boulevard just across the *Place de la Bastille,* so we grabbed our baskets and sallied forth to fill the larder. We had provisioned last at market day in Pont sur Yonne, but it hadn't prepared us for this. The vendors of fresh meat, fish, pastries, charcuteries, vegetables and fruits went on for a half a kilometer. Long lines of Parisians stood in front of their favorite vendors like conga lines during intermission.

We were sitting on a bench, our bulging shopping bags at our feet and munching on the remains of a pain au chocolate, when Linda said, "This is a great market. Is it every week?"

"Must be. Look at all the people lining up at their favorite butcher and cheese guy," I said.

"I want to have a favorite butcher in Paris."

"Well, the boat's just over there." I pointed toward the harbor. "This is your neighborhood. I imagine in a few weeks, you'll have a favorite butcher, and cheese guy, and a baker that knows exactly what you want when he sees you at his booth."

Krista looked at us and said, "Listen to you guys. Guess what, you made it. You live in Paris."

Linda started to cry.

We still have a lot of cruising to do on *Phaedra*, and we will be out there. But Linda's dream has come true. She now has a favorite butcher shop in Paris. It's a little place on the *Ile St. Louis* called *Boucherie Gardil*. It's just a five minute bike ride from the *l'Arsenal*. Check it out. Tell them the American lady off the *petite peniche* sent you.

A NOTE ON LEARNING FRENCH

I'd like to take a moment to address the language issue. I've been coming to France to chip the rust, fix the plumbing, and clean the bilge on our lovely *Phaedra* for several years now and the first thing people say to me when they hear about this is, "So, how's your French?"

After several classes, tutors, computer programs, and a French emersion course in Provence, the answer is, I get by. With a tenuous grasp of the present-tense-singular of some primitive words, hand gestures, drawings, and lots of mumbling, I can feed myself.

I'm not proud of my linguistic achievements here, but I have an excuse. It's not me. It's them. They've intentionally made it more difficult for foreigners to learn French by introducing sex into everything.

The French language is obsessed with sex. I'm as interested as the next guy, but I don't look at everything in the universe and try to figure out if it's a boy or a girl. Unfortunately, the French do. The Minister of Culture for France presides over *La Delegation General a la Francaise et aux Langues de France,* or, The DGLFLF. (Pronounced "d-gigl-af-laf"). The DGLFLF is the ultimate authority over the French language and has the power to definitively determine the gender of everything that appears in it, from apples (*pommes*) to zucchinis (*courgettes*). Which are both females bye the way.

It's hard enough at my age to learn a whole new vocabulary for everything without having to also remember if it likes pink or blue. A door, *porte*, is feminine. But a doorknob, *bouton de porte*, is male. A car, *voiture*, is female, but the carburetor in it, *carburateur*, isn't.

This is crazy making folks. It took me months to finally sort out the correct gender of *croissants (f)* and *baguettes (m)* so that the lady at the *boulangerie (f)* would serve me. If I didn't ask for my bread using the correct gender descriptor, I'd get nothing but a blank stare from *madame la patissier*. Who cares about the sex of a pastry at 7:30 in the morning? The French do.

This is just a holdover from their proud and ancient past you might say. A time when the world revolved around the simple things of life and everything was tied to the natural cycles of birth, death, and rebirth.

Afraid not folks. They're still doing it. The DGLFLF is constantly updating the French dictionary with new words, and each one gets a thorough examination and then it's sex is announced.

Did you know your computer (*ordinature*) was a male? Pick it up. Turn it over and really look closely. See? It's a boy! Of course the programming that's running it, that's feminine. But that's not so unusual I guess.

Mice are simple. You have boy mice and girl mice, Mickey and Minnie being the benchmark mice we all can picture. So, if you see a mouse running through your kitchen and it's wearing a polka dot skirt and a ribbon in it's hair, you know it's a girl mouse. Easy.

But what about that mouse in your hand? The one you fondle all day and tease all night with right and left clicks. Did you know it has a gender? Would you feel differently about your relationship with your mouse if you knew? The DGLFLF pondered long and hard and, after many late-night, closed-door sessions, determined that the computer version of a mouse, is definitely – drum roll - a female. (Maybe you should give it a name.)

Having cleared that up, it's pretty obvious what gender that mouse pad is, right? Yes, the DGLFLF is obsessed with sex, but the good old fashioned variety. They have bestowed the male gender on that mouse pad, which, I'm sure, makes both the mouse and the pad very happy. Particularly since in most cases, the mouse pad lasts much longer than the mouse.

So, I guess it could be said that there is a certain logic in the decisions made by the DGLFLF. It could be said indeed, but it wouldn't be completely true. I'll leave you with these memorable and incontrovertible gender decisions made by that esteemed agency and if you can point out their logic, please let me know.

Vagina, *vagin* in French, is masculine.

Viritlity, *virilite* in French, is feminine.

A bientot!

About the Author

Since 2003, Cris and Linda Hammond have been spending half of each year on their 56-foot Dutch barge *Phaedra*, exploring the canals and rivers of France, cooking, writing, painting and resetting their body clocks to a much slower pace. The rest of their time they are at home in Sausalito California, in their little Victorian studio by San Francisco Bay where he sells his paintings and she dotes on their new grandson.

Cris is a nationally known artist, cartoonist and entrepreneur. His comic strip, *"Speed Walker, Private Eye"* was seen daily in over 150 newspapers across the country. His paintings of ships and the sea have appeared in galleries in Sausalito, San Francisco, Tiburon, and Carmel California. He was a special effects designer and model maker for George Lucas' Industrial Light and Magic, where he contributed to Academy Award winning efforts in *Star Trek III, Star Trek IV, Innerspace* and *The Abyss,* among others. In 1994 he founded ABE, a company that specialized in defining the legal and tax liabilities associated with the contingent workforce. After eight years of wearing a tie, he left the company and created PaparazziH2O, a web enabled, on-the-water yacht photography business. After winning international attention for his innovative use of new, and not so new, technologies, Cris sold the business in 2004 so he'd have time to see how much trouble he could get into on that barge in France.

To that end, since 2003, Cris and Linda have meandered through more that 850 kilometers of canals and rivers and negotiated more that 1100 locks in their travels from the Rhone wine region, through Burgundy to Chablis and the Seine and into Paris. With *Phaedra* as their floating home base in Europe, they've struck out by car and train to explore Brittany, Provence, the Alsace, Northern Spain, Venice, Tuscany, Germany and the UK.

Back in 2001, when that V.P. of H.R. said to Cris, "Have a nice life," he had no idea what he started.

Made in the USA
Lexington, KY
06 July 2016